DENIS LAW

KING AND COUNTRY

DENIS LAW

KING AND COUNTRY

ALEX GORDON

First published in 2013 by
Arena Sport
An imprint of Birlinn Limited
West Newington House
10 Newington Road
Edinburgh
EH9 1QS

www.arenasportbooks.co.uk
www.birlinn.co.uk

ISBN: 978 1 90971 506 6
eBook ISBN: 978 0 85790 639 7

British Library Cataloguing-in-Publication Data
A catalogue record for this book is available from the British Library

Typeset by Iolaire Typesetting, Newtonmore
Printed and bound by ScandBook AB, Sweden

CONTENTS

DEDICATION

To my wonderful wife Gerda for her support throughout. Also, for getting the coffee going at the ungodly hour of 5am when I was working on this book. And for throwing a bacon butty into my den every now and again for some much-needed sustenance.

A massive thanks must also go to the man himself, Denis Law. What an inspiration to everyone. The glorious memories will always be treasured. Cheers, Denis.

ACKNOWLEDGEMENTS

There has been a lot of laughter along the way in putting this book together. A lot of hard work, too. Denis Law had a playing career that spanned 18 years and there wasn't too much this man missed on his way along life's highway, on and off the pitch.

There was so much to be discovered that hadn't already seen the light of day about a genuine Scottish football legend. I delved through newspapers, scrutinised cuttings, scoured magazines, checked out books, devoured matchday programmes, visited libraries, watched hours of TV, video and DVD footage and interviewed so many people who were happy to give their time to talk freely about the one and only Denis Law. Thank you everyone. There are too many to mention, but you know who you are. Also, I would like to express my gratitude to Neville Moir and Peter Burns at Birlinn.

A special round of applause must go to my good friend Fraser Elder, a stalwart of journalism for as long as Denis has been around. Thankfully my mate, by his own admission, is a hoarder. On his travels throughout the world, Fraser, working in all aspects of the media from TV and radio to the written word, has picked up a veritable treasure trove of football memorabilia. For instance, he magically produced the matchday souvenir brochure for the England v. Rest of the World FA Centenary celebrations at Wembley on 23 October 1963, when Denis Law played alongside his great hero Alfredo di Stefano. That's just one instance; there are so many more. Fraser became a man possessed as he unearthed gem after gem, facts and statistics of which, I have to admit, I didn't even realise existed. His help, professional dedication and kindness will never be forgotten; there is a lot in this tribute to Denis Law that would never have been seen if it wasn't for my pal. Thank you, Fraz.

AUTHOR'S NOTE

I was enjoying a welcome pint of cold frothing ale with my good friend Davie Hay in a quiet little pub one day when I mentioned I was thinking of writing this very book. Yes, I realised Denis had already been involved in at least three excellent autobiographies, but I was also aware that they, as you might have expected, majored on his time with Manchester United, a massive chunk of his career and life. A chapter in each tome had been set aside for his international experiences. To my mind, there was so much more to discover about Denis Law, as patriotic a Scot as you are ever likely to meet. One chapter per book on his playing days with Scotland was never going to be adequate. There had to be a full book on this colourful character's devotion to Scotland. As I dropped the idea on Davie, he looked at me, grinned and, without a flicker of hesitation, said matter-of-factly, 'Denis Law, Scotland's first football superstar.'

Just like that. Absolutely spot-on. Six little words. I smiled and ordered another drink for my mate – it was well worth it. The book came alive in that instant.

SIR ALEX FERGUSON

It's hard to say something about Denis Law that hasn't already been said by countless people over the years. Quite simply, he was the finest player that Scotland has ever produced and one of the greatest the world has ever seen. He was my idol as a player.

Denis Law is one of the all-time great stars of football and that opinion would have had a much broader base had he played in more international tournaments. World Cups and European Championships provide a huge profile and there are few great players who break into the world class category who haven't displayed their skills regularly in the big international contests.

To say that Denis is the finest talent to come from 'North of the Border' is in itself a huge accolade. The Scottish national side may not be the team it once was, but there were times when Scotland could boast numerous outstanding players. Richly-gifted individuals such as Alan Morton, Hughie Gallacher, Jim Baxter, Jimmy Johnstone, John White, Billy Bremner, Willie Henderson, Kenny Dalglish and Alex Ferguson (how did he get in there?), and that's just a few of the names that trip off the tongue.

It's no wonder that the fans of the Stretford End were quick to crown him as their 'King' when he moved to Manchester United from Italian club Torino in 1962. He was in the early years of his incredible career, but he had already stamped his mark on the game. Lightning quick, fearless, dynamic, good with both feet, spectacular – and sometimes unbelievably devastating – in the air, he was as near as damn it the perfect goalscoring individual.

Anyone who saw him in his halcyon days was privileged in the extreme to see a total footballing craftsman in action and I'm immensely proud to say that he's a Scotsman.

There are not a lot of years between Denis and myself, but I list him as one of my heroes, and a close friend.

SIR ALEX FERGUSON

THE PATRIOT

Playing for Scotland is, without doubt, the greatest honour anyone could have bestowed upon me. It really doesn't matter if it's football, rugby, athletics or whatever; it's a massive honour to represent your country, though, particularly in football as it's the national game. It was always a thrill to be informed that you were playing, no matter whether it was against Jutland, Norway or Brazil. As the old saying goes, you would play for your country for nothing: the money side of things doesn't even come into the equation. That certainly holds true for me at any rate.

DENIS LAW

INTRODUCTION

BY ROYAL APPOINTMENT

Artiste and assassin. Entertainer and executioner. Showman and swordsman.

Denis Law. The name simply shimmers and sparkles with charisma. It whisks you off to a golden, bygone era when football truly was the beautiful game. Performing for his country, he was the Dark Blue Pimpernel, a character with a rare and spectacular combination of elegance and menace; a debonair destroyer; a master of improvisation; a contortionist in the penalty box. He was the Demon King, clinical and nerveless, possessor of lightning, gravity-defying reflexes to unleash hell, or open the gates to heaven, depending on which side you were on.

Unique and uncompromising. Beguiling and brave. Flamboyant and fearsome.

Denis Law. Scotland's favourite footballing son, the offspring – the last of seven – of an Aberdeen trawler man and a school cleaning lady. A special talent whose daring deeds on the field of battle are the stuff of legend. A one-off, the genuine article, there will never be a replica. An exponent of danger zone spontaneity; a devotee of creating mayhem in packed defences. The millions who were fortunate to get a close-up view of this extraordinarily-gifted individual were swept along as he lived the dream.

Talented and tenacious. Performer and predator. Cavalier and controversial.

Denis Law. A free spirit who engaged your mind, emotions and ambitions. An individual who embodied and captured the very essence of a small and proud nation that was always up for the skirmish, always determined to punch above its weight. An icon who was never addicted to the spotlight; a man who never craved publicity. Try to give him the red carpet treatment and he'll head for the back door. Put him in a football strip, though, and things happened. Marvellous, exceptional and memorable things. He was the football hero's football hero.

And Scottish ... passionately Scottish.

He brought Hollywood to Hampden. The shock of blond hair, the arm thrust into the air, the cuff tightly gripped, the back ramrod-stiff, the jersey flapping outside the shorts and the magisterial strut after leaving another scene of devastation behind him.

He was the main attraction, irresistibly so. The quintessential Scotsman. There may have been imitators and even impostors, but Denis Law was the real deal. You really shouldn't compete with a legend. He was light years away from us mere mortals, but somehow had a relationship with us; some sort of captivating connection with the man on the terracing.

How else can you explain a collection of schoolboys congregating outside a tenement block at 54 Dougrie Road in Castlemilk, a council estate on the south side of Glasgow, on the freezing cold evening of 7 November 1963 preparing to walk almost two miles to Hampden Park to watch Scotland play Norway, hardly a world force and consisting almost solely of amateur players? It was a friendly encounter of very little importance, the game largely meaningless and the result, too, probably. But Denis Law was in town, in the team and around ten young lads – aged between 11 and 13 – weren't going to pass up the opportunity of witnessing their soccer god in action. Another 35,400-or so supporters agreed with us. The weather was dreadful and, in fact, the game had to be put back 24 hours after a blanket of fog had engulfed the city the previous evening. However, we trekked to the national stadium bursting with curiosity, wondering what Law might conjure up beyond the relative mundane, muck and nettles of ordinary football fare served up on a weekly basis in domestic football. There wasn't anyone to compare with the great man. Yes, we had Jim Baxter, Jimmy Johnstone, Willie Henderson, Billy McNeill, Alan Gilzean and so many other exceptional worthies. But they weren't Denis Law.

He possessed something extra that the others didn't have and, as an 11-year-old, obviously I would have found it impossible to define. Nevertheless, it was there alright. We could merely watch in wonderment and awe as he performed as only he could. Floating majestically in mid-air, a snap of the neck muscles like an angry cobra, pent-up energy released to perfection at the moment of impact, and the ball whizzing beyond another bewildered goalkeeper. Only the terminally stupid among the defensive fraternity ever eagerly anticipated confronting this combustible character.

My pals and I, a mixture of supporters of Celtic, Rangers, Clyde, Third Lanark, Partick Thistle, Queen's Park and, if I recall correctly, one Falkirk fan, met on that particular November evening in 1963 with the skies already turning slate grey; the fog being replaced with the very real threat of a downpour. Naturally enough, as you might expect, not one of us hardy souls would be the possessor of that wonderful invention, the umbrella. No matter. Off we went along Dougrie Road, passing St Margaret Mary's Secondary School and then the stretch of three-storied tenement buildings on Birgidale Road on our left, Castleton Primary School on the opposite side and eventually turning right into Carmunnock Road and heading down towards Croftfoot roundabout, passing the Bluebell Woods on our left, the vibrant summer colours having long since surrendered to the dark and dank conditions of an uncompromising change of season. Then we journeyed beyond a row of shops on either side and onto Aikenhead Road, with King's Park, very stately we thought, on the right.

Our determined trek would take us past the Wylie and Loch-head funeral parlour at the corner of leafy Southwood Drive. On the same trip a couple of years later, there was always a pause at this particular juncture among the Celtic-supporting fraternity. They would go through the 'we are not worthy' salutations directed towards a neat and tidy bungalow at the end of the stretch; home of the legendary Jock Stein. Some-how you always felt in awe of this particular pile of bricks and mortar. Jock Stein actually lived here. We couldn't have been more impressed if The Queen herself had invited us in for tea at Buckingham Palace. The voyage would continue along Aikenhead Road past the Territorial Army recruitment centre. We would pass the Beechwood Bar, bulging with Scottish sup-porters and obviously doing brisk business.

Our hearts pumped a little faster as the towering Hampden Park floodlights, at half-beam some 40 minutes before kick-off, loomed into view. Valhalla was a mere handful of minutes away. There was a great wee fish and chip shop on the way and some of my chums would look at their admission money and wonder if it was worth taking the risk of purchasing a poke of chips – 3d – and then relying on some kind supporters to give them a lift over the turnstile. It happened all the time back then and that was when you actually envied the wee guys. There never seemed to be a problem with them. Me? I think I came out the womb at six foot two inches, so there was little point in me making such a request to some bloke who came up to my navel. Denis Law or a poke of chips? There was only ever going to be one winner.

Then our travels would come to a halt outside Scotland's football fortress. We had arrived at our destination and we would soon be watching the Great Man in action. Exciting times, indeed. Even pre-match, Denis Law looked special. He was style personified. The way he caressed the ball, the manner in which he kicked it, the stabbed pass to a colleague. Then it was time for the 7.30 p.m. kick-off, the floodlights now on full-beam and lighting up the pitch, illuminating the frosty, glistening playing surface. We had our own little spot in the middle of the terracing about halfway up the West Stand, known commonly as the Rangers End. We didn't even think of such things back then. As far as religious matters were concerned, we were a motley crew from Castlemilk; Catholics, Protestants, believers, non-believers, don't-knows and don't-cares. We were football fans.

Once again, on the evening in question, our idol didn't disappoint. In fact, he sent a bunch of kids all the way back home with beaming smiles, the rain now drifting into our exposed faces. No-one complained as we had just witnessed one of those extraordinary one-man displays that Denis Law seemed to be able to produce with wondrous regularity. He thumped in four goals during a runaway 6-1 triumph, with Spurs' Dave Mackay helping himself to the other two. Drenched, we would get to our homes about an hour later; smiles still intact. Happy days.

Years later, on Friday 23 May 1975, to be exact, Denis Law impressed me once again. I was 23 years old at the time and working on the sports desk of the *Daily Record* as a sub-editor. The location had switched from Glasgow to London and the Scottish support had arrived mob-handed, as usual, for the bi-annual encounter with the Auld Enemy, England, at Wembley. Half of Scotland seemed to have poured itself into the two bars in the White House Hotel on Euston Road near Regent's Park. The bevvy was flowing, the hours were ticking down and it was clear to see that the alcohol was taking hold of a few who had probably saved up for two years for this event.

There was a great wee pub in York Street along Glasgow's Broomielaw called Dick's Bar. A lot of the *Daily Record* and *Sunday Mail* journalists used it as a favourite watering hole and there was a real eclectic mix in this establishment, which, alas, is no longer there. John Dick was the genial host, but he ruled with a rod of iron. There was such a thing as 'The Wembley Fund' and the book opened probably minutes after the final whistle at Wembley for another two years of collecting cash before the fixture came round again. If someone felt flush, had a win on the horses, fiddled their expenses or found a pound they would put some money behind the bar, saving for the trip across the border. Now, take it from me, they never saw a penny of that cash until they were ready to travel to Wembley two years later. It didn't matter that they might be about to be evicted or their kids hadn't eaten for days. They knew the score. John Dick put the cash away for them and told them it was under lock and key for the next 24 months. Then, and only then, would they get their money in full. Punters from that pub used to arrive at Wembley Stadium in stretch limos, they had so much disposable dosh.

Anyway, more than a few of the revellers in the White House Hotel the evening before the match must have had similar arrangements with their local pub owners. As so often happens, some of them had seen their senses washed away in a sea of booze. A few of them appeared to have parked their brains at the border. I detected friction among some of the supporters. It didn't matter they were all wearing kilts and looking like extras from *Braveheart*, they were more than ready for a little bout of handbags at dawn. It wasn't quite The McDonalds v The Campbells, but there was more than a hint of trouble in the air. It was about to turn a tad nasty when a bloke wearing a crisp white open-neck shirt, dark blue jacket, smart grey trousers and black slip-on shoes came in the front door. 'Now, boys', was all he said. They seemed to snap to attention, almost saluting in the process. Peace had broken out. Only Denis Law could have achieved that. Pity he couldn't turn out the following day; we were walloped 5-1.

It would be another 14 years before I was finally introduced to Denis Law, at Hampden of all places. The setting was another

Scotland v. England confrontation and, by this time, I was sports editor of the *Sunday Mail*. I went along to the game with the newspaper's two top sportswriters, Don Morrison and Dixon Blackstock. It was a glorious May day as we mulled about the packed pressbox. Don and Dixon, as you might expect as field journalists, had met Denis on numerous occasions but, having worked mainly as a production journalist, I had never had the pleasure.

I was reading the match programme when I received a tap on the shoulder. Don said, 'Alex, I would like you to meet someone.' I turned and smack in front of me was my all-time football hero. Denis Law was standing there, balancing a pile of sandwiches, sausage rolls and pies. Juggling with the eateries, he managed to shake my hand. 'Great to meet you,' I gushed, or it could have been, 'Meet to great you' I was so taken by surprise. 'Same here,' returned Denis with that cheeky grin of his. He told me he was covering the game for radio – the BBC's World Service – and I said, 'I see you are looking after your colleagues,' pointing to the mountain of grub he had selected. 'No chance. These are for me – the English can look after themselves,' he laughed. And with that he was off.

If Neil Armstrong will never forget landing on the moon, then it's an identical feeling for me meeting Denis Law. Sounds way over the top, I accept, but it's true. I would interview him several times after that and you will not be surprised to discover he was always a complete gentleman, helpful and courteous. A genuine rarity in that he would take the time to telephone you back, too, if you left a message. Denis Law telephoning Alex Gordon? Wonder of wonders.

The long and winding journeys for a primary school kid to Hampden on bitingly-cold winter evenings in the early sixties to witness first-hand a master craftsman going about his profession seem an eternity ago. Unforgettable, though.

CHAPTER ONE

THE MAN, THE MYTH AND THE MAGIC

George Best was often fond of telling the following tale about his great mate Denis Law. The Northern Irishman's eyes would twinkle with mischief as the story unfolded. He would reminisce about a happier time when he and his wife, Alex, went on holiday to Portugal and met up with Denis and Diana and the Law family.

Denis insisted on taking the Bests to a little restaurant he had discovered in the Algarve. 'When we arrived at this place, we thought it was some kind of joke played on us by Denis,' Best recalled. 'The place was called The Chicken Shack and it was just that – a shack that sold chicken. But Denis was deadly serious and played the good host by telling us about the food and introducing us to the manager. I had chicken and chips, Alex had chicken and chips, Di had chicken and chips and, would you believe, Denis went for chicken and chips. When the bill came, Denis waved it in front of my nose triumphantly and said, "Look at that, where else on the Algarve can four people eat for that price?" He continued smiling and added, "And it includes wine, you know."'

Denis Law? The stereotypical tight-fisted Aberdonian? Yes, they are canny with a penny in that part of the world. Denis does not fall into the category of a miser, though. Far from it. I can think of a few instances when he has gone out of his way to do a favour without any hint of recompense.

A few years ago a good friend of mine, a proud Yorkshireman

1

by the name of Alec Harper, was about to celebrate his 60th birthday. His lovely wife Judith had adopted MI5 and KGB tactics in keeping the big night quiet. It was a genuine surprise to my old mate when the evening of the party at a local hotel came round. Alec, for his sins, is a massive Huddersfield Town fan. There is only a seven-year gap between Denis and Alec, but my pal idolised that man. He could get misty-eyed of an evening and say, 'You know, lad, it was all downhill after Denis left.' He meant it, too. I have tried to remind him that Denis, in fact, hadn't been anywhere near the old ground at Leeds Road since the spring of 1960. Alec, however, would insist, 'We could have been a real force in Europe, lad, if he had stuck around.'

I contacted Denis and asked him if he wouldn't mind signing a replica 1950s Huddersfield Town top and a birthday card for my mate. There wasn't the merest hint of hesitation. 'Sure,' he said, 'I'll be happy to oblige.' Sure enough, a couple of days before my wife Gerda and I were due to fly to Manchester, the shirt and card arrived. On the big night, I handed the gifts to Alec. I swear he almost fainted. 'Is this really Denis Law's signature?' he asked. 'Is this a wind-up?' I assured him they were the genuine articles. He spent the rest of the evening mingling among the guests with his treasured presents, proudly showing them off. He may have turned 60 that day, but a gesture from Denis Law appeared to have swept the clock back about 55 years. When it came to making his speech in front of around 400 guests, all Alec could talk about was his shirt and card. Judith, who had worked tirelessly under cover to put the event together, didn't even get a mention! She forgave him; she was well aware of what Denis Law meant to her husband.

I have also got to point out that I have interviewed Denis several times for newspaper and magazine features over the years and not once has he asked for a penny. He has given his time freely. I can tell you there are other individuals, who shouldn't be talked about in the same breath as Denis Law, whose first words when you get in touch with them are, 'How much?' These guys are hardly on the breadline. Yes, if it's an exclusive story, done in a first person manner, then, of course, I believe there should be a payment. But if it's only for a couple of quotes about something relatively mundane? Every newspaper in the land would be bankrupt in double-quick time.

Pat Crerand knows Law better than most and insists his good friend has knocked back fairly hefty fees in the past for commercial enterprises. 'Denis made few public appearances and preferred his privacy to the fees he could have picked up,' Crerand said. 'When he was in a Manchester hospital recovering from a knee injury that would rule him out of the 1968 European Cup Final against Benfica, the BBC thought it would be a good idea to put cameras into Denis's hospital room. The game was being beamed live on television, of course, and they wanted to show his reaction and perhaps get his comments at the end. Matt Busby raised no objections to this idea and the hospital authorities were quite willing to allow a camera crew to set up at his bedside. The only person who didn't like the idea was Denis. He said, "No" and that was that.'

Crerand also revealed his mate could be a bit reclusive when he felt like it. 'He avoided public places where he would be quickly recognised and in many ways he was a lone wolf. He even had his own gimmick for not getting involved. If, after training, some of the boys asked him what he was doing in the afternoon, he would always answer "gardening" with a straight face. He wouldn't know one end of a weed from the other, but it gave him an excuse to go off on his own and earned him the nickname, The Gardener.

'Denis chose his company very carefully. He would rather have a beer in a quiet pub with ordinary blokes than mix it with celebrities at a cocktail party. If he liked you, then Denis could be great company, but there was no middle road with him. If he didn't like someone he wouldn't talk to them.'

3

Crerand's friendship with his fellow Scot didn't preclude him from getting it in the ear when Denis was unhappy. Harry Gregg, the Manchester United and Northern Ireland goalkeeping legend, recalled Crerand being on the receiving end of a verbal salvo from Law before a European Cup game against Benfica in Lisbon in 1966. 'We had won 3-2 in the first leg at Old Trafford, so obviously, we were all a bit uptight at meeting this great Portuguese side in front of their own fans at the famous Stadium of Light,' Gregg remembered. 'Before the kick-off, we were all sitting there going through our usual routines. I recall it was a lovely dressing room and one wall was completely covered with a mirror.

'Pat Crerand was standing around juggling the ball from foot to foot. The next thing we knew there was this tremendous crash. The mirror was on the floor, smashed to smithereens. Denis let rip at his fellow Scot. The language was choice. The last word was hooligan and I'll let you fill in the blanks before it. Some footballers can be a bit superstitious. What do you get for breaking a mirror? Seven years' bad luck? Crerand had taken down an entire wall! What could we now expect when we ran onto the pitch to face Benfica? Almost straight away George Best scored with a header. At half-time we were 3-0 up and I'll never forget what Crerand said to the Lawman in the dressing room during the interval. He looked at him and, completely stone-faced, asked, "Can someone else find another mirror?" The place just cracked up. We went on to win 5-1 and Crerand, in fact, scored a rare goal. It was a great night in Manchester United's history.'

Gregg remains a good friend of Law to this day and revealed, 'Off the field, Denis was a completely different person to the one who displayed such fire and bravado during his day job. Even now, when required to do after-dinner speaking or appear in company, he'll still come across as cheeky, chirpy and full of confidence. But it's an act, something he turns on, rather than it being his natural way.

'Denis is a quiet lad at heart, more of a thinker than his extrovert alter ego would suggest. He has always been his own man, even at United, where Matt Busby was the archetypal authoritarian. If Denis made up his mind about something, nothing – and I mean nothing on God's earth – would shift him. Take injuries, for instance. The rest of us might have been easy to talk into playing if we were carrying a knock. Not Denis.

'Matt's presence in the dressing room was enough to sway most at least to test their injuries in training. However, this tactic failed miserably with Denis. Matt would ask, "Would you not give it a go, son?" Denis would just stand with his back to the boss and say nothing. In his own good time, he would then change into his kit and stroll down the tunnel past Matt. Then he would return, change and leave – all this without a word being exchanged. I consider Denis Law a good friend. I respected him as a player and I respect him as a person. Denis is the sort of fellow you could really depend on. In fact, there are not many players I would say this about, but I would bet my life on him.'

Sir Alex Ferguson doesn't hesitate when he goes on record about Denis Law. 'Scotland's greatest-ever footballer,' the Manchester United legend emphasises in the Foreword. The managerial doyen goes on, 'He was my hero. He typified my idea of a Scottish footballer. He was dashing, he was mischievous. He was everything I wanted to be. There were occasions when you were just waiting for Denis to cause trouble. A lot of Scots can do that, you know. It was his way of telling the world, "You're not going to kick me." He had wonderful courage and daring. There is a lot in Denis Law that we Scots appreciate. He was pure theatre and knew how to work the crowd. I saw him make his debut against Wales at Ninian Park in Cardiff in 1958 and I watched him in his next game against Northern Ireland when he kicked their captain Danny Blanchflower up and down the park! He was told to mark the great Spurs player, but he took it too literally. He was only 18 years old at the time, too, and Danny was one of the best players in Britain. I think it was Pele who said Denis was the only British player who could get into the Brazilian team. That says it all.'

Bertie Auld played alongside Law in three international games and is still a close friend. 'He was a fabulous guy to be around, a real man's man,' Auld said. 'I made my Scotland debut against Holland in Amsterdam in May 1959. Denis was playing that day, too, and we hit it off. He oozed charisma, but he was far from being big-headed. He was just one of the lads and never came across as Billy Big-Time. We went for a wee walk through Amsterdam after a training session one afternoon and found it to be an interesting city – although possibly not as interesting as it is today! But I spotted that Denis was getting noticed by some of the locals. No wonder. He actually looked like a movie star. He was wearing this fabulous camel-haired coat, with a big collar and belt. Denis wasn't trying to attract attention, he just did. And this was before he went to Turin and caught up with the Italian fashion which was all the rage at the time.

'He was a dream to play alongside, too. Utterly unselfish. There was none of this superstar stuff with Denis. No chance. He was one of the boys and raced around and chased the ball all day. You watch some of the petulant prima donnas strutting around and preening themselves today and I can tell you they haven't got a fraction of the talent or the ability Denis possessed. He was genuine class, no argument. I wish I could say it was a thoroughly enjoyable experience making my first appearance for my country alongside Denis, but, sadly, I can't. I was sent off after a bit of a skirmish, but, on a happier note, we still won 2-1 with goals from my wee pal Bobby Collins and that great Aberdeen and Fulham player Graham Leggat.

'It got a bit untidy at one stage and I can assure you Denis wasn't slow to get in there with some Dutch heavyweights. There were tackles flying around everywhere and the Dutch fans were baying for blood. There were over 55,000 in the ground, as I recall, and it couldn't have been more competitive if it had been the World Cup Final. You look at Denis and there isn't a pick on him. He certainly didn't take one of those Charles Atlas courses that were around at the time. You know the ones I mean. The advertisement of this muscle-bound bloke, posing in tight swimming trunks, saying, "You, too, can have a body like mine. No-one will ever kick sand in your face." Denis would probably have made mincemeat of him. It was only too easy to be impressed by Denis. There wasn't an awful lot of him, but he really got stuck in. It's rare that a guy who is so obviously gifted gets involved in the physical side of things. There are some blokes out there who can play football alright, but they couldn't tackle a fish supper. Not Denis. I never saw him shirk a challenge in my life.'

Bobby Collins, who would leave Celtic for Everton for £23,500 in 1958, a massive fee at the time, played in the Scottish team against Wales on 18 October 1958, when Law, at 18, made his international debut. 'We had heard about the lad, of course,' Collins said. 'He was making a name for himself at Huddersfield Town, but you could only go by what you read in the newspapers. There weren't television cameras at every ground as there are today, so we were still a bit in the dark about this teenager. Sometimes the press can go a bit overboard and exaggerate a player's skills. Professionals like to make up their own minds. We saw him at first-hand against the Welsh that day and, boy, could that lad play. Within minutes you instinctively knew you were in the presence of someone special, very special.

'I was lucky enough to play another six games alongside Denis spanning seven years. A month after his debut against Wales, I scored in a 2-2 draw with Northern Ireland and the following May I was fortunate enough to net again in the 2-1 win over Holland in Amsterdam. A week later we lost 1-0 to

Portugal in Lisbon and, amazingly, it was another six whole years before we lined up alongside each other again. I came out of international exile to play in the 2-2 draw with England at Wembley where Denis scored a truly fantastic goal with a shot that completely bamboozled Gordon Banks. Believe me, it took a lot to surprise a goalkeeper of Gordon's calibre and ability. Denis could do it, though. That was in April and the following month we had a goalless draw against Spain at Hampden. Perhaps fittingly, Denis was on target against Poland in our 1-1 World Cup qualifying draw in Chorzow in the parting of our ways. It was his farewell gift to me. I can look back and realise how fortunate I was to play alongside Denis. He was the best, no argument.'

Former Rangers captain and manager John Greig performed alongside Law on 18 occasions for his country and is another with fond and treasured memories. 'When it comes to strikers, there was none braver or more aggressive than Denis Law,' Greig said. 'My Scotland teammate may have looked puny, but he had the heart of a lion and would have fought with his shadow. Denis loved to play against England – and hated losing to them because of the stick he took from his English teammates at Old Trafford. He was also deceptively strong and fought for every ball, but it was in the air that Denis really excelled. He seemed to have the capacity to hang in the air when he jumped for the ball. When I met him for the first time, Denis made an instant impression; he had an almost magical aura because of his personality. I remember early in my international career, when the squad was based in Largs on the Ayrshire coast, going to Denis's room just to chat to him. He sat with a pot of tea and a packet of fags and regaled me with fascinating tales. Denis is quite a private person, but he was a truly great player.'

Billy McNeill made his international debut alongside Law in April 1961. 'Nothing to do with Denis, but I would prefer to forget all about that particular afternoon,' said the Celtic legend. 'It was one of the worst days of my career. I was only 21 years old and making a wee bit of a name for myself when I was given the nod to face England at Wembley. Excited? You bet. However, if it could go wrong that day, it did. We were trounced 9-3 and it was a truly horrible experience. I am as proud a Scot as the next guy and that really hurt. My Celtic teammate Frank Haffey was in goal and he took the bulk of the blame, but we all contributed.

'Everything England attempted came off for them while every mistake we made was magnified and punished in the most brutal fashion possible. England took us apart and there was little Denis, myself or our colleagues could do about it. There was a lot of cruel humour afterwards. The ball was orange so it was said that the Rangers full-backs Bobby Shearer and Eric Caldow refused to kick it while Frank Haffey refused to touch it. Those versed in the religious divisions of the West of Scotland will require no further explanation, but for the uninitiated in the eyes of some people the Orange Order represents Protestantism.

'Back then, there seemed to be a Home Scots v. Anglo Scots confrontational situation. Some Scotland supporters actually wanted the international team to consist only of players plying their trade in Scotland. The Anglos, with Denis among them, were seen as some sort of defectors. Ridiculous, of course, and would be laughed at today, but in the fifties and sixties it was a contentious issue. If Scotland failed, the Anglos were the first to get the blame. I know Denis always detested the label Anglo-Scot. He made the point he was born in Aberdeen with a Scottish mother and father and had three Scottish brothers and three Scottish sisters. "How much more Scottish can you get?" he would say.

'In fact, Denis was a revelation when he played and he had few poor games for Scotland. His electrifying darts into the penalty box allied to his razor sharp reflexes were his strongest assets. He also had a wonderful sense of anticipation, which enabled him to snap up half-chances when the ball broke off the goalkeeper or a defender, but perhaps people were less aware of just how tough and durable Denis was. Denis was as hard as nails. He gave and took knocks without complaint. His incredible timing and his ability to appear to almost hover in the air meant he had to be brave when he jumped with a defender.'

George Best backed up McNeill's thoughts. 'I remember one day in training at Manchester United when Bill Foulkes, our big, strapping, powerful centre-half, knocked Denis to the ground. Now, remember, Bill had been working down the mines and only quit at the age of 20 when he broke through in football. He was an authentic tough guy. What happened next? Denis just got up and punched him. Bill hit him back and the next thing everyone was piling in. Denis gave as good as he got.'

The late and much lamented Bill Shankly, in his unmistakeable, porridge-thick Ayrshire accent, rasped, 'I had three years at Huddersfield Town with Denis. He was a young boy and we were giving him special food for energy. He did training sessions that he liked and on Saturdays in matches he'd give you everything he had. He'd run himself into the ground. So you couldn't ask him to do it on the field and off it at his size and weight. But he never held back in training, I can tell you that. Ray Wilson, who won a World Cup medal with England in 1966, was our established first-team left-back when Denis arrived. You should have seen those two go at it in training games. We could have sold tickets for the event.'

Wilson, five years Law's senior, recalled, 'We were staying at the same digs when Denis arrived. Honestly, we thought it must have been some mistake. He looked about 12 years old and he told us he would be training with us. The following day we saw what he could do with a ball. We realised then he was a player. And what a player.'

Later on, as manager of Liverpool, Shankly rarely discussed

at length the strengths of the opposition. Scottish internationals Ian St John and Ron Yeats were among the players sitting in the Anfield dressing room who witnessed a particular gem from their manager, who was in full flow before a game against Manchester United. 'The goalkeeper, Stepney. He's no good in the air and he's not much better on the ground,' Shankly said. 'He's so wee he's got to jump for the low balls. What's the difference between Stepney and Jesus Christ? Jesus saves. And the full-backs, Brennan and Dunne, a couple of clapped-out Paddies, that's what they are, should have been put out to grass years ago. Nobby Stiles, as blind as a bat, runs around the field like a headless chicken, not worth talking about, that lad. Foulkes? Ancient. Older than me. He wasn't even any good when he was young. Sadler needs watching, but no-one ever passes to him so no problems there. The boy Morgan can run a bit, but he can't beat an egg and the other lad, Kidd, can't hold the ball. Big girl's blouse. This team is a shambles. You'll take them apart. You'll run up a cricket score. No problem.'

The Liverpool captain, Emlyn Hughes, put his hand up at the end of the team talk. 'Boss, you haven't mentioned Best, Law or Charlton,' he said. Shankly glared at him. 'Christ, Emlyn, you're worried that you can't beat a team with just three players?' In a more reflective moment, Shankly would admit, 'If we were playing Manchester United, I'd never talk about George Best, Denis Law or Bobby Charlton. If we did, we'd frighten ourselves to death.'

Shankly followed Law's progress with interest. 'Denis was always full of enthusiasm for the game and full of awareness,' the Merseyside legend once recalled. 'He scored the goals he should score. It sounds funny saying that. A lot of players score spectacular goals, but don't score the ones they should score. Denis didn't blast the ball or try to burst the net. All he wanted to do was get the ball over the line. If Denis was through on his own with only the goalkeeper to beat you could get your tea out and drink it – it was going to be a goal. Every player should be taught what to do in any given situation; Law always knew what to do. If the keeper stayed on the line he would take the ball right up to him and say: "Thanks very much," before slipping it into the net. If the keeper came out, he sidestepped him, angled himself and put it into an empty net. Law was quicker than most inside the box. Very, very quick. He was lean and didn't carry any weight. No keeper stood a chance when he had a sniff at goal.'

It was Matt Busby who revolutionised Law's role in football. 'When Denis first arrived at Old Trafford he was all action, all over the pitch,' said Harry Gregg. 'He was, in my eyes, the complete inside-forward. Matt Busby, though, had other ideas and I remember the day he transformed Denis into a purely attacking weapon. We had been going through a rough patch, our performances did not match Matt's expectations. Then, during one team talk, he announced, "From now on, Denis Law does not come back over the halfway line." I thought to myself, "That's a waste, this guy's got so much to offer all over the pitch." In the end, Matt was right. Denis went on to become even more of a prolific goalscorer – his 236 goals in 393 games is all the evidence you need.'

It is ironic, then, that one man who did not believe the switch was for the best was Denis Law himself. He said, 'My favourite player was Alfredo di Stefano, the great Real Madrid star. He could score goals, but he could also perform all over the pitch. That's the way I wanted to play. I liked to play inside-forward. But Matt felt differently and I wasn't happy. Of course, I was delighted to score a goal or two but, in that role, you could miss a lot of the game. I always wanted to be involved. No, I wasn't happy.'

Busby never had any doubt about the devastating finishing ability of Law. 'When I signed Denis I knew that we had the most exciting player in the game,' the United manager said. 'He was the quickest-thinking player I ever saw, seconds quicker than anyone else. He had the most tremendous acceleration and could leap to enormous heights to head the ball with almost unbelievable accuracy and often the power of a shot. He had the courage to take on the biggest and most ferocious of opponents and his passing was impeccable. He was one of the most unselfish players I have ever seen. If he was not in the best position to score he would give the ball to someone who was. When a chance was on for him, even only half a chance, or in some cases, no chance at all for anybody else but for him, whether he had his back to goal, was sideways on, or the ball was on the deck or up at shoulder-height, he would have it in the net with such power and acrobatic agility that colleagues and opponents alike could only stand and gasp. No other player scored as many miracle goals as Denis Law. Goals which looked simple as Denis tapped them in were simple only because Denis got himself into position so quickly that opponents just couldn't cope with him.

'He was the first British player to salute the crowd. Early on at Old Trafford, the multitudes cheered him and he soon became what the crowd called him – The King. With his sharp reflexes, he became the most dangerous man in a penalty box I ever saw. Even in the ordinary scrimmaging for the ball, Denis could be spotted a mile off. With his arms and legs flailing about in a bid to get to the ball first, he looked twice as physically dangerous as he really was. He was brave, too. I have seen his legs after many a game, virtually slashed to ribbons, with blood and cuts all over the place. He never complained and always went back for more.'

Bobby Charlton, who, along with Law and Best, formed the awe-inspiring talent-laden trio which became known as the Manchester United Trinity, understood well the merits of his former teammate and dangerous international foe. 'There was a period around the mid-sixties when Denis was free from injury

13

and then we saw the full scale of his brilliance,' Charlton said. 'He was an awesome sight as he went into dangerous places, daring a centre-half or a goalkeeper to blink. He got up to incredible heights and when he did so the defenders knew they couldn't afford half a mistake. The semblance of a slip was all he needed. The ball would be in the back of the net and his arm would be shooting skyward.

'What the fans loved most about Denis, I believe, was his incredible aggression and self-belief. There were times when he seemed to define urgency on a football field and there was always a gleam in his eye. They never made a big centre-half who could induce in Denis even a flicker of apprehension. One of the most amazing things I witnessed was his decision to take on big Ron Yeats, the man once described as the 'New Colossus' by his Liverpool manager Bill Shankly. Denis scarcely came up to the man's shoulder, but he was in his face throughout the game, chivvying, needling, always at the point of maximum danger. I remember thinking, "This is ridiculous, impossible," and for anyone else but Denis it certainly would have been.'

England's 1966 World Cup-winning goalkeeper Gordon Banks has an interesting take on Law. He said, 'Denis could be arrogant, precocious, evil-tempered, hilariously funny and simply brilliant all in the space of a few minutes. Often, when the pressure of the match was at its peak, Denis brought a smile to my face with a sudden aside. That was at club level. When he was playing for Scotland, he didn't have a good thing to say to any of us Sassenachs.'

Law praised the England goalkeeper. 'If you scored against Banksie you knew you had earned it,' he said. Banks returned the compliment and rated the Scotsman in fourth place in his all-time Top Ten Strikers list. Pele came first, with Jimmy Greaves second and Gerd Muller third. Then came Law, ahead of George Best, Bobby Charlton, Eusebio, Johan Cruyff, and Jairzinho with Geoff Hurst and Roger Hunt joint tenth. 'I thought Denis was a great competitor,' Banks said. 'The press often referred to him as the Electric Eel. I think Electric Heel would have been more appropriate. He had such fast reactions in the penalty box that it was as if he was plugged into the mains. I will always remember – with mixed feelings – his remarkable performance for Manchester United against Leicester City in the 1963 FA Cup Final. He produced one of the greatest forward displays ever seen at Wembley and inspired United to a 3-1 triumph. Denis, a menace if ever there was one, scored one goal and was jumping in celebration of another when his header struck the bar. I turned expecting to see the ball in the back of the net and, gratefully, received the rebound into my arms. Denis threw both arms in the air and collapsed to his knees. He always was one for theatrical gestures.'

Nobby Stiles, Law's United teammate and another of Sir Alf Ramsey's world conquerors, laughed, 'We were good friends at Old Trafford, but you couldn't talk to him in the tunnel or during an international game. And you knew he was taking these encounters seriously when you noticed he was wearing shin guards. They weren't compulsory back then and Denis rarely wore them. But when he was facing England, they were in place and you realised, to your dismay, that he was up for a scrap.'

Another World Cup winner, Jack Charlton, had a few head-to-heads with Law during their playing days at club and country level. He recalled, 'We were drawn against Manchester United in the semi-finals of the FA Cup. The first encounter was at Hillsborough and was a bad-tempered affair which ended in a goalless draw. I had a number of clashes in the penalty area with Denis, nearly pulling the shirt off his back on more than one occasion. You had to hang on to Denis because he was so sharp and so good in the air. I used to hate playing against him, though I have always regarded him as a good pal of mine.

'Denis was a great competitor. I'll never forget going for a cross in a game at Elland Road and, as I went to volley the ball clear, suddenly Denis was diving over me and heading it into the net. I kicked Denis right in the mouth. I really walloped him – not deliberately, of course. Anyway, I remember Denis lying on his back and there's blood and everything coming out of his nose and mouth while the trainer was sponging him down. I was standing over him as he started to come to. He looked up at me and smiled, "Did I score, big fella?"

'There was talk of me having a little black book with the names of players I would be looking out for. I didn't really have such a thing, but I did have perhaps five or six players in mind who had committed nasty tackles on me and whose names I wouldn't forget in a hurry. You always remember the names of people who have done you wrong. I would get them back if I could. But I would do it within the laws of the game. A lot of people thought Chelsea's Peter Osgood topped my list, but that wasn't the case. Ossie and I had some good battles, but I don't remember doing anything untoward in my duels with him and I can't recall him ever doing anything untoward to me. The same was true of Denis. I've still got two or three of Denis's shirts at home that I ripped off his back.'

Charlton also recalled a funny moment minutes after another hectic confrontation between Leeds United and Manchester United. 'It was 1965 and I was sitting in the dressing room, caked in mud, when I got news I had been chosen by Alf Ramsey for the England team that was due to play Scotland in April,' he said. 'It was the first time I had been picked. I was so excited I knew I had to tell Bobby right away. I practically ran into our opponents' dressing room and said, "Hey, kidda, I've just been told I'm going to play for England against Scotland! What do you think about that?" Denis was far from impressed with my big news. I believe I was "invited" to leave the premises and he "would sort me out at Wembley". The international ended 2-2 and, yes, Denis scored.'

A teenage Bobby Lennox, who became a Celtic favourite who

would play alongside Law in the memorable 3-2 triumph over world champions England at Wembley in 1967, occasionally travelled through to Glasgow from the family home in the Ayrshire holiday resort of Saltcoats to take in games at Parkhead and Hampden. He remembered an outing at the national stadium in 1961: 'I went to see Denis Law, then at Torino, playing for an Italian Select in a 1-1 draw with the Scottish League. He was a glamorous player, almost godlike in comparison to the rest of the players. He stood out from the crowd.'

Lennox also recalled Law's generous side when he agreed to travel to Fife to play in a posthumous testimonial match staged in the winter of 1974 for John Lunn, the Dunfermline defender who had been diagnosed with leukaemia and had sadly died of the disease the previous year. 'A team was put together to play Dunfermline and there were five players each from Celtic and Rangers – plus Denis Law,' Lennox said. 'I thought it was a fine gesture from Denis, who had actually retired just three months or so before, to travel up to Fife for that occasion. That typified the man.'

Former Celtic manager and player Davie Hay admitted, 'Denis was my boyhood hero when I was growing up in Paisley. Back then, you didn't get anything like the media coverage we have these days. We knew Denis had gone off to play in Italy with Torino and that sounded very adventurous. A Scot playing in the Italian League? It was unusual back then and it's still unusual nowadays. The difference between, say, Joe Jordan playing for AC Milan and Graeme Souness with Sampdoria in the eighties, is that we knew what was happening with them. In the early sixties, Denis might as well have been playing on the moon. He had gone into uncharted territory, but I'm not surprised that he took on the challenge.

'Denis, quite rightly, had a great belief in his ability. It was a joy to spend some time in his company. Denis was just a down-to-earth character and it wasn't an act. I called him an ordinary superstar. He was liked by everyone and joined in with the lads when we went for a pint. You had to remind yourself sometimes that you were actually mixing with a true soccer great.

'Who could ever forget the high jinks in Largs one crazy morning – I believe it was around 4 or 5 a.m., but I can't be sure – in 1974 when my wee mate Jimmy Johnstone was cut adrift on a boat? It would be fair to say a few ales had been partaken by several of the lads, Denis among them. Someone mischievously pushed out the rowing boat – Sandy Jardine has since owned up – and there was Jinky singing his head off as he headed towards Millport. Then, suddenly, it dawned on Jinky he didn't have any oars. He was genuinely alarmed as the boat drifted away from the shore. Denis was one of the first to spot his pal was in trouble. "He's not joking," said Denis. "He needs help." Now, I know Denis isn't a big fan of water, so he was staying put on land. Erich Schaedler, the Hibs full-back, and I jumped into another of the little rowing boats. Our judgement was out a bit – this one had a huge hole in it. We didn't get too far. Eventually, the coastguard was called in to save wee Jinky. Denis, like the rest of us who were involved, can still laugh at that memory today.

'However, the SFA officials were far from pleased with us. We were due to play England at Hampden in a few days' time and they frowned on such behaviour. There was talk of Jinky being sent home. It didn't come to that, thank goodness. In fact, they would have been struggling to put out a team at Hampden on the Saturday because so many of us were involved. Willie Ormond played the Wee Man against the English and, as you might expect, my Celtic pal was unstoppable that afternoon. He put in a marvellous shift and we won 2-0. I recall Jinky swapping shirts with England goalkeeper Peter Shilton and then running to the trackside to look up at the press box. He was unhappy at their reporting of events in Largs and gave them the two-fingered salute. Or was he just reminding them we had scored two goals that day? Denis didn't play in that game which was a shame because it was a perfect setting for the Lawman.'

Johnstone, who sadly passed away at the age of 61 on 13 March 2006 after a five-year battle with motor neurone disease, once recalled a great act of kindness by Law. The little Celtic winger had played in a 3-2 Home International win over Wales at Hampden, but hadn't performed at his best. Rangers fans in the ground set up a chant of 'Willie Henderson ... Willie Henderson' for their own outside-right, a direct rival for Johnstone's position in the team. Johnstone, after winning only his sixth cap, was disillusioned. Injury prevented Law from playing that evening, but he was still at Hampden to watch the action. Afterwards at the Central Hotel, in Glasgow, where the Scots were staying, Johnstone recalled Law coming over to him, saying, 'Well done, Wee Man, you were brilliant.' The Celtic winger said, 'I knew otherwise, of course, but I will always be grateful to Denis for that gesture. I could have crawled into a hole and no-one would have noticed that night. But Denis tried to buck me up and it was a great tonic.'

Gigi Peronace, the Italian agent who lured Law and Joe Baker to Torino in 1961, said, 'They cost around £100,000 each, big money for British players in those days and they convinced the Turin public that their old great team was back. The speed and technical brilliance of Law reminded the supporters of their former hero, Valentino Mazzola. They had never seen anyone quite as quick-thinking as Denis. He was always two or three moves ahead. It was a pity he only stayed a year.'

Tommy Gemmell, Celtic's legendary left-back, has interesting memories of Denis. He said, 'When we were down at the Ayrshire resort of Largs preparing for international games I was always amazed at the amount of tea Denis consumed. He must have downed gallons of the stuff. He always seemed to have a cup in his hand and a wonderful old lady called Mrs Gamley used to run the Queen's Hotel where we stayed. She always made sure there was a fresh brew for "Oor Denis". If you saw someone wandering around with a pot of tea you knew who it was for. And did he like his lamb chops with mint sauce? I'm sure Denis would only ever have eaten lamb chops every day if he could have got away with it. What a staple diet – lamb chops washed down by oceans of tea. It certainly didn't do him any harm, did it?

'For all his fame, Denis was a very unassuming type of guy. He never wanted to take centre stage and was happy just to be a bit-part player off the field. That changed, though, when he crossed that white line and went onto the football pitch. Then he was in his element; that's where he was at his happiest. People have told me they thought he was arrogant. I don't believe that for a minute. He was very comfortable in what he did and he was most certainly a showman, but I don't think he was a show-off and I believe there is a massive difference between both. I never saw him belittle an opponent or rub their nose in it although he certainly possessed the ability and talent to do so. That wasn't his style.

'He was always a great teammate and I'll tell you something else, he had a brother, his name was Joe, who was also very handy to know. He just happened to be the buffet attendant on the Aberdeen to Glasgow rail run. When Celtic were coming back from games at Pittodrie, Jock Stein would let us have a couple of drinks, especially if we had won and we didn't have a midweek fixture. I'm not saying we went over the score, but Denis's brother made sure we were well looked after, if you catch my drift.

'As everyone knows, Denis is a proud Scot. He even made his wife Diana travel across the border to give birth to their kids to make sure they could play for Scotland some day. Remember, these were the years before FIFA relaxed the rule and allowed players to turn out for the countries of the origin of their parents or grandparents. Denis wasn't taking any chances and happily made that journey with a heavily pregnant Diana on a few occasions.

'How much would Denis be worth in today's transfer market? Think of an astronomical figure and multiply by any number you want. The £115,000 Manchester United paid Torino for him in 1962 must be the best money they have ever spent on any player in their history. They've splashed out millions in recent years, but, in terms of genuine ability, no-one can come anywhere near Denis. He was the bargain of the century. I'm told United weren't quite flush when they made their original move for Denis and they were offered a helping hand from a local bookie. If that's true, there should be a plaque somewhere at Old Trafford to honour that bloke.

'I loved playing in the same side as Denis. He never hid even if he wasn't having one of his most memorable outings. That's the sign of a great player. I've seen individuals disappear into an air pocket if they are struggling a wee bit. You are aware they don't want the ball. Not Denis. He always got stuck in and was always around to bail out a teammate if he was in trouble. He was one of the most unselfish players I have ever witnessed.

'We were both very upset one day following a 1-0 defeat from Northern Ireland in Belfast back in 1967 after his Manchester United pal George Best had taken Scotland apart. A photograph appeared on the front page of a national newspaper under the headline: 'WHAT ARE THEY LAUGHING AT?' There was Denis and I coming off the Windsor Park pitch looking as though we were actually smiling after getting turned over. Who says the camera never lies? I don't know if it was a trick of the light or whatever, but I can assure you we were not laughing. It was probably a rueful sigh after watching George Best go through his repertoire that afternoon. When George was in the mood he was unstoppable. Unfortunately for us he was well up for that match against Scotland. No doubt Denis would have had a word with his Old Trafford mate afterwards, possibly not a complimentary one, either. But if anyone looking at that photograph thought we didn't give a stuff about playing for Scotland they clearly didn't know Denis. Or me, for that matter. I've seen Denis unhappy in the dressing room afterwards following a win. He was a bit of a perfectionist and would run through walls for his country.'

Gemmell also recalled a story related to him by Joe Baker, Law's teammate during his unhappy spell at Torino. 'Joe was my assistant manager at Albion Rovers and he told me of his time in Italy where he shared an apartment with Denis. Joe had been driving when he and Denis were involved in a car crash in Turin, but, thankfully, they escaped without serious injury, although there were still little scars on Joe's face years later. Joe told me about just how desperate Denis was to quit the club and get out of the country. Torino, with FIFA's backing, were threatening to kick him out of the game if he didn't honour his contract which, Joe believed, was the same as his and probably bound them to the club forever! There was even talk of Torino selling on his contract to Juventus without his permission. At that time, according to Joe, Denis seriously thought about emigrating to Australia or South Africa and continuing his career in one of those countries. Back in 1962, neither of those nations were affiliated with FIFA, so there would have been no playing restrictions on Denis. However, it would have been helluva difficult, if not impossible, for Denis ever to get back into mainstream football. He could have been lost to the game for all time.'

Gemmell continued, 'Joe told me even he didn't know that his mate was about to do a runner. "I came back from training one day and there was no sign of Denis," said Joe. "There was a little scribbled note on the table informing me that he was going home. Just like that. Then I discovered he had taken a taxi to Milan before boarding a flight to London and then onto

Aberdeen. I was on my own. It wasn't long, though, before Arsenal came in for me and I would join Denis back in the English First Division.'"

Gigi Peronace was also involved in the deal to get Law to Manchester United, but not without the help of a journalist by the name of Jim Rodger. Known as 'The Jolly' to his colleagues, Jim was a bit of a Mr Fixit. Footballers called him 'Scoop'. I got to know him well during my career and I admit I was in awe of the man. He was with the *Daily Express* when I started at the *Daily Record* in 1967 and he seemed to have a fabulous exclusive every second day. He was a friend of Matt Busby and, with his stunning array of contacts, he got involved in trying to solve the Law predicament. Busby wanted Law, but also admitted he had thought of pulling out after being 'messed about' by the Italians. The Jolly was soon on the scene. A phone call here, a phone call there and weeks of anxiety and frustration were over for Law. My old mate telephoned the player to tell him Peronace was on his way to England and he was to meet him at the Midland Hotel in Manchester. A day or so later, Denis Law was a Manchester United player.

The Aberdonian in Law must have been in evidence before he signed for United in July 1962. Busby, of course, had unhesitatingly agreed to pay the £115,000 transfer fee to take him to Old Trafford. Everyone was only too aware that Law, after just one year, was thoroughly sick to his back teeth with football in Italy and was eager to return to Britain. But he wasn't going to sell himself short. Contract negotiations with Busby went on for two gruelling hours before personal terms were agreed. A weary Busby said afterwards, 'There's a lad who knows his own value.' Years later, the legendary Manchester United manager summed up the player best of all when he stated simply, 'Denis Law, an all-time great.'

George Best realised what Scotland meant to his mate. He once famously observed, 'I wouldn't have been surprised to hear Denis Law had been dressed in lederhosen and standing in the West Germany end at Wembley the day England won the World Cup in 1966. The Scots always support two teams – Scotland and anyone playing against England. Denis was no different.'

CHAPTER TWO

THE BOY WHO WOULD BE KING

This is the story of a gawky, short-sighted, skinny wee guy who would go on to conquer the world of football and become one of the most-loved sportsmen in his nation's history.

Denis Law had developed a dreadful squint in one eye in early childhood and was forced to wear corrective glasses from the age of five. All but one of his three brothers and three sisters suffered from the same affliction. 'Without the glasses my eye just went straight into the corner and I looked even worse,' said Law. 'I felt desperately self-conscious about my squint, so much so that I kept my glasses on as much as I could, even when I was playing football in the street. Every so often, though, the glasses would get smashed, exposing me to taunts and ridicule. Children, as we all know, can be the cruellest people in the world.'

Silver spoons were not in plentiful supply when Law was born on 24 February 1940 at the family home, a council-owned tenement block at 6 Printfield Terrace, Woodside, Aberdeen. He was the youngest of a family of seven. Back then, such a size of family was not unusual. His father, George, was one of 14, his mother, Robina, one of 12. Robina was already 41 years old when Denis was born. In family order, the Law siblings were Robina (known as Ruby) who was 15 years older than Denis, Frances, 13 years older, Georgina, 11, John, nine, Joe, seven, and George, five. Dad, who would serve his country in two world wars, worked as a trawler man, and his mum was a cleaner at a school. It was expected that Denis would automatically follow in his father's waders and make a living bobbing up and down on the North Sea catching fish. Thankfully, for football enthusiasts everywhere, that didn't turn out to be the case. In fact, none of the Law children would take that route of employment. George got a job in a paper mill, Joe worked for the railways and John on the buses. Ruby, Frances and Georgina all married and became housewives.

The Law family may have been poor, but they were proud. 'It's funny how common hardship seems to bind people together. None of us had very much of anything, but you certainly knew that the people next door were your friends,' Law would say. His father worked long and weary hours and could be absent for up to three weeks if the fishing boat was heading for the Faroes. The wages were not great. In 1958, when Law made his debut for the Scotland international team, the weekly pay packet for a trawler man was only £10. Law recalled that meals often consisted of soup and pudding. 'There was no middle course.' Meat was a luxury and when it was on the menu it was normally a Sunday and was reserved for Denis's dad. An infrequent treat for Denis and the family would be Scottish pies with a bit of gravy and mince. Mum was too proud and would never apply for free school meals or free boots that were available for people on low incomes.

Law remembered walking to school wearing only black canvas plimsolls even in the dead of a snowbound winter. And it can get cold in the Granite City. 'It was all we could afford.' Denis would be 14 years old before he would get his first pair of proper shoes and another year older when he got his first suit. Until then, it was all hand-me-downs from friends and relatives. However, Law recalled that he and his brothers and sisters were always clean, neat and tidy and well turned out by their mum. Sunday night was bath night because that was the only time there was hot water. Denis recalled that he washed and bathed in the sink most of the time. But he had the 'luxury' of an inside toilet while a lot of his pals had to go outside to the toilet in all sorts of elements.

Law nominated English, science, geography and technical drawing as his best subjects at school. He rated himself 'a fairly bright student' and thought he might seek employment as a draughtsman. However, football, by now, was taking an iron-like grip, almost to the point of obsession. Law would go everywhere with a ball. On his way to school he would kick it against walls and then it would be into the playground for a kickabout with his mates. Back from school, Denis recalled playing in the streets until it was dark. While representing his school teams, he had to remove his glasses and, remarkably, taught himself to play with one eye closed.

Well over half a century later, Denis Law returned to 6 Printfield Terrace as part of a Manchester United TV special, an hour devoted to, and entitled, *Denis Law – The King*. There was a playful glint in his eyes as he talked about his childhood. Law, standing outside the close, points to a downstairs window. Proudly, he states, 'This is where it all began. That's where I was born; in that very bedroom. There were three of us in a bed. We had three bedrooms, seven of us kids plus mum and dad.' The smile spreads and he is obviously enjoying the moment. He sweeps his arm around. 'This is where we played our football, on the streets. There was a lamppost here and that acted as a goalpost. We would put down a couple of jumpers over there and they would be another goalpost. About 50 yards over there (pointing down the street) we would put down another two jerseys. That was us ready to go.' Law looks around to point to the downstairs window again. 'Yeah, so that's where I was born. Nice to be back.'

The memories are cascading back now as he points to another tenement. 'That's where my friend George Geddis lived, at No. 4. You know, he gave me the money for my first pair of football boots. It was much appreciated, believe me. The next pair of boots I got were from my mother and she got them on tick.' He looks quizzically at the camera. 'You know what that means? On the drip? I think they were a Christmas present when I was about 15.'

George Yule, a friend from childhood, was also on hand to tell viewers, 'We played five-a-sides, seven-a-sides, 11-a-sides, oh, anything-a-sides. Everybody got a game and you had to fight for every scrap. I'm sure that came out in Denis when he was on the football pitch. I'm convinced of that.'

Before moving on, Law looks round once more and then faces the camera. 'We seemed to be happier back then. Kids get everything these days without doing anything. I don't know if there is the same enjoyment. When you have had to work for it, you appreciated it more and you really looked after it.' He laughs and adds, with a big smile, 'Oh, I don't know. Maybe I'm getting old and grumpy.'

He passed his 11-plus exams to allow him to go to grammar school. That presented a massive problem; unlike his first two schools, Hilton Primary and Kittybrewster, football was not played at the upmarket school, with rugby and cricket the favoured sports. The education authorities expected a young Denis to enrol at the grammar school, as was his right. He didn't want to go. No football, no Denis. His mother fought his corner and, after persuading officials that the family couldn't possibly afford cricket or rugby gear for their son, the authorities eventually relented. Denis would go to Powis Junior Secondary where they had several very good football teams. In fact, a huge debt of gratitude is due to a Mr Bill Durno who ran the school teams. He switched Law from full-back – 'where I had generally played at the time' – to inside-left. Would this have been a significantly different tale if it hadn't been for Mr Durno's intervention? It's not worth thinking about, is it?

On the MUTV tape, there is a scene when Law strides towards

a large, solid building. 'I'm back at my old school. It was called Powis Junior Secondary back then but, as you can see, it is now St Machar Academy. I remember it was a fantastic school.' He waves his hand, 'And they had those magnificent playing fields. They were right on our doorstep. It was a lovely time.'

Inside the school, Denis walks briskly along a corridor, past a framed Scotland international shirt and a stacked trophy cabinet before reaching a door marked 'PRIVATE'. Like a naughty school kid, he whispers, 'I've been summoned to see the headmistress.' He stealthily tip-toes towards the door, pushes it gently and pops his head round. There's the sound of laughter. He gives headmistress Isabel McIntyre a hug. 'Good to be back,' he tells her like he had just popped out last week. She asks him if he realises it is the school's 70th anniversary. 'Yes, I met some lovely ladies on my way in and they told me. Seventy years, eh? It's great the place is still here.'

Isabel shows him the register that tells him he joined the school in 1952. Law is surprised. 'I was here when I was 12? I thought I was 11. Maybe they didn't have a proper register in those days. Maybe they couldn't afford it.' Then, the eyes shining, he asks, 'Does it give my record of being a good pupil? An outstanding pupil? Anything like that?' He's laughing. The headmistress tells him, 'Oh, yes, we know you did well.' Law grins again, 'We had a good time here.' He reminds her, 'You do know I passed my exams to get to the grammar school, don't you? They didn't play football, so I came here.' The headmistress says, 'You made the right choice.' 'Exactly.' Later on, Law is taken to a big, open indoor area where ex-pupils are mingling. On a wall there is a photograph with the heading: 'ARE YOU IN DENIS LAW'S CLASS?' There are rows of youngsters posing for the camera – a team photo taken before term with everyone in their finery – and right at the back there is the cheeky image of a smiling youngster with round-rimmed glasses. Law moves closer to inspect the picture and fishes out his spectacles. 'I was a young boy then. Oh, dear. What about the glasses? That's a great picture, isn't it?'

As the day settles down, Isabel McIntyre thanks Denis for coming along to the 70th anniversary. 'He is the most famous former pupil by a country mile,' she tells the assembled company. Amid the applause, Denis is motioned to step forward and he plants a kiss on her cheek. 'If only I was 40 years younger,' he laughs. 'Oh, I've gone all red-faced now,' replies the flustered headmistress. Once she regains her composure, she goes on camera to say, 'He's thoroughly down-to-earth. He's not like someone famous at all. That's a sign of a great man.'

Back in the forties, Denis recalled, he and his friends used to play with tatty old tennis balls or tin cans if they didn't have a football. He would kick them against anything solid, collect the rebound and fire it back all the way to Hilton Primary, Kittybrewster or Powis. He would have a packed and bulky schoolbag slung over his shoulder making movement somewhat awkward. He admitted, 'It was good practice for control and balance.' The family radio was situated in the kitchen, along with a sink, cooker and a big drum where his mother used to do the washing. Everything was contained in an area of about three feet square. Particular radio favourites were *Dick Barton Special Agent* and *Appointment With Fear*. Another programme that was listened to avidly was *Quatermass*, a science fiction series. The only other source of indoor entertainment was provided by a ball of wool dangling from the pulley which was suspended from the ceiling and where the clothes used to hang out to dry. Denis would swing the makeshift ball around to make sure it didn't bounce off anything breakable in the kitchen. That done, he would jump up and head it for hours on end. His sister, Georgina, said, 'He would keep it at the same height for about an hour. Then he would shorten it and start again. After another hour he would shorten it again. By the end of the night the ball of wool was practically on the ceiling.'

It's difficult to comprehend that such a promising youth somehow slipped through the net of every Scottish football club and was allowed to be whisked south to sign for unfashionable Huddersfield Town. Aberdeen, in particular, must have been kicking themselves. Stories abound that the Pittodrie club were keen to make a move, but Law is adamant no such offer took place. Remarkably, not one Scottish club showed genuine interest in this precocious footballing talent. That's a fact. Maybe it would have been different if Law had played for Scotland Schoolboys but, for some unaccountable reason, that never materialised, either. The nearest he got to achieving that status was when he was taken with the schoolboy squad to Northern Ireland. 'The first time I had been outside Scotland,' said Law. But he never got a kick at the ball. Luckily for Denis, Archie Beattie, brother of Huddersfield's Scottish manager Andy, did a bit of scouting for the club and lived not far from the Law household. There were precious few talent scouts around at the time; it was far too expensive for clubs to even consider setting up such sophisticated networks. A lot of the recommendations were word of mouth and, eventually, Beattie took in a junior game and had his first look at Law. 'I used to score a lot of goals and I suppose that's what got me noticed,' said Law later. Beattie was suitably impressed and got in touch with his brother.

Andy Beattie wasn't quite in the same positive frame of mind when he first saw a five-foot three-inch Law, dwarfed while standing between his elder brothers George and John. He is quoted as saying to his brother, 'The boy's a freak. Anyone less like a footballer I have never seen. He's weak, puny and bespectacled.' So much for first impressions, then. 'A miserable bag of bones,' was Denis's own summing up of his physique at the time.

Law recalled that first trip across the border as a 'huge adventure'. The Aberdeen he had grown up in was a lovely city with nearby beaches and fresh air. Huddersfield, on the other hand, was an industrial town with huge chimneys and woollen mills. He admitted he was immediately homesick. Despite his hardly-inspirational first meeting, Beattie offered the youngster a week's trial. He did sufficiently well to be offered a contract as a ground staff apprentice which he duly signed on 3 April 1955. His first weekly wage packet was £4 14s. More than half of that – £2 7s 6d – paid for his board and lodgings. The Huddersfield Town manager later confided to his brother, 'I thought you were playing a joke on me, but as soon as I saw him kick the ball I realised he had it in him to be truly great.' He signed professional forms on 25 February 1957. Twenty months later, Law made his debut for Scotland. It was the start of something wonderful.

Another Scot was to give Law his first-team opportunity at Huddersfield Town. Bill Shankly had replaced Beattie, who quit the post in November 1956. Shankly, who would, of course, go on to become a legend at Liverpool, liked the gutsy, gritty, never-say-die spirit of the young Aberdonian. He admitted, 'He looked like a waif. I had to give him steak and milk to build him up.' But he had no hesitation in putting him in against Notts County at Meadow Lane on Christmas Eve 1956. A crowd of 9,165 witnessed Denis Law's first kick of the ball in senior first-team football. Law wore the No. 8 shirt and Huddersfield won 2-1 with both goals coming from Ron Simpson, wearing the No. 10 jersey, the number Law would wear with such distinction for so many years. Law only wore No. 10 in seven league games in his 81 appearances for Town. Amazingly, only two days after his first outing, Law played against Notts County again and netted his first goal at Leeds Road. His second league goal came in a 2-2 draw with Swansea and he opened his FA Cup account with one in a 3-1 victory over Peterborough.

Four matches after his debut, Law would come face-to-face for the first time with a man who would become a great teammate at Manchester United and a lifelong personal friend,

Harry Gregg. The Northern Ireland goalkeeper was turning out for Doncaster Rovers on 2 February 1957 at Leeds Road. Gregg remembered, 'I saw him and a more unlikely footballer was difficult to imagine. He was terrifyingly thin, like a leek, but it didn't take a genius to see that Denis Law was something special.' Gregg kept Law at bay as Rovers triumphed 1-0 in front of 17,888. In all, Law turned out in 13 league games and five FA Cup-ties during his first campaign.

Shankly was swiftly beginning to realise he had something special on his playing staff. By now, Law had undergone an operation to rectify the squint and he said, 'It was great to be able to look people straight in the eye. The confidence I got from that was enormous. That operation changed my life.' Shankly was suitably impressed by the consistently good displays from Law and said, 'Although he didn't look the strongest of boys, he was strong-willed and he had great strength of character. He fought with the heart. And the head, of course. Law was easy to teach. When he was just coming through, he never argued with the referee or the linesmen. He conversed with them in a different manner. In other words, he flannelled them. If a decision was given against him, he would cotton onto a linesman and have a conversation with him. And maybe the next decision went his way. He did the same with referees. He spoke to them politely and they must have thought, "He's a nice lad." He didn't show dissent. Instead of rushing over and telling them what to do, he would say, "Yes, you're right, ref." He was a very good actor.'

Shankly's influence would have a profound and lasting effect. Law said, 'The first day I met him I couldn't believe there could be a man so involved with football 24 hours a day, every day. It was his whole life. There will never be a man like him ever again in football. I've never met anyone before or since with the same passion and love for the game. He was obsessed with fitness, he absolutely hated players being injured even to the extent of ignoring those who were. He was an unforgettable man.' Law would later add, 'Mind you, he did my brain in sometimes. There are things to talk about other than football.'

Around the time of Law's second season, a local reporter noted, 'Law uses the match officials as props. They don't realise it, but he knows how to work them. He may be young, but he is learning the game very, very quickly.' The newspaper also informed us, 'Most of his goals come from nothing. He enjoys tidying up the penalty area to get goals that look simple. But their creation comes from deep reading, razor-sharp anticipation and, most of all, a willingness to go in where it hurts. Law often chases a lost cause and turns it into a winning one.'

Bill Shankly was adamant he would never sell Law. Bigger clubs were being alerted to the young, athletic, blond and stylish Huddersfield Town forward, particularly after his excellent first match for Scotland against Wales in October 1958. It seemed only a matter of time before he would move elsewhere. Shankly, who had formerly managed Carlisle United, Grimsby Town and Workington Town, left Huddersfield on 1 December 1959 for Liverpool, where he would spend 15 eventful years. He was 46 years old when he went to Anfield, with the club in the doldrums in the Second Division. His starting salary was £2,500 per year. Phil Taylor made way for Shankly and one of his last games in charge of Liverpool was a 1-0 defeat against a Law-inspired Huddersfield on 28 November that year. (In his video *The King*, Law thought the score was 5-1 and Shankly, in another book, believed it to be 5-0. The official Huddersfield Town book of history and stats, *99 Years And Counting*, gives it as 1-0 and the other league game between the clubs ended 2-2 at Anfield on 19 March.)

One manager who had taken note of Law's ability was Matt Busby, who would eventually pay the £115,000 fee to buy him for Manchester United from Torino in July 1962. He remembered, 'I first saw Denis at Heckmondwike in Yorkshire one night when he was playing for Huddersfield against United in a youth game. When we were losing 2-0 at half-time, I wondered who was taking us apart. Then I realised it was a little will o' the wisp called Law, who had scored both goals. After the match I offered £10,000 for him, but Huddersfield wouldn't listen, even though that was a high figure for a young player in those days.'

Eddie Boot took over from Shankly in a caretaker capacity before accepting the job on a full-time basis on 19 January 1960. Law would play only six games for Boot before being transferred to Manchester City on 15 March for £55,000, a record fee between two British clubs. Law left the Huddersfield fans with smiles on their faces in his last game, a 1-0 win over Hull City at Leeds Road. Alex Massie, another Scot who had been recommended to the club by Archie Beattie, scored the only goal. Law had played 27 games and scored eight goals in his last season. He also turned out five times for his country as a Huddersfield Town player.

Law, in fact, was informed of his first international call-up in the strangest of circumstances. He was in the city's town centre where a bloke called Eric sold the local newspaper, the *Huddersfield Examiner*, at the corner of a street. 'Hiya, Denis,' said Eric. 'Hi, Eric,' replied Denis. 'Congratulations, by the way.' Law looked at Eric. 'What for?' 'Don't you know? You've been selected to play for Scotland – it's here in the paper.' It was the first Law had heard of the astounding news. He was on his way. There was no spectacular fanfare of trumpets, but a legend was about to be launched.

CHAPTER THREE

ENTER DENIS

Scotland's urgent requirement for a consistent goalscorer manifested itself during the turmoil of yet another disastrous campaign in the 1958 World Cup Finals in Sweden. The Scots' feeble frontline, paraded in front of a global audience, could muster only four goals from their three games as the nation completed their ill-fated campaign anchored, once again embarrassingly, at the foot of their section. Three games, two defeats and a draw. As in Switzerland four years previously, victory at the highest level had eluded them. While the entire Scottish contingent could only conjure up a quartet of strikes, France's Just Fontaine completed the tournament with 13 goals – two against Scotland – in six games.

Sadly, the trip to Sweden proved to be a shambolic waste of time, to the torment of the Scottish fans. There had been supreme optimism after the qualifying stages which saw Scotland beat a strong Spain side, fancied by many to win the World Cup. Switzerland, who had reached the quarter-finals of the trophy in their own country, were the other group opponents. The first qualifier was against the Spaniards at Hampden on 8 May 1957. Real Madrid, triumphant in the inaugural European Cup the previous year when they beat French side Reims 4-3, had just won through to their second final where they would meet – and beat – AC Milan. The European masters provided five of the Spanish squad that would travel to Glasgow, including Denis Law's particular favourite Alfredo di Stefano. The jet-heeled outside-left Francisco Gento was also included. It seemed all they had to do was honour us with their presence at Hampden and the points were as good as theirs.

Scotland captain George Young, a giant of a man who achieved iconic status with Rangers, was not overawed. He said, 'If we are to believe all we hear, we are asked to meet a team of supermen. The Spaniards have been described as the greatest team in the world. We are expected to feel inferior when we meet them. They are just 11 men in jerseys. We are as good, if not better, than them. We'll see on the day.'

Stirring stuff. Scottish fans were roused and 89,000 turned out for the 6 p.m. kick-off as Hampden still hadn't installed floodlights. Blackpool's Jackie Mudie had the fans singing in the 24th minute when he scored with a header, but Ladislao Kubala levelled almost instantly. Hopes soared again when John Hewie's badly-struck penalty-kick foxed the Spanish goalkeeper, the much-vaunted Antonio Ramallets, whom many reckoned to be even better than the Russian, Lev Yashin. Ramallets got to the ball, but allowed it to squirm over the line. Back came Spain and they equalised again five minutes after the turnaround when Tommy Younger pushed away a drive from di Stefano and it fell perfectly for Luis Suarez to glide the ball in from close range. Was it to be another of those days? It was deadlocked at 2-2 with light beginning to fade when Bobby Collins, at war with his opponents throughout, set up Mudie and his shot dipped over the helplessly-exposed Ramallets. Ten minutes from the conclusion of an entertaining encounter, Collins again played the role of provider as he sent Mudie clear and he made no mistake once again. Scotland 4, Spain 2. The Spaniards were just 11 men in jerseys, after all.

There was a buoyancy about Scotland as they travelled to Switzerland for the second qualifier 11 days later. An unchanged team saw them concede an early goal, but come back to triumph 2-1 with headers from the diminutive Collins and the ever-dangerous Mudie. In the return against Spain in Madrid,

Scotland were brought back to earth. They were well and truly walloped 4-1 and didn't impress opposing coach Don Manuel Vallina, who sniffed, 'Scotland's defence was not compact enough. To my mind, it had no plan. It offered our forwards opportunities they should never have been given. I wasn't impressed at all.' No wonder. Spain were two ahead by the 20th minute after goals from Enrique Mateos and Kubala. Estanislao Basora claimed two after the interval with Hibs outside-right Gordon Smith hitting Scotland's consolation effort.

The situation for Scotland was now simple – a win over Switzerland at Hampden would secure a place in Sweden. It was a 2.30 p.m. kick-off to catch what would remain of the November daylight. Almost 57,000 turned out to see if Scotland could reach their second successive World Cup Finals. Clyde's enterprising Archie Robertson put the Scots ahead, but that was cancelled by Fernando Riva's effort. Mudie restored the advantage and Rangers' Alex Scott, looking yards offside, thumped in number three. The Swiss reacted angrily and surrounded the referee who refused to change his mind. The goal stood. Just as well, too. Scotland had to fight a rearguard action for the final 20 minutes as their opponents bombarded Younger's goal. Near the end they were rewarded when a close-range drive from Roger Vonlanden almost ripped a hole in the roof of the net. The Swiss were to be applauded, but it was the Scottish players who would be looking out their passports for Sweden.

The Scottish Football Association, in their infinite wisdom and not before time, decided that the national team should have a manager. On 9 January 1958 they turned to Matt Busby, achieving some wonderful things at Manchester United. He was offered the part-time post only days after his club side had defeated Red Star Belgrade 2-1 in the European Cup quarter-final first leg at Old Trafford. Busby said, 'I am delighted to accept the invitation. It is a great honour to be asked to manage my country. I hope I can do something to help Scotland win the

World Cup. I aim not to have a team content merely to put up a respectable show in Sweden, but one that will take the field with the aim of winning the trophy.'

Busby was fated not to lead his nation in those finals. On 5 February he was in Belgrade to see his United side draw 3-3 with Red Star Belgrade to claim a place in the European Cup semi-final. A day later on the flight home, the squad had a stopover in Munich. Their plane aborted one take-off attempt amid a blizzard. The captain tried again. The craft was barely airborne when it crashed and 23 people died, including eight Manchester United players. Busby was severely injured and lapsed into a coma. He was taken to intensive care at Munich's Rechts der Isar hospital. The staff were put on emergency alert and Busby, receiving regular blood transfusions, was placed in an oxygen tent. He was given only a 50-50 chance of survival by the surgeons. He pulled through although his journey to full recovery would be slow. Dawson Walker, the Scotland trainer, was put in charge of preparations as the national squad gathered at the Ayrshire resort of Turnberry. The players trained daily at Girvan Amateurs' ground and were told they would be paid £50 per game. They seemed happy with the arrangement.

The SFA selectors were putting together their final group of 22 players and an 18-year-old making a name for himself in England was mentioned. It was Denis Law, then with Huddersfield Town. He was selected in the initial squad of 40 in March after impressing an SFA official. As luck would have it, he had to withdraw only a few days later, sidelined for six weeks with an ankle ligament injury.

Possibly it was a blessing in disguise. The Swedish experience might have put his career into freefall.

Scotland, displaying incredible naivety, arrived in Sweden on 2 June, only six days before their opening game against Yugoslavia in Vasteras. Remarkably, they had even arranged to play a local side 24 hours before the first encounter. Thankfully, no-one was injured in a 2-0 win over the amateurs of Eskil-stuna. Collins and Mudie were the scorers in a full-strength 11. Six minutes into the real thing, Younger, who, along with Tommy Docherty, gave the team talks in the absence of Busby, was picking the ball out of his net, put there by Aleksander Pet-kovic. However, Hearts' Jimmy Murray headed in the equaliser after a neat ball from Eddie Turnbull, so often an opponent in Edinburgh derbies. It ended 1-1 and Scotland appeared quite satisfied with their point.

Next up were Paraguay in Norrkoping three days later. Some-one at the SFA had the foresight to send squad members Tommy Docherty and Archie Robertson to spy on the opponents. They came back with notes informing the selectors that the Paraguay-ans were 'rough, very fit, good on the ball and were excellent at passing'. Sadly, no-one took a blind bit of notice. Sammy Baird, Dave Mackay and Docherty, three muscular players who could mix it with the best of them, were ignored. A lightweight side was fielded and once again the dithering Scottish defence gifted their opponents an early advantage with Juan Aguero, a lively winger, racing in to poke the ball through the legs of Younger in the fourth minute. Mudie duly equalised in the 25th minute after a shot from Graham Leggat had been cleared off the line. So, it was stalemate with only seconds to go to half-time. Could Scotland hold out? Remember, this is Scotland we are talking about. Everton defender Alex Parker failed to intercept a pass from Jose Parodi and it was worked to Cayetano Re whose shot bounced off Younger, struck an upright and ended up in the net. The Liverpool custodian wasn't having the best of days and that was highlighted with 15 minutes to go when he allowed a routine cross to slip from his grasp straight to the feet of the delighted Jorgelino Romero who poked it home from close range. Collins pulled one back – the 500th goal scored in World Cup Finals – but it was too little, too late. The 3-2 defeat meant the Scots were bottom of Group 2.

Docherty, who didn't get a kick of the ball in Sweden, would often joke later that one thing was certain in World Cup Finals. 'The Scottish team will be home before their postcards,' he would grin. He was proved right again. Younger's abysmal performance against Paraguay saw him dropped, his international career ending there and then at the age of 28. Dundee's Bill Brown, only two years his junior, replaced him against France in Orebro on 15 June. The new man picked the ball out of the rigging twice in the first-half, beaten by efforts from Raymond Kopa and Just Fontaine. Scotland's plight wasn't helped when defender John Hewie squandered a penalty-kick just after Kopa's opener. The full-back clattered the post with his misjudged effort. Sammy Baird's strike just before the hour mark put a better complexion on the scoreline, but it didn't matter. Scotland, just as in Switzerland four years earlier, were out and were still waiting for a win at this level. It could hardly have been termed a glorious failure. There would be no thousands turning out to welcome them home on their return to Scotland.

There had been no replacement manager for the most important competition on the planet and there had been little or no supervision of the players at the team's hotel where they were given a full breakfast, two three-course meals during the day and cream buns and all sorts of pastries at 10 p.m., supper time in that part of Sweden. This was the international set-up in 1958, a country going in no particular direction except down, sucked into a whirlpool of mediocrity. A confused bunch of officials and footballers miserably lost in a maze of mistakes. There was little to inspire anyone, on or off the field. It was all very depressing. Optimism had been buried among the debris. A newspaper report at the time summed it up perfectly: 'Scotland learned nothing, absolutely nothing, from the World Cup Finals of 1954. Every mistake in Switzerland was repeated in Sweden.' Who would lift the sagging spirits of the nation? Was there anyone out there with an answer?

Enter Denis Law.

It's a preposterous thought in these enlightened times, but there was actually some opposition to the SFA selectors even considering the blond teenage attacker who was making such an enormous impact across the border. Matt Busby had the courage of his convictions to name an all-Anglo forward line against Wales at Cardiff on 18 October 1958. It read: Graham Leggat (Fulham), Tommy Docherty (Arsenal), Denis Law (Huddersfield Town), Bobby Collins (Everton) and Jackie Henderson (Arsenal).

Law said, 'The Scottish media weren't too happy about it and there was a great deal of controversy north of the border because one of the Anglos was only a young Second Division player with a team in England called Huddersfield. "Who?" they asked. I had not even played for the Under-23s before my full debut against the Welsh and, indeed, I had won six full caps before my first Under-23 game against Wales in Wrexham.' Huddersfield were due to play Ipswich Town at Portman Road the same afternoon as the Welsh match but Law, an ever-present since the start of the season, was allowed time off to represent his country. It probably helped that his club manager was Bill Shankly. Without Law's goal threat, Huddersfield settled for a goalless draw.

At the same time, another ambitious young player also wondered what international football had in store for him. Twenty-three-year-old Dave Mackay, then an old-fashioned, barrel-chested wing-half with Hearts, had played in the World Cup loss against France and pondered his immediate future. He was to be pleasantly surprised. Mackay recalled, 'I was selected to play in the Home International against Wales later that year. When I arrived at our hotel I was puzzled when I was told Matt Busby wanted to see me. He was weak and frail after suffering terrible injuries in the Munich air crash. The fact that not only was he back managing Manchester United, but had now also resumed control of the national side, was incredible. Matt told me he was appointing me team captain. Now captains are normally senior in years and have been long established in the side. I was preparing to play only my third international. Tommy Docherty, then playing at Arsenal, and Bobby Collins, of Everton, were both in the team and far more experienced and respected than I was.

'Busby was adamant, though. He told me, "Davie, you are the man for the job, be in no doubt. You are hungry. You never admit defeat. You inspire those around you and you have many years ahead of you. I want to build this Scotland side around you. You are an old head on young shoulders." I was extremely flattered and proud. Matt fielded an experimental side against the Welsh with four players making their debuts, John Grant, Willie Toner, David Herd and Denis Law. Denis was only 18 years old and was already receiving rave reviews in the English game. He was good and he knew it, but not big-headed. He was a cheeky chappie who could see fun in everything and his general good humour and mischievousness were infectious. We became pals straight away. I was not surprised that he became both one of the most admired forwards of his generation and one of the greatest Scottish players in history. You would be surprised how many former professionals rate Denis as the best player they have competed against or alongside when asked in private.'

Law was primed and ready to go as he raced onto the Ninian Park pitch in Cardiff to take his international bow. A healthy crowd of 60,000 turned out as English referee Eric Leafe blew his whistle to allow battle to commence. Mackay remembered, 'Denis scored on his debut – our second – after I had missed an early penalty-kick. Bobby Collins and Graham Leggat got the others. We played an excellent game of football and were comfortable 3-0 winners. Later in the game, goalkeeper Bill Brown, who would become a good friend and teammate at

Tottenham Hotspur, took a nasty knock in an aerial clash and was forced to have treatment off the field. It was the days before substitutes, so I went into goal. At one stage I charged from my line in an attempt to catch the ball, but I realised it was sailing over my head. I looked round expecting the inevitable. Never fear, the boy wonder, Denis Law, was standing on the line grinning as he cleared the ball away.'

There seems some confusion surrounding Law's historic first goal for his country and flickering black-and-white film footage is of little aid. Denis admitted, 'I scored – if I can use that term – my first international goal in the second-half when David Herd crossed the ball and I jumped for it with Dave Bowen, whose firmly-struck headed clearance hit me on the head and flew in past a startled Jack Kelsey.' Not a classic, then, but we'll take it, nevertheless. One down, 29 to go.

The modest Law was involved in the other two goals that day. A superb sweeping pass allowed Jackie Henderson to scamper down the touchline and the Arsenal winger swung in a superb cross for Leggat to bury a positive header beyond Kelsey. Law did it again when he nodded down a long ball from Grant into the path of Mackay and he teed it up for Collins to stroke in the third. Denis added, 'I had to read the newspapers the following day to see what I had done and how the goals came about. To me, it was all a blank. In fact, I had no recollection of Dave Mackay's penalty miss until he reminded me years later.'

Bobby Collins smiles at the recollection of Law's fairly memorable – well, to everyone else! – first game for Scotland. Collins, the original Wee Barra, said the raw teenager made an immediate impact on him. He revealed, 'Denis was even better than we had anticipated. He was one of those players who grew in stature the moment they stepped onto the football field. Some have that ability; some haven't. Denis had plenty of it.

'He was only 18 years old when he played at Cardiff. If he was nervous he didn't show it. His disguise was perfect. His chest seemed to swell as he raced out of the tunnel, preparing to go straight into folklore as one of the best players football has ever produced. He knew he had ability, he must have realised what destiny had in store, but this was no big-headed kid with a mouth to match. Far from it. George Best once said it was impossible to be miserable when you were in Denis's company and I couldn't agree more. The guy just has this rather special aura. It's apparent all the time; he doesn't switch it on and off. He thoroughly deserves all the good things and the adulation that have come his way. He was a special player and he's a special guy.'

Law, as expected, kept his place in the line-up for the next international against Northern Ireland at Hampden the following month. In fact, Matt Busby was so pleased with the performance against the Welsh that he announced an unchanged team. It was to be memorable for Law – for all the wrong reasons. He said, 'The Irish team was a strong one and had reached the last eight in the World Cup Finals that year. Undoubtedly, their star performer was Danny Blanchflower, of Spurs. He was a majestic and influential player who could take complete control of a game. Matt Busby naturally asked us to keep a close eye on him, but sometimes, when you are young, you can take things too literally. Matt said to me before the game, "Make sure you stop him because he is the guy who starts everything for them." To be honest, I am embarrassed to this day by what I did to that great player.'

The 72,732 fans who turned up on 5 November, Guy Fawkes Night, were looking for fireworks from the young Huddersfield player whose reputation was beginning to soar in his native land. It was Hampden's first look at Law and if those supporters were in attendance to witness his marvellous and deadly prowess in the penalty box or his all-round excellent play elsewhere on the pitch, they were to be sadly disappointed. In Law's own words he gave Blanchflower 'a good kicking' as he followed him around for 90 minutes. It was effective for a time as the Scots, with goals from David Herd and Collins, were leading 2-0, but, after more defensive lapses, they had to settle for a 2-2 draw. Law admitted, 'I didn't play any football. I've apologised to Danny many times since that game.' Fortunately, the Northern Ireland purveyor of perfect passes was also a gentleman and accepted the young Scot's apology. Later on, they would become good friends.

Blanchflower noted, 'Denis could have done with a bit more experience. Nearly every tackle was a foul. But he wasn't kicking me so much as always coming in late. I knew he had ability or he wouldn't have been in the Scotland team. He wasn't a tough player, but he had strength and vital energy and was direct and determined. When I came out of the Hampden dressing room afterwards, Bill Shankly, who had taken over as manager from Andy Beattie at Huddersfield, was standing there saying what a great player Denis was. I decided not to argue and walked away. I wasn't bitter. However, I would give him credit. For a skinny kid with a squint to develop into such a magnificent striker who was fast and fierce was like growing from a toad into a prince. It was a tribute to his determination.'

Law's mother and father were in the Hampden stand that day to watch their son as a professional footballer for the first time. Like all the other witnesses they saw a different player from the one expected. Remarkably, neither ever saw their son in action again for club or country. Law added ruefully, 'To cap it all, my parents were injured in a car crash on their way home.' Thankfully, not seriously.

Overall, it had been a good year for Denis Law. And it would be even better in 1959.

CHAPTER FOUR

HISTORY-MAKER

Denis Law is unique among Scottish footballers. He is the only player to make his debut for the Under-23 side after playing six times for the full international team. Remarkably, Law had faced Wales and Northern Ireland in 1958 and Holland, Portugal, Northern Ireland and Wales in 1959 before his call-up to play against the Welsh Under-23s at the Racecourse Ground in Wrexham on 25 November later that year.

A teammate that evening was a slimly-built inside-right called John White who had already made such an impact at Falkirk that he had been transferred to Spurs for £22,000. Law and White would combine 17 times in the full international team. Celtic's Dunky McKay, a right-back many thought was ahead of his time because of his attacking instincts, was also in the line-up in Wrexham and he would be a colleague of Law's on six occasions at the highest level.

Alex Young, who would later join Everton from Hearts, scored the only goal of the game in front of 10,966 fans. The Scotland team was: Adam Blacklaw (Burnley); Dunky McKay (Celtic), Andy Milne (Cardiff City); Jimmy Gabriel (Dundee), Jackie Plenderleith (Hibs), Billy Higgins (Hearts); Willie Hunter (Motherwell), John White (Spurs), Alex Young (Hearts), Denis Law (Huddersfield Town) and Andy Weir (Motherwell).

Blacklaw, Gabriel, Plenderleith, Hunter and Weir, along with Law, White, McKay and Young, would go on to represent their country in full internationals. Higgins would play three more

Under-23 games before disappearing off the scene. Milne never represented his country again at any level.

England's Jimmy Greaves stole the show in Law's next Under-23 appearance, a rollicking 4-4 draw at Ibrox on 2 March 1960. It was the first time Law had a close-up look at the frontman he later came to admire and name as the 'complete striker'. Greaves fired three into the Scottish net, but it ended all-square with Ian St John (2), Alan Cousin and Dunky McKay, with a penalty-kick, scoring for the Scots while a crowd of 25,012 looked on. The team was: Blacklaw (Burnley); McKay (Celtic), Ian Riddell (St Mirren); Gabriel (Dundee), John Martis (Motherwell), Higgins (Hearts); Hunter (Motherwell), Cousin (Dundee), St John (Motherwell), Law (Huddersfield Town) and Weir (Motherwell).

Law's big moment came the following year against the English on 1 March in front of 21,858 spectators at Middlesbrough's ground, Ayresome Park. Law grabbed the only goal of the encounter with a typical effort, but he didn't have similar good fortune a month later in the full international against England at Wembley. Scotland scored three; unfortunately England netted nine. The Under-23 team lined up: John Ogston (Aberdeen); John Hogan (Partick Thistle), Riddell (St Mirren); Pat Crerand (Celtic), Billy McNeill (Celtic), Ian Ure (Dundee); David Hilley (Third Lanark), Denis Law (Manchester City), John Hughes (Celtic), Alan Gilzean (Dundee) and Johnny MacLeod (Hibernian). McNeill and MacLeod would also suffer alongside Law in London. Celebrations and commiserations are never far away from each other in football.

Interestingly, the goalkeeper in the victorious Under-23 team was John Ogston – nicknamed 'Tubby' because of his girth – and who was well-known to Law. They had played alongside each other for Aberdeen Colts and the keeper went on to have a sound career at Pittodrie. Two weeks before the 1-0 win over England, Law played for the Under-23 side in an unofficial match against the British Army on 15 February watched by a crowd of 12,003 at Motherwell's ground, Fir Park. Ogston was in goal for the Army and Law stuck two goals past his pal as the Scots triumphed 3-2. Ian St John got the other. Billy McNeill beat his Celtic teammate Frank Haffey to put through his own goal with Jimmy Kearns (Coventry City) claiming a second for the Forces. Ron Yeats (Liverpool) and Jim Baxter (Rangers) were among those who turned out for the Army.

The Scotland team read: Frank Haffey (Celtic); Pat Delaney (Motherwell), George Simm (Aberdeen); Frank McLintock (Leicester City), Billy McNeill (Celtic), George Miller (Hearts); Johnny MacLeod (Hibs), David Hilley (Third Lanark), Ian St John (Motherwell), Denis Law (Manchester City) and Bertie Auld (Celtic).

Law's appearance against England in March 1961 was his last as an Under-23 player. Partick Thistle's John Hogan and St Mirren's Ian Riddell shared the same distinction. However unlike Law, they would never represent their country again at any level.

CHAPTER FIVE

AFTER THE BRAWL WAS OVER

Denis Law went on his first trip abroad with Scotland in May 1959 after injury forced him to miss the first two internationals that year, a 1-0 defeat against England at Wembley and a 3-2 victory over West Germany at Hampden. The tour started with an unofficial match against Jutland that ended in a 3-3 draw in Aarhus, Holland. Law scored the first goal in what transpired to be a fairly uneventful 90 minutes. Then it was on to Amsterdam to play the Dutch national side and the Huddersfield teenager remembered it 'being a rough, tough game'. Celtic winger Bertie Auld, who had also played against Jutland, was sent off near the end.

'That was my introduction to international football,' said Auld, who, years later, would be likened to Desperate Dan, the character in the *Dandy* comic paper, by Law. 'The Dutch were trying to kick lumps out of us and the Portuguese referee didn't want to know. He gave us precious little protection. A couple of their defenders had a kick at me and if they were trying to show me who was the boss, they were up a gum tree. I had played against harder guys on the streets of Maryhill when I was just a kid. They were wasting their time. One of their defenders, a thug called Jan Notermans, thought it might be fun to use me as a football throughout the game.

'Denis wasn't intimidated, either. He was putting it about with the best of them, much to the consternation of the Dutch. Far from being terrified, Denis looked as though he was actually enjoying it. My wee pal Bobby Collins played and scored in that game, too. Bobby was a mere five foot four inches and if their defenders thought they could boot him around all day, too, they were in for a shock. The Wee Barra never took any prisoners when he played. There might not have been much of him, but what was there was genuine Glasgow grit. As I recall, he was outstanding in that game.'

Centre-half Bobby Evans, another Celtic player who became a huge favourite and lifelong friend of Auld, was skipper and said, 'Aye, that was a hard game. I haven't a clue what triggered off the Dutch, but they were determined to give us a good kicking. We had young lads like Denis Law and John White in the team and it must have been a real eye-opener for them. At the same time, though, it would have been a bit of an education. It certainly toughened them up because no team can carry passengers at that level.'

Cornelius van der Gijp put Holland ahead in the 19th minute with an effort that whizzed past Blackpool keeper George Farm, who was representing his country for the second-to-last time. Bobby Collins equalised in the 61st minute and the Olympic Stadium was in uproar when Graham Leggat notched a second four minutes later. Auld said, 'Someone must have forgotten to tell the Dutch players and fans it was a friendly game. No medals would be getting handed out after it; no huge cash bonuses for the winners. The remaining 25 minutes were pandemonium. The supporters were throwing cushions onto the pitch; they must have had particularly comfy seats at Ajax's old ground! I went over to take a throw-in and they were snarling and screaming at me and making all sort of rude gestures. When you have sampled the heat of a Glasgow derby then you can overcome anything. I just smiled at them. That seemed to make them even madder.

'There was a massive bust-up about three minutes into injury time. Everyone seemed to be involved and certainly Denis and Bobby were in the thick of it. Punches were thrown and I was astonished when I was singled out by the match official and sent off. Apparently, my sparring partner Notermans had taken a sore one on the chin. I tried to protest my innocence, but the ref was having none of it. I looked into his eyes and I could see he had "gone". He was burbling away in Portuguese and I might have said something in my Scottish brogue about his parentage before I walked off. Once again, the fans were hissing and booing. I smiled back.'

Law and Auld teamed up again a week later for a meeting with Portugal in Lisbon. A crowd of 30,000 at the Estadio Jose Alvalade witnessed their nation's 1-0 win with Lucas Matateu the solitary marksman in the 25th minute. Auld looked back, 'Thankfully, there were no fisticuffs during that encounter. It was tough, but quite tame in comparison to the Dutch game. The fans, though, seemed rather animated and, as in Amsterdam, they were throwing cushions onto the field. Some fabric manufacturer must have been making a fortune at the time!'

Law and Auld were back in tandem in November for the visit of Wales to Glasgow. John White was one of three Spurs players on display, the others being Bill Brown in goal and Dave Mackay at right-half. Only two other Anglos were in the team; John Hewie, of Charlton, and Denis Law, of Huddersfield Town. Almost 56,000 paid to watch the action and, but for a small section of visiting fans, they were silenced in the eighth minute when John Charles scored from a free-kick. Scotland won 20 corner-kicks in this confrontation and had success from one. Auld flighted in a swirling cross that was met perfectly by Leggat and keeper Jack Kelsey was well beaten. For the second time in two years, Mackay had to answer the SOS to take over in goal when Brown was forced to go off with a head injury with 15 minutes to go. As in Cardiff in 1958, Mackay proved a capable deputy and didn't concede a goal.

It was the last time Law and Auld would play alongside each

other. The legendary Celt sighed, 'That was a pity because I really liked Denis's company, on and off the pitch. He was a real character and you could see he was going to make a genuine impact on the world of football. It was when he changed his style to play mainly within sight of goal that he really came into his own. As a youngster he would roam all over the place. He would even go deep into his own half to take the ball off the full-backs. He just wanted to be involved all the time. But when he switched to taking care of business in and around the penalty area he was something else altogether. I called him a predator; that's exactly what he was. Denis was onto rebounds in a flash and would punish any lapse in concentration from a goalkeeper or his defenders. What a player to have in your team. He had a great sense of humour, too, and he still thought he was 16 when he was 60!'

As in the previous year, Law would turn out for his country four times in 1960, the first of which was the 1-1 draw with England at Hampden which is covered in 'THE AULD ENEMY' chapter elsewhere in this book. Poland provided the opposition for a friendly match on 4 May and the game was noteworthy for one reason; Law's first goal at Hampden in front of his own fans. The historic moment came in the 21st minute and levelled Krzytof Baszkiewcz's effort in 11 minutes. Sadly, the arrival of the goal didn't inspire Law's teammates and the Poles went on to win 3-2. Lucjan Brychczy gave the visitors the advantage just before the half-hour mark and Ian St John replied immediately after the interval. Ernest Pohl got the winner in the 60th minute. Pohl would return to Hampden five years later to play in the team that severely dented, if not destroyed, Scotland's hopes of reaching the 1966 World Cup Finals in England. Law would describe his country's 2-1 defeat that night as 'the biggest disappointment of my life'. Pohl and right-back Henryk Szczepanski were the Polish survivors who would come back to haunt Scotland and celebrate a second victory in Glasgow. Bill Brown and Denis Law were the sole remaining Scots who would seek, and ultimately fail to achieve, revenge.

Law and Brown were also in the side that travelled to Austria for a friendly at Vienna's world famous arena, the Prater Stadion on 29 May. It was the first of a three-match ten-day tour. Over 60,000 saw the Austrians ease their way to a 4-1 victory against a Scottish team that offered little in the way of resistance. Law had a good excuse; he lasted only 12 minutes before going off following an ankle injury and Alex Young came on in his place. The hosts were 3-0 ahead by the time the interval arrived. Gerhard Hanappi netted twice in the first half-hour and Erich Hof added the other. He scored the fourth in the 63rd minute and Dave Mackay hit Scotland's consolation 14 minutes before the German referee, Helmut Dusch, mercifully blew for time-up to put the Scots out of their misery. Law summed up, 'We were thumped.'

The brief appearance in Vienna was to be Law's only input to a tour that saw the Scots draw 3-3 with Hungary in Budapest – Willie Hunter, George Herd and Alex Young on target – and collapse 4-2 to Turkey in Ankara. Eric Caldow, with a penalty-kick, and Young were the Scottish goalscorers. Remarkably, 172,500 spectators watched the three games. Goodness knows what the players had to celebrate, but the newspapers were filled with stories of a wild party – or 'shenanigans' as Law called it. To be fair, there were banquets after all three matches and one player, wishing to remain anonymous, told a reporter, 'The game in Ankara was played in unbelievably difficult conditions. It was hard to draw breath and the pitch was baked solid. Most of the players were dehydrated. There was some wine available at the after-match reception and it went straight to our heads.'

Denis Law, after completing his £55,000 British transfer record move from Huddersfield to Manchester City, was back in place for the meeting against Northern Ireland in Glasgow that November.

There were three debutants; one who would make a bit of a name for himself, one who would score eight goals from as many appearances and one who would vanish from the international scene after only 90 minutes. In came Rangers' strolling left-half Jim Baxter, Manchester City centre-half Jackie Plenderleith and the Ibrox side's prolific frontman Ralph Brand. Baxter would take centre stage in many internationals, Brand netted his eighth goal in his last outing – a 3-2 defeat from Uruguay 18 months later – and Plenderleith was ignored for all time.

Law was eager to show he was well worth the massive fee shelled out by City and he underlined that value with a typical strike in eight minutes. Eric Caldow slotted in a penalty-kick before the interval and Danny Blanchflower did likewise for the visitors three minutes after the turnaround. Then came a four-goal avalanche in the last 12 minutes, with Alex Young kicking off the scoring storm. Brand made it 4-1 in 81 minutes, Peter McParland pulled one back almost instantly and Brand called a halt to the whirlwind activity by beating Harry Gregg for the fifth and final time in the last minute.

Denis Law was on cloud nine. How that number would become so significant to him five months later.

CHAPTER SIX

WEMBLEY WOE

Denis Law will never forget his first visit to Wembley as a Scottish international. It might be accurate to say he would require dynamite to remove it from his memory banks. The Manchester City forward was keenly anticipating his 11th full cap and, as a footballer who never needed any extra motivation, he was eager to make an impact on this occasion.

On Saturday, 15 April 1961, Law and his unsuspecting teammates made their way down the lengthy tunnel from the visitors' dressing room, onto the track and emerged onto the plush and immaculate playing surface of England's national stadium. The Scottish fans had once again turned out in force among the 97,350 crowd. Lion rampant flags were fluttering in the gentle breeze, and tartan tammies and scarves were well in evidence as both teams strode purposely towards the centre circle where they would meet the dignitaries, go through the usual handshake routines and then have a quick limber up before French referee Michel Lequesne blew for the game to commence bang on 3 p.m.

The Scottish team that fateful day was: Frank Haffey (Celtic); Bobby Shearer (Rangers), Eric Caldow (Rangers); Dave Mackay (Spurs), Billy McNeill (Celtic), Bert McCann (Motherwell); Johnny MacLeod (Hibs), Denis Law (Manchester City), Ian St John (Motherwell), Pat Quinn (Motherwell) and Davie Wilson (Rangers).

Not a lot went according to plan during a horrible experience for Scotland. Forty-five minutes later, heads down, the players trudged disconsolately back to the relative safety of the dressing room. They were 3-0 adrift and, painfully and obviously, were being ruthlessly humiliated and punished by their fiercest rivals. Bobby Robson, the Fulham midfielder who would later manage his nation, had netted inside ten minutes. Jimmy Greaves, as natural a goalscorer as the world will ever see, added another two. Dave Mackay recalled, 'Recriminations flew during the break. We were devastated to find ourselves in this position at half-time. I remember thinking that if we did not pull ourselves together, we were in danger of being really massacred – the thought was not one I could entertain. I ran back onto that hallowed Wembley turf like a man possessed. We were determined to pull the game back by sheer force of will if nothing else.

'I scored within three minutes and Davie Wilson netted a second five minutes later. Suddenly it was 3-2 and we were right back in it. The relief was palpable. Then England got a free-kick and Bryan Douglas took it quickly. Too quickly for our goalkeeper Frank Haffey, who caught the ball and then dropped it and watched it bobble into the net. That was it. We buckled and England scored five goals in 12 minutes. Somewhere among the mayhem we managed to score once more through Pat Quinn. It was inconsequential. We were routed like we had never been routed before. It was like we were a Sunday park side who happened by some quirk of fate to be playing Brazil at their peak. We were spectators of our own destruction. Jimmy Greaves, my Spurs teammate, got another and Bobby Smith and Johnny Haynes got two each. I prayed for the final whistle.

'In footballing terms, it was the worst day of my life. Afterwards, in the dressing room, there was no inquest. There was simply nothing to say at that point. We were all in shock. It was like being hit by a car. History has blamed our goalkeeper Frank Haffey, but this is far too simplistic. For a goalkeeper to concede nine goals, his defence must have failed at least nine times, too. That was us. We played crap. Frank played double crap. I felt such a shame for letting my country down so dramatically and did not know how I could face anyone. After the game, Denis Law and I decided we needed to take solace in alcohol and sneaked into the West End for drinks at a club. Alcohol began to deaden the senses until we turned and looked over our shoulders to see half of the England team, all smiles and bathed in the glow of victory, walking in the door.'

Law recalled, 'What a strange game that was – my blackest day and it never should have happened. We never felt out of it even when they were leading 3-0. Then Dave Mackay and Davie Wilson scored after the interval. At 3-2, England were rocking and we were back in the driving seat. We were still trailing, but we had our tails up. Then we conceded a stupid fourth from a free-kick and suddenly they were back in command. We were, to say the least, dodgy at the back with Celtic goalkeeper Frank Haffey having a nightmare game. Don't forget this England team were on a roll having scored 23 goals in their previous four matches. Sure enough, when that fourth goal went in they ran away with it.

'Can you imagine being in a Scotland team that has been beaten 9-3 by England? It might be just about acceptable in a schoolboy match, maybe even in a club match, but certainly not in an international game and most definitely not at Wembley. For the rest of our careers that result made the Scottish players all the more determined on the pitch, because we continually had to live it down.'

Celtic's Billy McNeill, who made his international debut that wretched afternoon, recalled, 'I felt sorry for Denis because there was no greater patriot. However, like the rest of us, his performance at Wembley had not matched his true abilities, but he had certainly not lacked passion and commitment. Indeed, I am sure Bobby Robson would have testified to that. He was on the receiving end of a challenge from Denis smack in front of the Royal Box that left a lasting impression. I felt it was especially unfair of the selectors to point the finger at Denis because, such was his loyalty to the national team, that he angered his club by choosing to play for Scotland. The club game he missed was a league match between Manchester City and West Ham which had a significant bearing on City's First Division survival prospects.

'The selectors were savage after our Wembley mauling. Hardly surprising, Frank Haffey had played his second and last international. Bert McCann, the Motherwell wing-half, also paid the ultimate price. It was Bert's fifth Scotland appearance and he must have known in his heart of hearts there would not be a sixth. On the evening following the game, Bert, Ian St John, Pat Quinn, Dunky McKay, my Celtic teammate, and myself had sought refuge in a backstreet London pub in an effort to escape the attention of the media and the fans. The intention was to drown our sorrows with pints of overpriced beer in the hope the effects of the alcohol would dull the pain sufficiently to allow us to sleep free from nightmare images of Johnny Haynes, Jimmy Greaves and company scoring for fun.

'More seriously, we wondered about our international futures – if, in fact, we had any. We knew there would be a backlash. As I recall, Denis was dropped for the next match against the Republic of Ireland the following month. Rangers' Ralph Brand and David Herd, then of Arsenal but later to become a colleague of Denis at Manchester United, were brought in to spearhead the attack. As luck would have it, they scored two goals each as we won 4-1. Four days later we played a return match against them in Dublin and once again there was no sign of Denis. Everton's Alex Young led the attack and scored twice as we triumphed 3-0. Brand got the other. There was no reprieve for Denis, either, in the World Cup qualifier against Czechoslovakia in Bratislava a week later. We were trounced 4-0 and paid a heavy price for leaving one of our best – if not *the* best – players kicking his heels at home. Four months later we played the Czechs at Hampden and, thankfully, the selectors saw sense and brought back Denis. He responded with two goals in a 3-2 victory. Welcome back, Denis.'

Years on, Bobby Robson did, indeed, recall being clattered by Law. He said, 'In fact, I will never forget when we clashed right in front of Her Majesty Queen Elizabeth at Wembley. I know Denis blamed me for the incident, but I still have the bruises. Kick Denis first? I should be so lucky! He was a real will o' the wisp player, as sharp as a needle and lightning fast in his movements, with a brain to match. The advice I always used to give to anyone who had to mark him was track, mark and tackle … and always wear shin pads!'

Goalkeeper Frank Haffey bore the brunt of the flak. However, if it upset him he certainly disguised it well. Law, as you might expect, was fuming when he heard singing coming from the corner of one of the baths. Haffey recalled, 'Yes, that was me. I always enjoyed a wee sing-song. So, it is a fact that I did a bit of warbling as we got a soak after the game. The baths at Wembley are quite huge. Remember, I was just 22 years old at the time, I was still a Celtic player and I had my whole career ahead of me. I could sing or I could melt into the deepest, darkest depression. I chose to sing. I was sitting there in the bath and all around me was doom and gloom, so I just started singing. Denis Law came over and said, "Damn it, Big Man, for a goalkeeper, you are a great singer." Don't get me wrong, though. I wasn't indifferent to what had happened to Scotland and a 9-3 defeat at Wembley was a very sad situation. I could have sung all night, but I was still shocked and stunned. I might have been trying to laugh it off – or even sing it off – but inside I was completely burned up.

'Yes, I posed for photographs as the press followed me around the following day. There's a picture of me in front of Big Ben with the hands at three minutes past nine. There's another at King's Cross station with me standing under the sign for platform nine. It was just my way of dealing with it. If someone had a problem with that it was their problem and not mine. Obviously, the defeat wasn't all down to me, but I was the goalkeeper and they always get the blame. Back home, I had people practically stalking me with cameras wanting me to pose in front of houses with the numbers nine and three. I had photographs of me taken all over Scotland.'

Haffey never played for Scotland again after the Wembley debacle and when his footballing career was over he emigrated to Australia. In 1989, Denis Law and George Best did a tour Down Under as they took their after-dinner chat show on the road. Best recalled, 'We were performing in Sydney and Frank Haffey turned up. Afterwards, he was engaged in a conversation with my old mate in the car park of the hotel where we were staying. He asked, "Tell me straight, Denis, is it safe for me to come home now?"

'Solemnly, Denis thought about it for a moment, stroked his chin, shook his head and answered, "Not yet, Frank. Not yet."'

CHAPTER SEVEN

HAILED . . . AND FAILED

Denis Law was missing in action when the qualifiers kicked off for the World Cup Finals in Chile in 1962. He had toppled into an international void after the 9-3 humiliation against England at Wembley. Law wasn't helped by the fact that he had moved to Italian side Torino and they weren't sympathetic to Scotland's cause and would only allow their player to represent his country in World Cup-ties. As it turned out, the SFA selectors overlooked Law for the squad for the opening World Cup encounter against the Republic of Ireland at Hampden on 3 May 1961.

'I was dropped for the games against the Irish and Czechoslovakia,' recalled Law. 'I was stuck in Italy with Torino, away from the eyes of the selectors, and I began to feel I'd had it as far as Scotland was concerned.' Ralph Brand, Rangers' livewire frontman, took his place and scored twice in the 4-1 triumph. Arsenal's David Herd, the only Anglo-Scot in the side, also notched a double. Four days later, the Scots beat their Irish opponents again, this time 3-1 at Dalymount Park, Dublin, where Brand scored once more while Everton's Alex Young, a late replacement for flu victim Herd, bagged two.

The World Cup activity continued with a game against Czechoslovakia in Bratislava only a week after the Dublin encounter. Scotland were again without Law. Ian McColl, only 34 years old and still registered as a Rangers player, combined managing Scotland with running a garage business. For whatever reason, he decided to drop Young after his two-goal performance against the Irish. The Goodison forward – known on Mersey-side as 'The Blond Vision' – wouldn't play for his country again for five years. David Herd returned from illness to lead the line. The need for Law's finishing qualities was underlined in this lopsided affair. The Czechs, roared on by a partisan crowd of 51,590, ran amok as they dismantled Scotland 4-0 after sweeping nonchalantly to a three-goal half-time advantage.

All eyes were now on Hampden on Tuesday, 26 September when Scotland attempted to claim back some pride against Czechoslovakia. A crowd of just under 52,000 made it to the famous old stadium and Law, thankfully, was back in his rightful place in the Scotland frontline. The SFA, though, were forced by Torino to insure the Lawman for £200,000. As it turned out, it was worth the risk. Torino pleaded with Law to remain at the club, but were told, 'No chance' – or the Italian equivalent. To many, this was the game that Denis cemented his unique relationship and intimate rapport with the Scottish support. Only five players remained from the nosedive in Bratislava four months earlier – Eric Caldow, Pat Crerand, who somehow sidestepped a suspension after being sent off against the Czechs, Billy McNeill, Jim Baxter and Davie Wilson, the solitary forward to escape the axe. Into the frontline came Alex Scott, Wilson's Rangers team-mate, Spurs' elegant John White, Ian St John, who had just left Motherwell for Liverpool, and Law.

The scene was set for an epic encounter. Could Scotland come back from their bloodied nose in Bratislava? With Denis Law around anything was possible. Czechoslovakia arrived in Glasgow in a relaxed and confident mood. They knew a draw would suit them with two games against the Republic of Ireland still to be played. Three out of four points against the Irish would propel the Czechs towards Chile the following summer. Scotland couldn't expect any favours from their near-neighbours. They knew they had to do it on their own. And so it proved.

A report at the time stated, 'Given the hype and the fact that the match was to be staged under Hampden's new floodlight pylons, it was hoped the elements would smile. Instead, a vicious wind gurgled round the stadium, marginally favouring the Czechs in the first-half. Early goals had detonated all Group 8 games to date and this was to be no exception. In the sixth minute a back-heel from Josef Masopust, a layback from Kadraba and a fierce shot from Kvasnak put the visitors in front. It was an incisive goal and the white-clad Czechs danced a ghostly tango in delight. Like all east European teams, Czechoslovakia had been scathingly dismissed as dour, one-paced, unimaginative. The stereotype had its source in political propaganda, not footballing analysis, and was hopelessly misplaced. The Czech forwards constantly interchanged and the whole side bristled with imagination and power. Not for one moment had they come to defend. Now, a goal behind, the calibre of the Scottish team was held up for inspection.'

The observer continued, 'The Scots could not compete with their opponents' technical wizardry, but they could, and did, combat Czech steel. The game surged from end to end. One moment Brown was leaping at the feet of Scherer, the next, shots from Scott and White were charged down in front of Schroiff. Scotland levelled when Law back-headed White's cross to St John, whose header squirmed under Schroiff's body in the 21st minute. The goal was hardly memorable, but it was all Scotland needed. They powered forward, though the Czechs continued to break out at lightning speed. Scherer's slide-rule pass set up Kadraba for a shot that Brown turned behind for a corner. Soon after the break, Scotland lost a dreadful goal. Jan Popluhar's belted clearance found Scherer, who, to his disbelief, was permitted to stroll 40 yards into the Scottish nerve centre and beat Brown with ease. It was the sort of goal to have coaches and managers tugging at their hair.

'With the wind at their backs and the Hampden Roar in their ears, Scotland dug deep for a spell of frenzied attacking. St John tussled with the giant Popluhar and Law was a constant thorn in the Czech rump. It was Law who equalised in the 62nd minute, drilling White's cross into the net. Hampden was a cauldron, Scotland turning the screw against a cool, calm defence that refused to panic. Falling rain could not dampen Scotland's ardour. St John was felled in the box, but the referee merely awarded an indirect free-kick and not a penalty-kick. Wilson collided with Schroiff and was then crudely flattened by Kvasnak. Czechoslovakia seemed as impressive on the defence as the offence, but with seven minutes to go Scotland took the lead for the first time. White was again the instigator, sparking the move that climaxed with Law swerving clear of two tackles and rifling the ball past Schroiff at the far post.'

Law said, 'The forward line that day was Alex Scott, John White, Ian St John, Davie Wilson and myself. I thought it was good enough to give any defence in the world a hard time. I celebrated by having one of my best matches for Scotland. As well as scoring two goals, I reckon I covered every blade of grass on the pitch during that game.' A nation celebrated an excellent victory. A new star had arrived and manager Ian McColl surprised his own players by moaning about the opportunities they had missed and the goals they had conceded!

Scotland now sat back with bated breath to see if the Czechs would falter against the Republic of Ireland. They might have guessed the outcomes of the matches. The Irish were turned over 3-1 in Dublin and were thrashed 7-1 in Prague. That meant a play-off between Scotland and Czechoslovakia to see who had the right to travel to Chile. A neutral ground was required for the 29 November fixture. Someone at the SFA helpfully suggested Wembley, possibly hoping the Czechs didn't have a great grasp of geography and the fact Scotland played there every second year. Unsurprisingly, the motion was kicked into touch.

Brussels was elected as the destination for the two countries to challenge for a place in the World Cup Finals.

The kick-off was brought forward to 1 p.m. because the Heysel Stadium didn't have floodlights. The BBC beamed the game live and industry in Scotland just about ground to a standstill. Apparently, a one-day flu epidemic swept through the country that decisive Wednesday afternoon. There was the usual wrangle between Law and Torino over his release. The player had missed the two previous games, a 6-1 triumph over Northern Ireland in Belfast and a 2-0 win over Wales in Glasgow. However, at the eleventh hour, the Italians relented and once again Scotland were told they would have to put up £200,000 in insurance for the player. The Italians even sent three officials with Law to Belgium to protect their investment.

Unfortunately, Scotland were forced to make changes for the Brussels encounter. Dunfermline's Eddie Connachan took over in goal and Dundee's Hugh Robertson played at outside-left. Regulars Bill Brown, of Spurs, and Rangers' Davie Wilson were injured. Connachan would only appear once more for his country, in a 3-2 defeat from Uruguay in a friendly in Glasgow six months later. Rangers' Billy Ritchie replaced him at half-time. Neither goalkeeper figured in the future. Robertson's international career ended with the referee's final whistle in the Belgian capital. Alex Scott was also sidelined and his place on the right wing was taken by Rangers colleague Ralph Brand, playing out of position. Celtic's inspirational captain Billy McNeill was missing, too, after picking up a strain playing a league game the previous Saturday. Manager McColl also fielded the Dundee defensive double-act of Alec Hamilton and Ian Ure, who were winning only their second caps. The average age of the side was just 23. Preparations could have been better for such a crucially important confrontation. The full Scotland team read: Connachan; Hamilton, Caldow; Crerand, Ure, Baxter; Brand, White, St John, Law and Robertson. A mere 7,000 turned out for the game, played in monsoon conditions with the pitch cutting up badly throughout two hours of football.

'The Czechs,' as one reporter so ably put it, 'were equipped for all contingencies. If they needed to play, they could play; if they needed to kick, they required no lessons from anyone.' He added, 'Denis Law's electric showing at Hampden guaranteed he would be securely padlocked on this occasion.' Law was shadowed everywhere he went, but Scotland still made the breakthrough as half-time approached. Popluhar, a fine defender who would never become famous for hesitating before dishing out some ruthless punishment, dumped Ian St John, not for the first time, on the muddy surface. Jim Baxter, with comfortable ease, strolled forward to take the free-kick. He sent it into the danger zone and, as goalkeeper Villiam Schroiff was caught in two minds, St John launched himself forward to thump a header into the net. Scotland kept the lead for the following 10 minutes to go in at half-time a goal to the good.

Annoyingly, the Czechs did manage to draw level with 20 minutes remaining. The game had got rougher as the rain continued to pour down from the heavens, just about neutralising the ball-playing skills of the slight John White, so important in the Scottish engine room. These were not his conditions and the Spurs man struggled to make an impact. From a fifth consecutive corner-kick, right-back Jiri Hledik joined in with the attack and planted a header beyond the grasping Connachan. Remarkably, Scotland regained the lead within a minute. The quick-thinking Brand took a free-kick and picked out St John who only had to side-foot the ball past Schroiff for his second goal.

Agonisingly, the clock ticked towards the end of a gruelling, hard-fought encounter. With a mere eight minutes remaining, Scotland were heading for Chile. Then Dame Fortune, as she did on so many occasions, snarled in their direction. The ball ricocheted around the packed goalmouth before landing at the feet of the unmarked Scherer, who fired high past Connachan, the effort striking the underside of the crossbar, bouncing down and out. Law, and every other Scottish player, was convinced the ball did not cross the line. Right-back Hamilton got a good view of the incident and said, 'That ball never went in; no way. It hit the line, but the whole of the ball did not go over it. The referee couldn't have seen it properly from where he was standing, but he gave it, anyway. It was a real sickener.'

So near and yet so far. Scotland would have to do it all again in extra-time. Did they have the stamina to see off a powerful opponent? Law came close to providing an instant answer when he sizzled in a drive that had Schroiff frantically scrambling, but the ball flew just over the crossbar. Then White somehow summoned up the power in his slender frame to wallop in a ferocious 20-yard drive that thundered against the junction of bar and post. It was not to be Scotland's day. Pospichal volleyed one beyond Connachan in the 95th minute and 10 minutes later Scherer beat the Scottish goalkeeper with a long-range effort. The second period of extra-time meant little. The Czechs shut up shop and there was nothing Denis Law or his teammates could do to unlock their blanket defence. Game over. World Cup hopes obliterated.

There was a remarkable incident just before extra-time kicked off when two Scottish players were seen rolling around on the ground, grappling with each other. Pat Crerand, two years before he left Celtic for Manchester United, and Old Firm friend and rival Jim Baxter were the men involved. Crerand explained, 'We gathered around before the restart. The trainer passed me a sponge and Jim tried to grab it out of my hand. We finished up on the ground trying to punch each other. We were about to play the most important half-hour in Scotland's football history and yet we were fighting with each other over a sponge. We were both pals, but we were so angry because they had equalised so late on that we took it out on each other in the heat of the moment.'

Law added, 'Mine was a very depressing and lonely journey back to Turin. A few of the guys in the Torino side played for Italy. They knew they were going to Chile, so they, too, were disappointed for me because they'd thought we would all be going together.'

CHAPTER EIGHT

JUST HEAVEN! ELEVEN IN SEVEN

A Scottish international team without Denis Law was unthinkable by the time 1963 arrived. After making his goalscoring debut against Wales in 1958, Law had appeared in another 15 internationals in four years and had added nine more strikes to his growing tally to leap into double figures. Along the way he celebrated seven triumphs, suffered five defeats and was forced to settle for three draws. Law played only three internationals in 1962, including the 2-0 success over England at Hampden.

The most memorable scoring feat of that year was his four-goal haul as he almost single-handedly demolished Northern Ireland in Glasgow. Billy Bingham put the Irish ahead early on before Law embarked on a personal assault on Bobby Irvine's goal. He equalised five minutes before the interval and netted a second after an hour. He completed his hat-trick in the 77th minute and Willie Henderson added another two minutes later. Law, at his ruthless best, thumped in number five with three minutes to go. A fortnight before that sparkling performance, Law had been on target again in a 3-2 victory over Wales in Cardiff where Rangers pair Eric Caldow and Willie Henderson also scored.

The Jim Baxter-inspired 2-1 victory over England at Wembley on 6 April was the first of Law's seven games in 1963. The Manchester United marvel sat out only one match through injury – a 2-1 defeat against Northern Ireland in Belfast where his rapier-like thrust up front was sorely missed. One observer put it this way, 'The Scottish forward line was as sharp as a sausage.' A frustrated Ian McColl, the manager, was even more succinct. His reason for the defeat? 'Non-triers, as simple as that.' In the seven games in which he had turned out, Law had claimed an astonishing 11 goals. It was to be an eventful year for Scotland's national treasure.

Law was settling back into his natural habitat following the turmoil of Turin. It was obvious to all that Denis Law and Italian football was not a marriage made in heaven. That it lasted only one season before the inevitable divorce surprised no-one. 'I have one thing to thank it for, though,' said Denis. 'It taught me all about man-marking. I hadn't encountered that before in English football. However, it was an accepted fact in Italy that you would be shadowed everywhere you went by an opponent; sometimes two. That sharpens your game. When I came back to play in England it was like I wasn't being marked at all.' Matt Busby paid £115,000 for Law in July 1962 and the Scot immediately earned a place in the affections of the Old Trafford support by scoring 23 goals in 38 games. He was also on target in the 3-1 FA Cup Final success against Leicester City. The following season he averaged a goal a game with a haul of 30. These were exciting times for Law at club and country level.

After the Wembley triumph, Scotland were involved in a remarkable encounter against Austria at Hampden; a rough-house that saw the concerned English referee Jim Finney abandon the contest in the 79th minute with the Scots leading 4-1, Law and Rangers winger Davie Wilson claiming two apiece. Spurs wing-half Dave Mackay was captaining his country for only the third time and admitted the confrontation stuck in his mind because of 'the uncharacteristically filthy play by the Austrians. On this night in Glasgow, I could have sworn they were on a mission to injure Denis Law. We really had to look out for him. Denis could well look after himself, of course, but with five or six maniacs chasing him around the field the odds were not good.'

There was only quarter of an hour gone when the Rangers double-act of Jimmy Millar and Davie Wilson combined with the outside-left firing in the opening goal. They worked a neat one-two ten minutes later and once again Wilson plonked the ball into the net. In the words of Law, 'all hell was let loose' shortly after that. 'The Austrians started to put the boot in.'

Horst Nemec was booked for a vicious foul and then looked as though he was going to have a go at the match official. He was immediately sent off. A seething mass of Austrians, led by their manager, suddenly surrounded Finney. At that stage a visibly shaken English referee threatened to call it quits there and then with a bemused crowd of 94,596 looking on. When proceedings calmed down, Law fired in a third just after the half-hour mark. It didn't get any better following the turnaround and, as Dave Mackay observed, Law had been singled out for some 'special' treatment from opponents who had clearly lost the plot. His colleagues weren't faring much better. Millar was pole axed following a challenge from behind and Willie Henderson was scythed down after a dreadful tackle from desperate defender Erich Hasenkopf. The chirpy little Rangers outside-right later quipped, 'If I had known I was going to spend so much time up in the air in that game I would have brought my parachute.'

It was no laughing matter, though, as the Austrians continued to chop at the Scots; Law, in particular. They lost winger Henreich Rafreider through injury and, with only a substitute goalkeeper on the bench, had to soldier on with nine players. Law made it 4-0 in the 71st minute before Anton Linhart pulled one back almost immediately. The visitors' ranks were further depleted when Erich Hof was ordered off for another dangerous lunge at Henderson. A report noted, 'Law had to avoid a flying boot and then he retaliated. Linhart crumpled to the floor and referee Finney decided enough was enough.' Law was lying on the ground when he looked up to see the Englishman from Hereford walking off the pitch. 'No-one knew what was happening,' admitted Law. Willie Allan, the SFA secretary, then appeared on the pitch to tell the players the game had been abandoned and Finney had no intention of returning. There were only 11 minutes left to play and the match official explained afterwards, 'What could I do? I felt that I had to abandon the game or someone would have been seriously hurt. I ordered off Nemec for spitting and Hof for a diabolical tackle at waist height.'

Jock Stein, then the Dunfermline manager, was in the crowd that evening. He said, 'For too long British teams have been pushed around and booted all over the park by foreigners who continually disobey the rules. I know that in some quarters Mr Finney has been criticised, but, to my mind, he showed great courage. He was right to be concerned about the safety of the Scottish players.'

FIFA, the world's governing football body, later agreed. They backed Finney who then went on to become a senior referee in their international set-up. He returned to Hampden to offici- ate in 1965 when Scotland again won 4-1, this time against Wales. Thankfully, the game lasted the entire 90 minutes on this occasion. Finney was back a year later for the 1-1 draw with Brazil, who were preparing for the defence of their World Cup in England, and he was in charge again as the Scots beat Wales 3-2 in 1967. Scotland remained unbeaten in his four games in Glasgow. Denis Law had competition for his role as his nation's talisman.

It was a bit more sedate a month later when Scotland trav- elled to Bergen to take on the amateurs of Norway in the first of three friendlies in the space of ten days early in June. Denis Law walloped in a hat-trick, but does not remember the game fondly; Scotland lost 4-3 in a genuine shocker. No-one saw this one coming. Possibly Scotland were showing a reaction from the bone-shuddering ordeal of facing up to Austria, but Law, never a man to shirk responsibility, said, 'No excuses.'

Captain Dave Mackay took a knock and was replaced by Leicester City's Frank McLintock in the 78th minute, by which time the Scots were leading 3-2. In fact, it turned out to be a fairly exciting game, a bonus for the 23,000 supporters in the Brann Stadium. Olav Nilsen shot the Norwegians ahead in the fifth minute, but Law responded with the equaliser in the 14th minute and added a second eight minutes later. Erik Johansen had the fans celebrating wildly with the leveller on the hour mark, but that merely sparked another retaliatory strike from Law who hit a third in the 76th minute. Then off went Mackay and McLintock came on to make his international debut. It was one he wouldn't forget with Norway netting twice during the 12 minutes he was on the pitch. Arne Pedersen swept a third past Adam Blacklaw in the 81st minute and, horror of horrors, the Norwegians, with the supporters whipped up to a frenzy, got the winner through John Krogh seven minutes from time.

After the full-time whistle, Denis Law looked at Ian St John who looked at Jim Baxter who looked at Davie Wilson who looked at Willie Henderson who looked at Alec Hamilton. Class players, every one of them. Law and Baxter, in fact, would play in the Rest of the World Select against England in the English FA's centenary match at Wembley in October later that year. Quality counted for nothing in Bergen where raw exuberance from an eager bunch of amateurs won the day. Dave Mackay missed the next game against the Republic of Ireland in Dublin five days later with McLintock making his first start. Manager Ian McColl handed the captaincy to Denis Law, the first of five times he would lead his country. It wasn't a pleasant memory for Law, McLintock or any of the other Scots. They had slipped into a deep lethargy and not even a wake-up call from Noel Cantwell, scoring in the sixth minute, could stir them for the rest of the encounter. Two games, two unexpected defeats and the mini-tour would end with a match against Spain in Madrid on the evening of 13 June. A few years ago I asked Law for his recollection of that game. Here is the interview in full.

'We were due to face the might of Spain in the Bernabeu Stadium, home of Real Madrid, and I thought we were going into this encounter like lambs to the slaughter. I was asked to continue as skipper with Dave Mackay still injured. It seemed I might always recall the occasion for all the wrong reasons. But history books will now show we hit one of the world's top nations on their own ground for six.

'We weren't expected to do too much against the Spaniards. To a lot of people it might have looked like a lost cause, but they reckoned without our fire and spirit. We went out and hammered them 6-2 in front of their own fans and showed anything was possible in this wonderful game. I recall scoring that night. In fact, we played five forwards and we all netted. Willie Henderson, Davie Gibson, Ian St John and Davie Wilson all grabbed goals and the other came from Frank McLintock, then an old-fashioned right-half. As I recall, Spain scored first, but I was lucky enough to get an equaliser shortly afterwards. Then we ran amok and scored three before the interval!

'It was an amazing night altogether because we had virtually no tactics. Ian McColl wasn't a tactician in the Jock Stein mould. So, there we were turning up in Madrid to take on Spain who, as you would have expected, were massive favourites to finish the job before half-time. Thankfully, it didn't quite work out like that. Actually, looking back, that was a very strong Scotland side – we had some exceptional players kicking around at that time. Billy McNeill played against the Spaniards as an emergency right-back. As far as I am aware, he never played in that position again. He was a centre-half, but the No. 5 shirt was taken by Ian Ure, the Dundee player who went on to play for Arsenal before becoming a brief teammate of mine at Manchester United.

'Billy might not have fancied playing out of position, but

he was like myself and so many other players around at that time – we just wanted to play for our country. Okay, I know it sounds corny, but it just happens to be true. I have always insisted that it was a real honour to play for Scotland. Of course, we had a guy called Jim Baxter at left-half against Spain. It didn't seem to matter if Jim was playing the world champions or the local boys' team – he was utterly nerveless. I made a rare appearance as captain in Madrid because that role normally went to a defender or a midfield player. It was highly unusual to have a forward as captain. So, it was just marvellous to be out there and really enjoying the occasion of turning over one of the greatest sides in Europe in their spectacular stadium. Memories are made of this!

'We played them again two years later and only yours truly, Billy McNeill and wee Willie Henderson were the survivors of the team that shook the world. Scotland and Spain fought out a goalless draw at Hampden on that occasion and, before you ask, I wasn't the skipper. Big Billy, back playing centre-half, was the captain – and what a good job he made of it, too.'

For the record, the Scotland team in Madrid on 13 June 1963 was: Blacklaw (Burnley); McNeill (Celtic), Holt (Hearts); McLintock (Leicester City), Ure (Dundee), Baxter (Rangers); Henderson (Rangers), Gibson (Leicester City), St John (Liverpool), Law (Manchester United) and Wilson (Rangers). The line-up that drew 0-0 on 8 May 1965 at Hampden read: Brown (Spurs); Hamilton (Dundee), McCreadie (Chelsea); Bremner (Leeds United), McNeill, Greig (Rangers); Henderson, Collins (Leeds United), Gilzean (Spurs), Law and Hughes (Celtic).

The international scene reawakened on 12 October with a Home International against Northern Ireland at Windsor Park, Belfast. Would Scotland be buoyed up by their scintillating six-goal display against Spain in Madrid? No is the quick answer. Scotland, after fielding Liverpool's Tommy Lawrence against the Republic of Ireland and Burnley's Adam Blacklaw against

Spain, selected their third goalkeeper in as many games with Spurs' Bill Brown returning to the fray. Unfortunately, Law was injured and his No. 10 shirt was taken by Leicester City's Davie Gibson. Brown picked the ball out of his net twice, beaten by Billy Bingham and Sammy Wilson, as the Irish won 2-1. Ian St John claimed Scotland's consolation in the 49th minute. The Lawman returned a month later, on 7 November, for his wonderfully unforgettable four-goal performance against Norway as the Scots responded to the poor show in Belfast with a rousing 90 minutes at Hampden. Frantic negotiations were made to play the game on Thursday after fog wiped out the original date, 24 hours earlier.

Norway, still elated after their victory over Scotland in June, must have thought they were heading for another evening of glory when Per Kristoffersen beat Brown with their first effort on target in the eighth minute. Law then embarked on a demolition job on the unsuspecting Nordics. He levelled in the 19th minute and had the 35,416 supporters cheering again – me and my mates included – just before the interval. The Law Show continued with his third in the 59th minute and then returning captain Dave Mackay thundered in two rapid-fire long-range salvos in the 74th and 76th minutes. It was left to Law to take centre stage just before full-time to tuck the sixth into the net. That brought Law's total to seven against Norway, a tally that would prove to be his biggest haul against any nation during his international career. It is not known if Norwegian keeper Sverre Anderson ever recovered from his meetings with Law.

Denis Law was still enjoying the spotlight when he notched the winner against Wales in a 2-1 triumph 13 days later at the same venue. It was a strong Welsh team that turned up in Glasgow, with Leeds United's Gary Sprake in goal, the centre-backs Terry Hennessey and Mike England propping up the defence, the speedy Cliff Jones on the left wing and the legendary John Charles in attack. John White scored the opening goal a minute from the break and Law joined in with the second in the 47th minute. Barrie Jones scored the Welsh counter just before the hour mark.

With 11 goals from seven international games, Denis Law was well on his way to being named European Footballer of the Year in 1964. Prior to that, the only other Briton who had received the honour was England's Stanley Matthews, the Blackpool and Stoke City outside-right who picked up the inaugural trophy in 1956. Law's personal favourite Alfredo di Stefano won it a year later. In quick succession, it went to Alfredo's Real Madrid colleague Raymond Kopa, di Stefano again, Luis Suarez (Barcelona), Omar Sivori (Juventus), Josef Masopust (Dukla Prague) and Lev Yashin (Moscow Dynamo) before Law was recognised. He is still the only Scot to achieve this accolade.

CHAPTER NINE

ON TOP OF THE WORLD

England, Denis Law's deadliest foes on the football field, made a dream come true for the Scot on Wednesday, 23 October 1963. The English FA decided to mark their centenary with a spectacular all-star exhibition game at Wembley; England would face a Rest of the World Select and various Football Associations around the globe were asked to nominate players who would grace the occasion. The SFA put forward two names; Denis Law and Jim Baxter.

And at 2.45 p.m. in London on that crisp October afternoon, Law found himself rubbing shoulders with his hero, Real Madrid maestro Alfredo di Stefano. My friend Fraser Elder supplied me with the official matchday programme that marked the event. It sold for one shilling (five pence) and informed us the game would take place at Wembley's Empire Stadium. It's hardly the glossy type of memento you would expect today. There are only 20 pages – and five of them are full-page advertisements for the *Radio Times*, Woodbine cigarettes, Booth's Gin, Double Diamond beer and Bovril. Three pages are taken up with photographs (including the England team), the double page spread displays the names of the line-ups and the substitutes (called reserves back then) and there is a full page story under the headline, 'WARM WELCOME TO OUR VISITORS' in a variety of languages including German, Spanish and French.

The lead item is on page five, 'ONE HUNDRED GLORIOUS YEARS' penned by Geoffrey Green. It stated, 'It was October 26th, 1863, that the Football Association was formed at the

Freemason's Tavern, Lincoln Inn Fields, London. We are thus at a point of history – the celebration of the first centenary of any governing body in football.

'All of us here at Wembley today are part of the fiesta; the myriads watching on television are part of it, too; and the 22 players on this national stage of ours are at the heart of it. Heirs of the creators, the visionaries, and the players of a bygone age, they have sprung from the very ideas and loins of the historic giants like C.W. Alcock, Lord Kinnaird, Major Marindin, Sir Charles Clegg, A.T.B. Dunn and a departed host.

'More than that. The talented actors we now see before us somehow symbolise the whole essence and growth of the game, for the story of the Football Association is the story of Association Football. A hundred years ago a pebble was dropped in a pond. The ripples have widened ever outwards and still move towards some unseen shores. It was that initial act of the FA that released all the ensuing flood of energy and now the game spans the five continents of the globe. Like the British Government itself it has "just grow'd", a signal compliment, indeed, in its imitators to the original pioneers and missionaries of these islands.'

All very fanciful and probably meant very little to the seventh child of an Aberdeen trawler man. However, you can imagine a young Denis Law in that Wembley dressing room, a bundle of pent-up energy, pulling on the unique blue shirt and white shorts of the FIFA Select and preparing to display his abilities to the world. Law admitted he had marvelled at the performance of Real Madrid when they won the European Cup in front of 127,261 fans at Hampden Park in 1960. 'I had watched them on television beating Eintracht Frankfurt 7-3. I was enthralled by the quality of play, the goals and everything about this fascinating spectacle. It opened my eyes to the possibilities of football outside Britain. Scotland had played England the week before, but this game was on a different planet. Puskas scored

ON TOP OF THE WORLD

four and di Stefano hit three. I watched that game in awe, little realising that only three years later I would be playing alongside them in the Rest of the World side.'

The souvenir brochure devoted a two-page spread to pen pictures of the Rest of the World team. It told us, 'Denis Law (Scotland) inside-right: A schoolboy international, he first came south from Aberdeen to play for Huddersfield Town. Manchester City paid a £55,000 fee for him in 1960 and Torino £100,000 a year later. In July 1962 he returned to Manchester to sign for United at a £115,000 fee. Dynamic if somewhat erratic genius of inside forward play. Aged twenty-three and has twenty-one caps.'

It also informed us that Russian goalkeeper Lev Yashin was nicknamed the 'Black Octopus', Brazilian right-back Djalma Santos was 'a strongly-built coloured defender of much culture', and West German left-back Karl-Heinz Schnellinger was 'blond-haired, fast and fearless' while Czechoslovakia's Jan Popluhar was a 'tall, dour twenty-eight-year-old stopper'.

French outside-right Raymond Kopa was a 'delicate and versatile artist who has struggled much with injuries to his ankle'. Portugal's inside-left Eusebio, we were informed, was nicknamed 'The Black Panther' and possessed a 'tremendous shot allied to guile and speed', adding, 'He comes from Mozambique and once excelled as a sprinter.' Spanish centre-forward Alfredo di Stefano was 'an Argentinian-born, naturalised Spaniard who has scored over 500 goals for Real Madrid in 10 years. Known as the 'White Arrow', he has thirty-one caps for Spain and seven for Argentina. Expert at screening the ball.' West German centre-forward Uwe Seeler 'excels at scoring from acrobatic angles'. The programme gave Pele his full title of Edson Arantes do Nascimento and told us of the great Brazilian, known as the 'Black Pearl', that he 'first hit the headlines as a seventeen-year-old in the 1958 World Cup and has continued to stay in the news. Brilliant individualist with remarkable ball control and soccer sense. He now has thirty-eight caps and was 23 two days ago!'

Di Stefano's Real Madrid team mate Ferenc Puskas, another much admired by Law, was the 'Galloping Major' who had 'scored a record 85 goals in 84 internationals. Now 37 and, though tubby, is as astute as ever with superb positional sense and lethal left foot.' And another Law favourite, the third from Real Madrid, was Francisco Gento who was 'one of the world's fastest wingers and a difficult proposition to contain by defenders.' Jim Baxter, although only a 'reserve', got a mention, too. We were told, 'Nicknamed "Slim Jim" he is a classical player in the true Scottish tradition. Unhurried, hard-working and displays ample powers of strategy. One of Rangers' few really big transfer signings, he was added to the Ibrox staff in 1960, having been with Raith Rovers earlier in his career. A 24-year-old with 17 caps.'

So, there was Denis Law poised to stride forth onto the world stage ready to strut his stuff alongside the 'Black Octopus', the 'Black Panther', the 'White Arrow' and the 'Galloping Major'. And a Fifer who answered to 'Slim Jim'.

Pele was nowhere to be seen when this Rest of the World team, in a 3-2-5 formation, took the field: Yashin (USSR); Santos (Brazil), Popluhar (Czechoslovakia), Schnellinger (West Germany); Pluskal (Czechoslovakia), Masopust (Czechoslovakia); Kopa (France), Law (Scotland), di Stefano (Spain, captain), Eusebio (Portugal) and Gento (Spain). Reserves were listed as: goalkeeper Soskic (Yugoslavia), defender Eyaguirre (Chile), midfielder Baxter (Scotland) and forwards Seeler (West Germany) and Puskas (Spain).

England went for a 2-3-5 system that read: Gordon Banks (Leicester City); Jimmy Armfield (Blackpool, captain), Ray Wilson (Huddersfield Town); Gordon Milne (Liverpool), Maurice Norman (Spurs), Bobby Moore (West Ham); Terry Paine (Southampton), Jimmy Greaves (Spurs), Bobby Smith (Spurs),

George Eastham (Arsenal) and Bobby Charlton (Manchester United). Their stand-by players were goalkeeper Tony Waiters (Blackpool), defenders Ken Shellito (Chelsea) and Ron Flowers (Wolves), midfielder Tony Kay (Everton) and striker Joe Baker (Arsenal). Four of England's starting line-up – Banks, Wilson, Moore and Charlton – would win World Cup medals at the same venue three years later, much to the annoyance of a certain Denis Law. There were two Scots on the Wembley pitch at the kick-off; Law and referee Bobby Davidson from Airdrie. Or R.H. Davidson, as he appeared in the programme.

A goal in the fading moments by Jimmy Greaves – 'the most natural goalscorer I have ever seen' according to Law – gave England a 2-1 triumph. It was one Law would have been proud to claim. Reserve goalkeeper Milutin Soskic spilled a shot and Greaves was onto it in a flash to tuck it away. The script was written for Law to score on this momentous occasion and he duly served up the equaliser after Terry Paine had given the celebrating home side the lead. Law recalled, 'It was Puskas who opened the way for me to score my goal; his pass was a dream and I found myself beating Gordon Banks for the second time in a few months at Wembley. (Law had netted in Manchester United's 3-1 FA Cup Final success over Banks's club side Leicester City at the same venue on 25 May.)

'Playing with such outstanding players is a memory I will always cherish. To be picked to represent the Rest of the World was a singular honour, as it was for my great mate Jim Baxter, who came on for the brilliant Josef Masopust in the second-half. And it just wasn't on the pitch that it was special. We mixed with those greats in our London hotel, too, and watched the likes of di Stefano and Puskas knocking back the whisky along with Jim Baxter and lighting up their cigarettes. I wouldn't have been surprised if it was Jim who'd introduced the two superstars to his favourite alcohol.'

Law added it was the first time he had met Eusebio and he was 'impressed with this lovely gentleman'. Many years later, the Portuguese legend returned the compliment. He said, 'I admired Denis Law as a player because he was exceptional and very different from a lot of British players from his era. Then British football was characterised by stamina and the determination of the players, who have excellent physical fitness. This is true, too, of other European countries – including the Germans, who are superbly prepared physically. But the British and the Germans, generally, both lacked technique. I have played against Denis Law quite a few times and have also played with him for FIFA and UEFA representative teams. Law is a very fine footballer and thoroughly deserved the European Footballer of the Year award he gained in 1964. He was a good team man with fine individual skills.'

Gordon Banks, rated by Law as 'the best goalkeeper I have ever played against', was another who would never forget the English FA's 100th birthday bash. He said, 'Here was a game I would willingly have paid to play in. It was a big, prestige affair and the Wembley pitch was graced with a procession of the true greats of the game. Jimmy Greaves emerged as the giant of this particular game. He scored one marvellous goal and had an even more spectacular one disallowed because he had been fouled on his way through their defence. Denis Law, my old adversary, was in sparkling form for the Rest of the World team and scored to equalise a well-taken effort by Terry Paine. But it was Greavsie who conjured up the winner with just three minutes of a memorable match left to play. I was like a kid at a Christmas party at the aftermath banquet and unashamedly went round with my match programme collecting autographs of all the players who had made it such a day to remember.'

After the Wembley extravaganza, the much-decorated Brazilian defender Djalma Santos, winner of two World Cup medals in 1958 and 62, was asked who he believed was the most accomplished performer in the game. In a hesitant combination of Portuguese and English, he answered, 'Number eight. Law. Buenos. Muchos.'

Anyone who had ever witnessed Law going through his unrivalled repertoire at his unsurpassable peak would have known exactly what Santos meant. No translation was required.

CHAPTER TEN

ARRIVEDERCI ENGLAND

The 1966 World Cup came to a conclusion with Denis Law wildly hurling his clubs around a golf course. He had just been informed that the host nation England had beaten West Germany 4-2 in extra-time in front of 93,802 fans in the final on the afternoon of 30 July at Wembley. It could have been such a different story.

Law got off to a flyer in the competition with a second-minute goal in a 3-1 victory over Finland in the opening qualifying tie at Hampden on 21 October 1964. After an absence of eight years, Scotland had a genuine reason for believing they could advance to the finals, especially as the tournament was being held across the border. Italy and Poland were the other barriers to the Scots' progress.

Ian McColl was in charge when the World Cup campaign began, but his only involvement was against Finland before he was replaced by Jock Stein in a caretaker capacity. McColl was blissfully unaware that the knives were being sharpened as he prepared for the visit of the Finns. A crowd of 54,442 watched Law open the scoring with his quickfire goal and Celtic's Stevie Chalmers and Leicester City's Davie Gibson pitched in with the other two before half-time. Juhani Peltonen got one for the visitors in the 70th minute, but Scotland were not to be denied their ideal introduction to the tournament. It was one of 16 wins enjoyed by McColl in his 27-game reign as Scots boss. Stein was in the dug-out by the time Scotland would play their next World Cup-tie under the Hampden floodlights, when

Poland provided the opposition a year later. It was not to be a memorable occasion.

Denis Law played in the three games in the run-up to the Polish encounter. Goals from Davie Wilson (2) and Alan Gilzean gave Scotland a 3-2 victory over Northern Ireland at Hampden on 25 November 1964. Law and Ian St John were on target in the 2-2 draw with England at Wembley on 10 April 1965 and a month later the Scots, with Billy Bremner, of Leeds United, and Celtic's John Hughes making their debuts, sparred to a creditable goalless stalemate with Spain in Glasgow. There was controversy when the Spanish side appeared to have rugged defender Severino Reija ordered off by English referee Ken Howley for launching Rangers' tricky winger Willie Henderson into orbit on one occasion too many. New boy Bremner was never convinced the Spaniard did, in fact, go off. He recalled, 'He lay there writhing on the ground, obviously feigning injury. The match official didn't know what to do next. He allowed their physiotherapist to come onto the pitch to give the player treatment. For a few minutes it was bedlam, Spanish players were arguing with the referee and a linesman and it was obvious that neither of them had a clue what was being said to them.

'There was all the usual shrugging of shoulders, arms outstretched and so on from the Spaniards. All the time this was going on, their player was receiving treatment for an injury that didn't exist. Eventually, everyone calmed down, the game restarted and I'm sure both teams still had 11 players on the pitch. The referee either forgot or ignored the fact that he had sent off the Spanish defender and I believe he remained on the pitch for the rest of the game. What a palaver to be involved in on your full international debut. It did give me an insight into the mentality of European footballers and what some of them were capable of. We were able to have a good laugh about it afterwards. What else could we do? As for the referee, well, despite his major cock-up, I don't think anything happened to him. The standard of refereeing didn't really improve through-out my career.'

McColl had seen 1964 begin with a 1-0 victory over England at Hampden on 11 April, when 133,245 supporters saw an Alan Gilzean header from a right-wing corner kick soar past Gordon Banks 18 minutes from the completion of another gruelling duel with the nation's fiercest foes. A month later, the rangy Dundee frontman, with Law alongside him, struck twice in a 2-2 draw with West Germany in a friendly in Hanover. Gilzean claimed the first with a trademark header to pull it back to 2-1 after the hosts had led with two goals from Uwe Seeler. And Gilzean, later to join Spurs in a £72,500 deal in December that year, smuggled in the equaliser after a shot from Law had hit the woodwork. Wales interrupted the sequence of good results with a surprise 3-2 win in Cardiff, when goals from Stevie Chalmers and Davie Gibson weren't enough to salvage a point. The Scots were undone by two goals from the appropriately named Ken Leek in the last four minutes. Normal service was resumed in the World Cup victory over Finland and then came the run of three games without defeat leading up to the match against Poland in Chorzow on 23 May 1965. McColl, given the post in November 1960, might have had every right to believe his job was safe. He would be wrong. Originally, he had been appointed on a game-by-game basis. However, after one season that was changed to a year-by-year contract.

McColl, in fact, was at the team's usual HQ in Largs prepar-ing for the World Cup-tie in Poland when he was asked by the SFA to resign his position. In other words, he was sacked. The timing was certainly odd, but Jock Stein, only six months into his managerial career at Celtic, agreed to take over on a temporary basis until after the World Cup run. The immediate problem for the much-vaunted Stein was to find a strike partner for Denis Law. Alan Gilzean had been on the receiving end of some roughhouse tactics by Spain's thuggish defenders only a fortnight before the trip to Poland. Stein continued to mull over the problem position until the day before the kick-off. Neil Martin, a consistent marksman Stein had known from their days together at Hibs, got the nod. Only three of the team – Denis Law, Alec Hamilton and John Greig – survived from the line-up that had beaten Finland in Glasgow seven months beforehand. Stein sent out this side: Brown; Hamilton, McCreadie; Greig, McNeill, Crerand; Henderson, Collins, Martin, Law and Hughes.

A partisan crowd of 67,462 rolled into the all-seater stadium in Chorzow's Park of Culture. Their spirits must have been somewhat dampened as rain came down by the bucketload. An observer said, 'The Poles were surging through the puddles like power-driven swans.' Stein pulled Law back into midfield for the first-half with Martin, willingly it must be said, going it alone up front. Bill Brown was forced to make a good save in the opening minute as a shot from Ernest Pohl slithered goalwards. Scotland, with Bobby Collins, of Leeds United, and Manchester United's Pat Crerand teaming up with Law in midfield, and John Hughes being asked to hug the left touchline, looked in reasonable control up to the halfway stage. Goalless at the interval, the job was half done. Disaster was to strike, however, five minutes after the restart. The speedy Roman Lentner escaped challenges from Greig and Hamilton before rifling the ball beyond the grasp of the unguarded Brown.

That sparked an immediate response from Jock Stein. Law was thrown into his more recognisable position up front and Hughes, who could also play at centre-forward, came in from the left for a three-pronged attack alongside Martin. The switches worked. Willie Henderson zipped down the right wing before flinging over a cross that was met solidly by Law's forehead, but goalkeeper Edward Szymkowiak touched the effort onto the upright. Only 14 minutes were left on the clock when a flighted Collins ball created confusion in the Polish rearguard. It was cleared to Henderson who headed it back into the mix and once again Law reacted quicker than friend or foe to knock in the equaliser. Not for nothing was the Scot the current European Footballer of the Year. Scotland were content with a point. Italy, too, had to be satisfied with a draw on the same ground.

Four days later, Finland provided the opposition in Helsinki. The Scots had been forced to embark on a 13-hour stamina-sapping trip by bus, train and aeroplane to reach their destination. It proved to be worthwhile although it didn't seem so after five minutes when the Finns opened the scoring through Martti Hyvarinon. Law, who had completed the season as the English First Division's leading scorer with 28 goals, temporarily lost his golden touch when he smashed a 15th-minute penalty-kick against the inside of the post. Undeterred, Law set up the leveller eight minutes from half-time. He collected a ball from Pat Crerand and lashed it into the penalty area, where it was superbly dummied by the astute Hibs playmaker Willie Hamilton. It sped to Davie Wilson, in the team in place of Old Firm rival John Hughes, and he clubbed it behind helpless keeper Lars Nasman. Scotland, playing in white shirts, surged forward as they sensed victory and it duly came their way when John Greig fired in a 25-yard shot five minutes after the turnaround. Greig would later claim that effort as the best goal of his career. Finland couldn't come back from that and the points were on their way to Scotland. Law was voted Man of the Match and won a silver spoon for his efforts.

Five months down the line, Poland again provided the opposition at Hampden. So much rested on this game that Jock Stein had several selection dilemmas to think about. Alan Gilzean, a player lauded and respected by his fellow professionals – Denis Law among them – had failed to start in the away ties against Poland and Finland, but Scotland's temporary manager remained among his admirers. Stein, always a deep thinker and expert strategist, once again pondered long and hard about the line-up and brought Leeds United's battling bantam Billy Bremner into midfield to the exclusion of Hibs' thoughtful, but one-paced, Willie Hamilton. Still looking for thrust up front, the Scotland manager raised an eyebrow or two by giving a debut to 18-year-old outside-left Willie Johnston, of Rangers, while overlooking his own Celtic player John Hughes. The team read: Brown; Hamilton, McCreadie; Crerand, McNeill, Greig; Henderson, Bremner, Gilzean, Law and Johnston.

Wednesday, 13 October 1965 was a bitterly cold evening at Hampden Park. There was a hint of fog in the air. A crowd of 107,580 turned up and for once the mood was more of confident anticipation rather than optimistic expectation. Even at this early stage, it appeared Poland's chances of qualification were remote. They had lost 2-0 to Finland in Helsinki in their previous encounter and Scotland had the opportunity to seal their elimination and propel themselves towards two back-to-back confrontations with Italy to complete the group. At that stage, Jock Stein believed both nations would cancel each other out when they met in Glasgow and Naples therefore making it even more critical there would be no slip-up on this occasion. Poland arrived at the national stadium in the realisation that only a victory would breathe life into their fading hopes.

It was Celtic captain Billy McNeill who settled the nerves of the Scottish players and the onlookers with the breakthrough goal in only 14 minutes. McNeill hit a ferocious shot that was in the net before Konrad Kornek could move. The goalkeeper, under pressure from the towering Gilzean, had failed to deal with a corner-kick from Willie Henderson. His feeble slap directed the ball to McNeill's chest where he controlled it in an instant and first-timed a 12-yard right-foot effort into the inviting net. Scotland's hopes soared; Poland's spirits slumped – for the time being, anyway.

Stein roared from the touchline as half-time approached, claiming a penalty-kick as Jacek Gmoch sent Henderson toppling in the box after a clumsy challenge. The referee wasn't so convinced and merely awarded an indirect free-kick that came to nothing. Scotland refused to go into gung-ho mode as they probed for the second goal. Stein, unusually, was counselling caution from the dug-out. Still, Law had a snap-shot diverted after good service from Bremner and Kornek went some way to atoning for his miserable attempt at a clearance for the Scottish goal when he twice denied Gilzean.

Half-time: Scotland 1, Poland 0. The Scots, with Johnston displaying devastating turns of speed on the left flank, looked in control. What could go wrong? If the Poles were heading for the World Cup gallows, they weren't going without a fight. They had 45 minutes to turn things around. For 39 of them they failed, although they had their moments. The dangerous Ernest Pohl gave goalkeeper Bill Brown, a steady and unfussy custodian, two frights as the visitors, unbelievably, started to boss the game. The Spurs goalkeeper held on grimly to a vicious shot from Pohl and had to be content with saving with his knees when the same player thumped in a wicked angled drive. Scotland were being overrun in the middle of the park; the rhythm built up by Bremner and Pat Crerand in the first 45 minutes had all but ebbed away.

Johnston, so dangerous early on, was starved of service on the left, as was his Rangers teammate Henderson on the opposite flank. Law tried to help out by moving into midfield, leaving Gilzean as the lone target up front. It was torture on the terracing as the minutes ticked down. The Scottish players were now content to hoof the ball anywhere and everywhere to keep the revitalised Poles at bay. The visitors sensed they could get something in enemy territory and they went for it. Frantic whistles from the anxious six-figure crowd implored Swedish referee Kurt Carlsson to blow for time-up. No such luck. The tension was unbearable and something just had to give – and it did in the 84th minute.

Hamilton, the Dundee right-back who was normally such a good user of the ball, was caught in possession by outside-left Eugeniusz Faber, who delivered a dangerous cross into the Scottish box at the far post. Chelsea's Eddie McCreadie was caught unawares as Jan Liberda came thundering in, brought the ball under control and left Brown without an earthly chance as he walloped an unstoppable drive high into the roof of the net. Silence. Mathematicians in the crowd were trying to work it out: was it a point dropped or a point gained? Their mental arithmetic meant little when, with four minutes to play, Jerzy Sadek was allowed to run through and almost casually beat Brown with a neat effort. More silence. Moments later, traumatised and disbelieving, the Scottish supporters, their spirits sapped, filtered out of Hampden, trudging wearily towards the exits. We didn't know it at the time, but Scotland's World Cup ambitions were heading in an identical direction.

Law ended this bizarre and perplexing confrontation with a damaged right knee, limping off at the end as Scotland tried to fathom how they had come to lose their first World Cup-tie at the national stadium for 11 years. What on earth went wrong? Law looked back some time later and said, 'Of all the games I've played in around the world for club or country, this one was the biggest disappointment of all time. I'm still trying to work out how the Poles could score two goals in six minutes against us and win the game. We had control of it for long periods. Maybe if there is an explanation, we relaxed too much. But the dressing room afterwards was like a morgue. We had blown it and we couldn't understand why.'

It was a desperate night to forget for just about everyone – not debutant Willie Johnston, though. He said, 'Despite the result, I will never forget my first appearance for Scotland, especially as it was the first time I played alongside my hero Denis Law. He is six or seven years older than me and as a schoolboy I worshipped him. It was never in my wildest dreams that a few years later I would line up alongside him as I won my first international cap for my country. Throughout the years I have listened to many an argument among fans on just who is the greatest Scottish player of all time. For me, there is only one name that fits the bill – Denis Law. He is a true living legend, the striker who had everything. He had flair, bravery and was the ultimate goalscorer. So many of his strikes were spectacular. He was The King!'

Law, though, was dropped for the next game when Italy arrived at Hampden on 9 November. By his own admission, he 'was going through a quiet patch'. Stein decided to pair Alan Gilzean and Neil Martin, the first time the two six-footers had teamed up together. Law was out and so, too, were Alec Hamilton, Pat Crerand and Willie Johnston. Hamilton would figure only once more for his country. Billy McNeill was injured and Rangers' Ronnie McKinnon was one of two players taking his international bow; Celtic's Bobby Murdoch was the other. Left-back Eddie McCreadie was suspended and Rangers' Davie Provan took over. John Greig was moved from his midfield berth to right-back. Stein sent out this line-up: Brown; Greig, Provan; Murdoch, McKinnon, Baxter; Henderson, Bremner, Gilzean, Martin and Hughes. The Italians had amassed seven points from their first four games and Scotland's mission was simple – a win was an absolute must. A draw wouldn't have meant much at the end of the day.

It was time for heroes. Step forward John Greig. The Rangers powerhouse was magnificent against the Italians. He hogged the headlines for his excellent winning goal two minutes from the end, but his contribution throughout the evening as he relentlessly drove Scotland on under the piercing Hampden floodlights should be neither forgotten nor overlooked. Twice he rescued Bill Brown, who played most of the game with a heavily bandaged thigh. In the first-half, Paolo Barison looped a header over the stranded goalkeeper, but Greig materialised on the line to clear it to safety. He staged an action replay after the interval when Giovanni Lodetti threaded the ball beyond Brown and the Ranger scampered back to boot it to safety. His evening's work was not done, though.

With the clock against them, the fans groaned when Ronnie McKinnon, unchallenged on the left, decided to pass back to Brown. Precisely 11 seconds later they were cheering wildly after a sublime passage of play. The goalkeeper wasted no time in rolling the ball to the twinkle toes of Jim Baxter. The former Rangers player, by now performing with Sunderland and given the responsibility of captaining his country by Stein on this occasion, brought it under control in an instant and strode purposefully forward. He knocked a pass to Billy Bremner who slotted it in front of the galloping Greig, surging menacingly ahead on the right. He switched it back inside to Baxter whose casual pass into space behind the Italian defence was perfection itself. Greig charged through on the blind side and the Ibrox stalwart didn't hesitate as he battered a ferocious left-foot drive from six yards inside the box. Italian keeper William Negri was helpless as the ball zipped in low to his left. There was only one destination for the ball once it left Greig's boot and that was the rigging. Scotland were back in the World Cup. The fans in the 100,393 crowd demanded a lap of honour. Jock Stein told his players to savour the moment and they took a collective bow.

Denis Law, far removed from the action, said, 'I was as thrilled as if I had been playing.' Now there was the last game of the section to be played against the same opposition. Would it be a case of 'See Naples and die?' A nation would discover its fate on a Tuesday afternoon on 7 December. Disaster after disaster dogged Jock Stein's attempts to put together a side that would make the trip worthwhile. As it turned out, even the most optimistic of Scotland's followers could not have held out much hope before the kick-off that was beamed live by the BBC. The performance should have carried an x-certificate.

Bill Brown and Billy McNeill were the first to withdraw through injury. Jim Baxter, so influential against Italy in Glasgow, was next. Intriguingly, though, he was fit enough to turn out for Sunderland in a friendly against Dukla Prague the same day. Stein's friendship with Manchester United's Matt Busby and Liverpool's Bill Shankly was put to the test when these two proud Scots, of all people, were trying to block their players travelling because of league commitments. Law admitted, 'I don't know if I would have been selected for this one, but injury ruled me out, anyway, so I had to sit through the game in utter frustration as Italy got the win they needed.'

A campaign that had started so promisingly at Hampden on 21 October 1964 – with Denis Law scoring only two minutes into the World Cup – was in serious jeopardy. It was swiftly going off the rails and on the morning of the game Rangers outside-right Willie Henderson had to call off after failing to overcome injury. Even back-up defender Billy Stevenson, of Liverpool, was forced to withdraw. In all, Stein's original squad of 22 had been stripped to 14 by the time the game was due to be played. No-one would have dared to believe the Scots could gain a second victory over an Italian side who had won 6-1 against Poland, Scotland's Hampden conquerors. They boasted some of the best players on the planet in Giacinto Facchetti, Gianni Rivera and Sandro Mazzola. Mission Improbable? Sadly, this was Mission Impossible. Even Stein admitted afterwards, 'Until then, we had enjoyed a good year. We had beaten the Italians in one of the best international games ever witnessed at Hampden. However, by the time we got to Naples, we had no chance.'

Stein handed giant Liverpool centre-half Ron Yeats the No. 9 shirt. If it was meant to confuse Italian manager Edmondo Fabbri, it didn't work. Yeats retreated into central defence alongside Ronnie McKinnon as soon as the match kicked off. Stein sent out this side: Blacklaw; Provan, McCreadie; Murdoch, McKinnon, Greig; Forrest, Bremner, Yeats, Cooke and

Hughes. So, it meant Davie Provan moving from left to right in defence and centre-forward Jim Forrest, his Ibrox teammate, playing wide on the right in place of Henderson.

Burly Adam Blacklaw, of Burnley, was the only recognised goalkeeper left for Stein to choose; Spurs' Bill Brown and Kilmarnock's Bobby Ferguson were both injured. Naples would be Blacklaw's third and final cap. His previous appearance for the international team had been two-and-a-half years earlier. Amazingly, it was the 6-2 hammering of Spain in a friendly in Madrid on 13 June 1963. His debut was the same month as the Scots were embarrassed by the then amateurs of Norway 4-3 in Bergen. Blacklaw's record at this level would be largely undistinguished. Three games played and nine goals conceded.

A crowd of 68,873 in the San Paolo Stadium saw Scotland retreat into massed defence from the first moment. Italy, infamous for their deep rearguard strategies that strangled the life out of the game, were on the receiving end for a change. It was their turn to try to pick the lock. The Scottish defence wasn't too fussy how it dealt with their probing. The Italians actually looked ill at ease with the white shirts ranked in front of them. Only seven minutes remained until half-time when Eddie McCreadie made the mistake that, ultimately, would put Scotland out of the World Cup and dump our hopes on football's rubbish tip once again. The Chelsea defender swiped at a pass from Rivera and got nothing but fresh air. The ball ran to Ezio Pascutti who lifted it over the startled Blacklaw. The referee could have put the Scots out of their misery and blown for time-up there and then.

Giacinto Facchetti, the elegant left-back of Inter Milan, doubled his nation's advantage in the 74th minute. Blacklaw made a hash of an attempted punched clearance. It went straight to the feet of the defender about 25 yards out and he lobbed the ball in with ease, sending Blacklaw scrambling furiously and vainly to get back onto his line. Bruno Mora brought down the curtain with the third goal five minutes from the end. The tournament ended in despair and defeat and the patched-up Scotland side must have been relieved to get off that pitch. Italian goalkeeper Enrico Albertosi was asked about his most anxious moment during the game. He thought for a moment before answering, 'When Yeats fell on me.' That just about summed up Scotland's goal threat.

The first thing Jock Stein did when he got home was to hand in his resignation. The SFA had hoped he might continue in the caretaker role, but he said, 'I've got enough on my plate with Celtic. I'll be concentrating everything on my club from now on.' The SFA advertised the vacancy on a part-time basis and stated, 'The job might suit a man with other business interests.' Willie Waddell and Eddie Turnbull both said no. Clyde boss John Prentice, however, took over the job. He lasted eight months before being sacked.

There was to be no happy ending for Edmondo Fabbri and his Italian players. Sensationally, they collapsed to a Park Doo-Ik goal as the unknown semi-professionals of North Korea overcame them 1-0 at Ayresome Park, Middlesbrough, on 19 July to send them spinning out of the 1966 World Cup Finals. Their supporters, who expected so much from their favourites in England, turned out at the airport in their thousands to let the manager and his squad know exactly how they felt. They were greeted by a barrage of rotten fruit.

CHAPTER ELEVEN

THE AULD ENEMY

Denis Law played against England nine times – eight on the trot from 1960 to 1967 – and was on the winning side four times, sampling defeat on three occasions with the other two ending in stalemate. Scotland scored 17 goals and the English claimed 20, including nine in the hammering of Ian McColl's side in 1961. Interestingly, they would score only three goals against the Scots in the next four Home Internationals, being beaten on three successive outings before claiming a draw in 1965 at Wembley.

An awesome total of 1,040,667 fans – averaging almost 115,630 per game – watched the action in Glasgow and London; the highest attendance being the 133,245 who turned out for the 1964 match at Hampden and the lowest was the 'mere' 97,350 who witnessed the rout of Scotland at Wembley three years earlier. Law scored three goals against the Auld Enemy, a total that was a source of irritation to a soccer perfectionist.

The Lawman, playing in only his seventh international, debuted in the Scotland v England encounter at Hampden in 1960. Intriguingly, he had fired five successive blanks after scoring on his debut against Wales in Cardiff in 1958. He had failed to register in games against Northern Ireland (twice), Holland, Portugal and Wales again. Now he was hoping, at the third opportunity, to strike his first goal at Hampden in front of the home support. England, after defeating Scotland 1-0 at Wembley the previous year with a 59th minute header from Bobby Charlton, arrived in Glasgow confident of another victory. Law and his colleagues had other ideas, of course. Joe Baker, who would become a teammate of Law at Italian side Torino a year later, was chosen to lead the English frontline. Bizarrely, Baker was a Hibs player at the time and was one of ten home-based Scots on display that afternoon.

As usual, there was the tussle between club and country to get players released. Spurs manager Bill Nicholson, who made one appearance for England in 1951, was as English as Law was Scottish. He refused to allow goalkeeper Bill Brown and the inspirational midfield duo Dave Mackay and John White to play for their nation on this occasion. Airdrie's No. 1 Lawrie Leslie was injured and Celtic's Frank Haffey won his first cap. Hearts centre-forward Alex Young also made his debut and there was a recall for his Tynecastle teammate John Cumming, the wing-half making his return after a five-year absence; his last appearance coming in a 2-2 draw with Yugoslavia in a friendly in Belgrade. Manager Andy Beattie, who would quit the post six months later to concentrate on club football with Nottingham Forest, also brought in three Motherwell players – Bert McCann, Ian St John and Andy Weir – as well as naming Denis Law at inside-left. Celtic defenders Dunky McKay and Bobby Evans, Rangers left-back Eric Caldow and Fulham forward Graham Leggat were the survivors from the team vanquished at Wembley 12 months earlier.

The Hampden game had no chance of becoming a spectacle with ruinous gusts of wind creating havoc when the ball was in the air. However, Hungarian referee Jeno Szranko saw fit to award England two penalty-kicks, three if you include a retake. With the Scots leading 1-0 after a ferocious angled strike from Graham Leggat left Ron Springett helpless in 17 minutes, Dunky McKay was adjudged to have pushed Bobby Charlton shortly after the interval. The Manchester United icon nonchalantly stroked the spot-kick past Frank Haffey who went right as the ball flew in the opposite direction. With the tartan-bedecked fans howling for justice, the match official awarded England another penalty. Haffey saved the first from Charlton, but Szranko spotted an infringement – the goalkeeper claimed it was because Law had rushed into the box before the kick had been taken – and ordered the ball to be placed on the spot again. This time Charlton fired past the keeper's right-hand post.

So, honours even and Denis Law had Wembley in his sights a year down the line. As we've covered that disastrous 90 minutes in a previous chapter we can swiftly move on to happier memories.

Scotland had been deeply embarrassed by the 9-3 thrashing from their old foes in 1961. Six years earlier, Law, then a schoolboy, recalled feeling extremely hurt when Scotland toppled 7-2 to the same opponents at the same venue, especially as the goalkeeper had been Fred Martin, then playing for Denis's local favourites Aberdeen. Ian McColl, who had replaced Andy Beattie 18 months earlier, prepared for the visit of England on 14 April 1962. He kept faith with five players who had been on the receiving end of a footballing nightmare the previous year. Rangers' Eric Caldow and Davie Wilson, to figure prominently on this occasion, Celtic's Billy McNeill, Ian St John, who was by now a Liverpool player, and Law were the men given the opportunity to get their own back on the English with 132,441 watching inside a heaving Hampden Park.

Bill Brown, with Spurs boss Bill Nicholson finally relenting and giving the go-ahead, replaced Frank Haffey in goal and there were also places for Dundee right-back Alec Hamilton, Pat Crerand, Celtic's forceful midfielder, Jim Baxter, the elegant Ranger, John White, the equally stylish Spurs player, and Rangers' pacy outside-right Alex Scott. Unsurprisingly, England manager Walter Winterbottom kept the same attack that had gone goal crazy at Wembley: Bryan Douglas, Jimmy Greaves, Bobby Smith, Johnny Haynes and Bobby Charlton. They had shared eight goals among them; Greaves with three,

Smith and Haynes with doubles and Douglas with a single. Midfield player Bobby Robson, who hit the opener past Haffey that bleak afternoon for the Scots, was injured. Sunderland's Stan Anderson replaced him and his international career was over after only two appearances.

England had devastated Scotland at Wembley with Robson scoring in the eighth minute and Greaves adding another two before the half-hour mark. This time it was England who were on the receiving end in the early moments. The lively Wilson, who had netted a hat-trick for the Scottish League against their English counterparts a few weeks beforehand, was on target in the 13th minute to the joy of his teammates and the relief of the supporters. Wilson's shot flew past the stranded centre-half Peter Swan, who was on the goal-line. He made a valiant effort on the line to kick clear, but he only succeeded in diverting the ball high into the net. Billy McNeill recalled, 'Denis Law was the architect of the goal after dribbling round goalkeeper Ron Springett and presenting Davie with the simplest of chances. Denis was outstanding and his darting runs and constant movement pressurised the English defence throughout the 90 minutes. I think he took the 9-3 defeat personally.'

As the Celtic captain pointed out, Law was in the thick of the action throughout proceedings as he challenged menacingly in the air and on the ground at every opportunity. England thought they had equalised when a shot from Haynes battered against the underside of the crossbar and came down on the line. Dutch referee Leo Horn waved play on. The match official awarded Scotland a penalty two minutes from the end when Swan, threatened by Law, handled the ball and Caldow made no mistake with the spot-kick. McNeill added, 'England were fortunate to hold us to two goals. Significantly, it was the first time for 15 games that England had failed to score. In truth, we completely outclassed them.'

Law's former Huddersfield boss Bill Shankly was in the

crowd at Hampden and said, 'England had been favourites to win, but Pat Crerand and Jim Baxter conducted the orchestra brilliantly. It was a typical bone-hard end-of-the-season playing surface, but it made no difference to those guys. They pulled the ball down and utilised it so well. Denis Law was also brilliant. What a display from him and his teammates. However, it riles me, frustrates me and annoys me to think of all the great players Scotland have had over the years and yet they haven't done anything. It's criminal after all that talent we've had that there's not been a really successful Scottish international team.'

Scotland returned to the scene of the crime in 1963 and five players remained in position from the calamity two years earlier – Eric Caldow, Dave Mackay, Ian St John, Davie Wilson and, of course, Denis Law. Willie Henderson took over from Alex Scott on the right wing from the line-up that had been successful in Glasgow 12 months earlier. Otherwise it was the same forward line. Law was buzzing and had already become the darling of the Scottish support. In the previous Home International, against Northern Ireland five months earlier, the Manchester United menace had banged four past goalkeeper Bobby Irvine, who played his club football in Northern Ireland with Linfield. Law had gone into that game after rifling in four goals for United in the previous league game. Eight goals in five days – not bad by anyone's standards.

The Wembley confrontation was only five minutes old when there was a sickening collision between Eric Caldow and England's bulldozer of a centre-forward, Bobby Smith. Willie Henderson claimed, 'I heard the crack above the din and I was over on the other wing.' That was the end of the contest for the Rangers defender, who was carried off with a broken leg. Smith continued, hobbling on the left wing with a knee injury. Substitutes had yet to be given the go-ahead by FIFA and Dave Mackay offered to take over Caldow's role on the left-hand side of the defence. Manager Ian McColl puzzled everyone, including the player, by nominating Davie Wilson. The Ibrox outside-left agreed to the switch, but insisted, 'I told the boss I would play in the position, but only if he remained on the touchline to offer advice. He had been up in the stand at the kick-off, but came down to see the extent of Eric's injury. Then he told me of the switch. I had never played there in my life. However, he agreed to remain trackside and I took confidence from that.' McColl explained, 'On my way down from the Royal Box, I had been wondering what to do if Eric had to go off as was, sadly, the case. Even though the game had only gone five minutes, I could already see that our half-back line of Mackay, Ure and Baxter had settled. I didn't want to disturb the situation. I knew Davie Wilson very well, so I asked him to play left-back.'

Jim Baxter then took centre stage. I recall a conversation I had with Rangers legend John Greig, who would make his international debut against England a year later, when we were discussing the merits of this extraordinary individual. Greig smiled, 'He does things with that ball others can only dream about. Do you know, he calls his left foot "The Glove"? When he's playing all you can hear are cries in that Fife accent, "Gie the ba' to The Glove." He's a one-off, alright. I remember a game against Partick Thistle at Firhill. It was the dead of winter and they had no undersoil heating at the time. The playing surface was treacherous, just like an extended sheet of glass. All of the Rangers players were changing their studded boots for rubber moulds. Well, everyone except one – Jim Baxter. He had already put on his usual boots with leather studs and he wasn't changing them for anyone. We implored him, but he just grinned and said, "'The Glove' will be okay." You can guess what happened next. He went out and didn't put a foot wrong while the rest of us slid around on our backsides for the entire game.'

The Baxter Glove was in full working order against the English. The eccentric left-half rarely made a tackle if he didn't believe the situation merited it. However, England right-back and captain Jimmy Armfield would later testify that Baxter could, in fact, tackle with the best of them. In the 29th minute the Scot robbed the defender as he foolishly tried to dribble round him. His timing in the challenge was impeccable. Then he elegantly strode into the danger zone and flashed an unstoppable drive between Gordon Banks and the right-hand post. The lurking Denis Law, in a good position, might have expected a pass from his pal, but Baxter's only intention was to plant that ball behind the goalkeeper. This he managed with a certain amount of aplomb. And Law was the first to congratulate him.

Leo Horn, the referee who had awarded the Scots a penalty-kick at Hampden the previous year, was to do so again two minutes later. The panicking Ron Flowers felled Willie Henderson and there was only one man to take the kick – Jim Baxter. He placed the ball on the spot and sauntered forth before casually and almost contemptuously rolling it into the net with the England goalkeeper guessing wrong. Baxter's slide-rule left-foot drive swept to Banks's left as he moved to the right. Law, hands on hips, watched from the 18-yard line, obviously confident in his teammate's prowess from the spot. Henderson said, 'I was fond of a cigar back then, the bigger the better. People used to see me with these massive things and comment, "Mind you don't fall off that, Willie." If I had a cigar in the back pocket of my shorts that afternoon, I would have lit up when Jim went forward to take that kick. He was never going to miss.' Blackburn Rovers' nippy raider Bryan Douglas beat Bill Brown with a fine effort with 11 minutes remaining. However, this was to be ten-man Scotland's day. The awful memory of 1961 was beginning to dissipate. Veteran sportswriter John Rafferty noted in the *Scotsman*, 'Bewhiskied Scottish fans weaved onto the field and kicked their tartan bonnets into the goals and planted standards on the greenest turf in Britain. Impatient policemen chased them, but they were not to be moved.'

We always were a nation to do things with a certain amount of élan and panache. At least the crossbars, on this occasion, remained intact.

Bobby Charlton knew how much beating England meant to his Manchester United teammate. 'When Nobby Stiles and I were helping England win the World Cup, Denis made a point of playing golf. Whenever we played Scotland, Denis would kick us both and call us "English bastards" within the first minute or so of the match. It was as though he felt obliged to make a statement and, having done so, he could then get on with the game.

'When I played my first match for England in Scotland I remember the bus journey from Troon up to Glasgow. It seemed there was scarcely a house where someone wasn't hanging out the window shouting the Scottish equivalent of, "You'll get nowt today." Sometimes we did, sometimes we didn't, but there was always one certainty – if there was a Scottish deficit, it would never be one of the heart. Down the years I formed the impression that no-one embodied this national pride more strongly than Denis and on my visits to his country there was always at least the hint that he was regarded as the most patriotic Scottish player of them all. I know that this image for him will always be the matter of deepest pride.'

Law was in his usual No. 10 berth a year later when England visited again on Home International duty on 11 April 1964. Manager Ian McColl made five changes from the triumphant Wembley line-up, some enforced through injury. Bill Brown, the unfortunate Eric Caldow, Dave Mackay, Ian Ure and Ian St John were replaced with Campbell Forsyth, a promising young goalkeeper at Kilmarnock, Celtic's stuffy left-back Jim Kennedy, a defender who rarely crossed the halfway line unlike his eventual successor Tommy Gemmell, Rangers' reliable John Greig, Billy McNeill, now captaining Celtic and Scotland, and Dundee's Alan Gilzean, a towering presence in the middle of the attack.

Facing Law that day was his former Huddersfield teammate Ray Wilson, who had since moved on to Everton. The left-back said, 'I saw Denis in the tunnel, smiled and said, "Hi, Denis." He just looked me up and down and said nothing. In fact, he looked at me as though he hated me.'

The game, played in driving rain and swirling winds, was still deadlocked until the 72nd minute. Match official Leo Horn, beginning to be recognised as a lucky omen to Scotland, awarded the home side a corner-kick on the right. Davie Wilson skipped over to take it before sending the ball arcing into the penalty area. It seemed to be held up in the air by an invisible hand in the gusty conditions while there was the usual pushing and shoving as the England defenders bellowed the time-honoured cry, 'Get a jersey.' Whoever was supposed to be marking Alan Gilzean – probably Spurs' giant centre-half Maurice Norman – wasn't listening. Gordon Banks appeared to hesitate as Gilzean propelled himself forward to score with a near-post header. Once again, for the third consecutive Auld Enemy encounter, the Scottish fans were celebrating. It remained 1-0 and most of the 133,245 fans repaired to the nearest hostelries. It was a good time to be a publican in the Mount Florida area.

Goalkeeper Banks recalled years later, 'That was my first game in Glasgow and it's no exaggeration to say that a Hampden crowd in full voice can be terrifying when you first hear it. For me, it was like hearing an explosion of guns from the enemy lines. I am sure the Hampden Roar could have been heard way down over Hadrian's Wall. Before their goal, I had Bobby Moore to thank for preventing me from giving away another. I miscued a throw right to the feet of Denis Law, of all people. He was so surprised to have it presented to him that he delayed his shot and Moore made one of those interceptions of his that were to make him a world-renowned defender. As I came off leaden-footed at the end, all I could see were thousands of Tam O'Shanters waving in the air like a field of tartan flowers. There is no celebration to match the one when the Scots have got the better of England on the football field.'

It was the third time Law and Gilzean had spearheaded the attack – they would play together on another six occasions – and later on there were suggestions of a rift between the pair. Law had a firm take on the rumours. 'Gillie is a friend. As for us not blending, he was ideal for me. I like to play it quick and sharp and Alan has this great ability to play one-touch stuff. There's nobody better to give you that half-yard extra space. Had he played for Scotland more often, we would have had a better team. He also has the sort of wacky good humour that keeps up morale. You get to know to check the salt and pepper pots. I'm not the only guy who has found the lid slackened and got the lot in my soup.'

The so-called fall-out between Law and Gilzean appears to have no substance. In the games where they dovetailed, Scotland scored 18 goals and the players shared ten strikes equally between them. Scotland won four of the nine encounters – against Norway (6-1), Wales (2-1), England (1-0) and Northern Ireland (3-2) – drew three – against West Germany (2-2 and 1-1) and Spain (0-0) and lost two – against Northern Ireland (2-3) and Poland (1-2).

Denis Law, with Ian St John replacing Gilzean, at last got on the scoresheet at the sixth time of asking against England on 10 April 1965. Alas, there was to be no victory parade at Wembley as a dour, tense struggle ended in a 2-2 draw. Spurs' Bill Brown was reinstated in goal with Chelsea's adventurous Eddie McCreadie replacing the pedestrian Jim Kennedy at left-back. Pat Crerand, Law's Manchester United mate, came in at right-half with John Greig moving to the left and Billy McNeill commandeering the role in the middle of the defence. Leeds United veteran Bobby Collins wore the No. 8 jersey. Spurs inside-right John White, at the age of 27, had tragically died after being struck by lightning while getting caught in a storm on a golf course in the summer of 1964. Law lamented at the time, 'He was killed in the prime of his life. It was a tremendous loss, not solely for his family, but for all of his teammates at club and international level. He was a super player who had still to reach his peak. He was wonderful to play alongside. John White was a favourite player of mine.'

Denis Law must have been the first name on Ian McColl's team sheet at the time. His four goals against Norway in the 6-1 win at Hampden in November 1963 brought his total to 15 in his last nine internationals. He had also netted four against the vulnerable Northern Ireland, another three as he waged a one-man campaign against Norway, two against Austria before the game was abandoned with 11 minutes remaining, and singles against Wales, Spain and Finland. The Manchester United attacker was also on target against Wales in a 2-1 victory 13 days after his virtuoso performance against the Norwegians. Alan Gilzean swept round lunging goalkeeper Gary Sprake to set up Law with a simple tap-in, his 21st goal in 22 internationals. Law, only 23 at the time, was well within sight of Hughie Gallacher's 23-goal record for Scotland. It was phenomenal finishing from an exceptional player. Law added another with a second-minute effort against the Finns as the Scots triumphed 3-1 at Hampden on 21 October 1964.

Law was now sitting on 22 strikes for his country. Could he equal Gallacher's feat at Wembley? The guy's timing was perfect and, yes, he scored his goal as Scotland came back from two down to claim a point. Bobby Charlton netted the opener in the 25th minute with a drive that flicked off Alec Hamilton and left Bill Brown flapping. McColl's men were in disarray by the time Jimmy Greaves had doubled the advantage ten minutes later with a shot that went in off a post. Thankfully, Law managed to pull one back four minutes before the half-time break, when he tried his luck with a dipping shot from 30 yards that left a befuddled Gordon Banks stranded on his goal-line. The

England custodian, normally so reliable, tried to kick the shot away and didn't look too clever as it zipped under his foot and sliced into the net. A crestfallen Banks said, 'I don't know what on earth happened with that goal. Denis simply scored with a shot that deceived me. He didn't get a lot of goals from outside the box and he really surprised me that day.'

England were severely handicapped in the second-half with injuries to defender Ray Wilson and West Ham forward John Byrne. In the circumstances, Scotland piled into attack and duly levelled with an Ian St John counter in the 59th minute. The Scottish press weren't ecstatic about the final 2-2 scoreline or the display. One said, 'England were clearly toiling with their injuries and, to all intents and purposes, they only had nine fit players on the field. They were there for the taking. Everyone saw it apart from Ian McColl and his players.'

At Hampden a year later, the Scottish fans had three goals to cheer. Unfortunately, England, with their players eager to prove to manager Alf Ramsey that they were good enough to be selected in his World Cup squad, netted four at the other end. John Prentice was now in charge of the international side and put out this team: Bobby Ferguson (Kilmarnock); John Greig (Rangers), Tommy Gemmell (Celtic); Bobby Murdoch (Celtic), Ronnie McKinnon (Rangers), Jim Baxter (Sunderland); Jimmy Johnstone (Celtic), Denis Law (Manchester United), Willie Wallace (Hearts), Billy Bremner (Leeds United) and Willie Johnston (Rangers). The Scots went into the match with plenty to prove. They were still disappointed at failing to reach the finals in England. Jock Stein had said during the ill-fated campaign, 'It will be like playing home games if Scotland can get there.' It wasn't to be, so hammering England 'to send them home to think again', in the words of the Tartan Army, would be the next best thing.

For 34 minutes there wasn't a murmur; the Hampden Roar stifled, for the time being, anyway. Geoff Hurst scored in the

18th minute and Roger Hunt added a quickfire second. However, it was Denis Law who gave the Scots hope with an unforgettable corkscrew header three minutes from half-time. Willie Johnston flashed over a left-wing corner-kick and Law rose majestically at the near post, moving in front of Bobby Moore. With one athletic twist of his slight frame, his head made perfect contact to send the ball hurtling into the net. Gordon Banks didn't even move; there would have been little point. Law's future Manchester United teammate Martin Buchan later said, 'That's as near to perfection as you will ever see in a football game.'

Goalkeeper Bobby Ferguson looked as though he was suffering stage fright in front of the 134,000 audience and he was left flat-footed when Hunt rattled in England's third only two minutes after the turnaround. Celtic's marvellously-entertaining Jimmy Johnstone zipped one past Banks ten minutes later, but Ferguson was again rooted to his line when Bobby Charlton fired in a long-range drive for number four in the 73rd minute. Again, the stubborn Johnstone replied with eight minutes remaining. Astoundingly, Scotland almost levelled in the fading moments. Willie Wallace swept a close-range shot past Banks, but dreams of a dramatic comeback were dashed when Nobby Stiles materialised to head the ball off the line. England would, of course, go on and win the World Cup and in doing so only concede three goals in their six games; one against Portugal in the semi-final and two against West Germany in the final. Uruguay, Mexico and France drew blanks against the English in Group One, as did Argentina in the quarter-final.

Scotland had managed in one match something that took another six nations to achieve in the World Cup. Unfortunately, in the grand scheme of things, it meant very little.

CHAPTER TWELVE

WEMBLEY WONDERS

Denis Law produced a spellbinding, enthralling, magisterial performance in Scotland's 3-2 triumph over England, then the world champions, at Wembley on 15 April 1967 in front of a crowd of 99,063. There might have been some English fans in attendance, but they were rarely seen and certainly not heard. Law scored a typical smash-and-grab goal and generally led the forward line with a perceived arrogance born of supreme talent. Bewilderingly, that was to be his last international appearance at Wembley. Even more puzzling is the fact that there would be an absence of five years before he figured again in this fixture; a 1-0 loss at Hampden on 27 May 1972. That, in fact, transpired to be the last time he kicked a ball against England.

However, that particular afternoon in London in 1967 is one of Law's favourite memories. His passion for his country was never doubted, but to play England 'on their own midden', as he once put it to me, while they were the World Cup holders stirred his patriotic emotions to the point of spontaneous combustion. Here was a man with something to prove. This was a professional footballer about to make a statement. It didn't matter a jot that Denis's Manchester United pals Bobby Charlton and Nobby Stiles had helped in conquering the best players in the world the previous year. Law just didn't appreciate the team known dismissively as Sir Alf Ramsey's 'wingless wonders' or 'Ramsey's Robots'. They became the first country in history to play all their World Cup games at the same venue, Wembley, and largely performed in a football style barren of flair and flamboyance. So, they were in Denis Law's line of sight when he strode onto Wembley that day. There was one snag, though. No-one gave Scotland a snowball's chance in hell of winning.

Bobby Brown had taken over as the new international boss, the first-ever full-time manager appointed by the Scottish Football Association. Celtic keeper Ronnie Simpson was making his debut at the age of 36. A relatively unknown forward who had failed to make the grade at Chelsea, Jim McCalliog, at the age of 20, became the first Sheffield Wednesday player to be capped by Scotland in 47 years.

There was even the possibility of Denis Law missing the occasion. Sir Alex Ferguson recalled, 'I was included in the Scotland squad for that game as stand-by in case Denis failed to recover from a knee injury that was bothering him. The remote possibility of running out at Wembley encouraged me to book flights for my dad, brother Martin and my mate Billy McKechnie to go to London. It was my dad's first England v Scotland match and he loved it. I didn't make the team, but we were there to celebrate a famous victory with a performance from Jim Baxter that could have been set to music.'

Tommy Gemmell, Celtic's buccaneering full-back, takes up the story. 'You could have written Bobby Brown's pre-match tactics on the back of a stamp and still have had space left over. In short, there weren't any. That suited Denis Law. Denis used to tell everyone that he hoped Matt Busby, his Manchester United manager, would leave his tactics talk to just before the kick-off and then he wouldn't have time to delve into too much detail. However, if Busby gathered the players around him on a Friday afternoon he had hours to spare. Denis just didn't want to know. All he wanted to do was get out there and play.

'As a Celtic player, of course, I was used to Jock Stein meticulously planning for all our games. It didn't matter if it was Real Madrid or Raith Rovers, you knew exactly what you had to do when you went on the pitch against your opponents. To be fair to Bobby Brown, if we didn't already know what we were about to face at Wembley that day we must have been living on the moon for a year. We got England rammed down our throats constantly after they won the World Cup – or 'borrowed' it for four years, as Denis might have said. According to the scribes across the border, we were wasting our time even turning up for the game. Apparently, it would be easier to nail jelly to a wall than to believe we would win. It was a foregone conclusion. Try telling that to someone such as Denis Law. Or Jim Baxter. Or Billy Bremner. Or me, for that matter.

'The bookmakers rated us as 7/1 against and, as we all know, these guys rarely got it wrong. They might just have lowered those odds had they been in the Scottish dressing room that day. I sensed a real "we'll show them" attitude from my team-mates. Absolutely no disrespect to Bobby Brown, but we didn't really need a manager that wonderful afternoon in April. The atmosphere was electric. We were in London to do the business and shut up the English once and for all. Denis was never convinced they deserved to win the trophy, anyway. There was all that controversy about Geoff Hurst's second goal that crashed against the underside of the crossbar and came down and bounced close to the line. Was it over? The Russian linesman nodded his head and England were 3-2 ahead in extra-time. No Scot, or neutral apart from that Russian, was ever convinced the entire ball had crossed the line. Newfangled technology has since proved that it did NOT go over the line. A bit too late to rewrite the history books. My English pals – and, believe it or not, I do have a few – keep insisting that the discussion over that effort doesn't mean a thing because Hurst scored a fourth with virtually the last kick of the ball. Oh, really? Well, the pattern of play wouldn't have been the same, for a start. But there were also fans on the field of play when Hurst charged through on a ball from Bobby Moore. It gave us the famous line from

TV commentator, Kenneth Wolstenholme, "They think it's all over – it is now."

'There are no ifs and buts about that one. If there are supporters on the pitch the game must be stopped. Why wasn't it on that occasion? Could it have something to do with England playing a World Cup Final in their own country? Would they have got away with it if the game had been in Brazil, Argentina, Italy, oh, anywhere? Of course not. Certainly not in Scotland! So, I have to admit there was a bit of simmering resentment as we prepared for the match against the Auld Enemy. We didn't need anyone to stoke the fires in our belly for this one. There was no point in any motivational speaking. In fact, there was no point in tactics. Every single Scot in that dressing room was puffed up and ready to go long before the kick-off. We all knew what we had to do, none more so than my old Manchester United mate. I had a bit of a reputation as being fairly laid back just before games. It was pretty much the same on this occasion, but I do admit the adrenalin was pumping a wee bit fiercer than normal. I looked around and I saw Denis. Slim Jim. Wee Billy Bremner. There was our Celtic goalkeeper Ronnie Simpson preparing for his international debut in his thirties. And then, at the other side of the age scale, there was young Jim McCalliog, of Sheffield Wednesday. Talk about a baptism of fire!

'There was John Greig, my old Rangers adversary, Chelsea's Eddie McCreadie, in at left-back with me on the right, Ronnie McKinnon, a sturdy, reliable centre-half, and two more Parkhead colleagues in Willie Wallace and Bobby Lennox. I looked at all of them – they were raring to go. Slim Jim was going on about showing England "a thing or two" in this encounter. He didn't rate them, either. And yet they had gone 19 games unbeaten until they came up against us that afternoon. No doubt they were confident of extending that run against a bunch of no-hopers.

'I remember the Scotland squad went to a cinema in London

an evening or two before the game at Wembley. Would you believe it – the England squad turned up to watch the same movie? I think it was a James Bond film. Denis, Billy Bremner, Jim Baxter and Eddie McCreadie played their football in England, of course, so as you could imagine there was a fair bit of banter flying around. Needless to say, I joined in. Goodness knows what the other patrons in the cinema thought. But I detected the English might not have been as confident as those who were saying we shouldn't have bothered turning up for the game. If they thought we were going to face the underdog then they got a different impression that night. My quick-witted teammates had them on the ropes. England 0, Scotland 1, without a ball being kicked!'

Willie Wallace answered an SOS to join the international squad only two days beforehand when his Celtic pal Jimmy Johnstone took a knock in the 3-1 European Cup semi-final first leg win over Czechoslovakian champions Dukla Prague at Parkhead. The man who still answers to the nickname Wispy rattled in two goals against Dukla on Celtic's way to making history that season and he was immediately invited to join the team preparing to take on the world champions. 'Amazed? You could say that,' recalled the likeable Wallace who now resides in Queensland in Australia. 'I hardly had time to draw breath. It was unfortunate for Jinky, but it opened the door to me and presented me with a truly memorable occasion. I was playing through the middle at Celtic, but I was asked to take Jinky's place on the right against England. That might have seemed strange to some, but I had played outside-right on a few occasions for Hearts before moving to Parkhead.

'Slim Jim Baxter was outstanding, England could do nothing to close him down. Wee Alan Ball snapped at his heels like a furious little terrier, but Jim simply ignored the attention from one of the world's greatest midfielders. He would even taunt the fiery little redhead who had a squeaky voice. "Hey, Wispy,"

Jim would shout, "what do you think he'll sound like when his balls drop?" There was a veteran comedian around at the time called Jimmy Clitheroe. He dressed up as a schoolboy and played this character "The Clitheroe Kid". He had this annoying, silly voice. Just to rub it in, Jim started calling the Englishman The Clitheroe Kid! Ballie didn't look too impressed. But it was a fabulous display from Jim and certainly not the sort I had witnessed too often during our two years at Raith Rovers when we started out together.

'A packed Wembley against the World Cup holders was his sort of stage. The same goes for Denis. These spectacles were where they did their best work. Yes, Denis had a few words with Jim during the game when he started to take the mickey, with all the keepy-uppy stuff and the like. Denis had been in the Scotland team that had been gubbed 9-3 six years earlier and he wanted to inflict as much pain on them as possible. He urged Jim to think about getting more goals, but my old mate was too busy enjoying himself to think of the practicalities. It finished 3-2 and I suppose that scoreline might make some people believe it was a tight confrontation, but, of course, that wasn't a true reflection on the gulf between the two nations that afternoon.

'Slim Jim had commandeered the dressing room before we walked out onto the pitch to be greeted by thousands of fluttering Scottish flags and tartan scarves everywhere. I had to remind myself we were actually playing at Wembley and not Hampden. Jim kept saying all the way down the tunnel, well within earshot of our opponents, "World champions? England? Don't make me laugh!" He had been telling everyone he was going to thoroughly enjoy the day and he would be looking forward to "nutmegging" a few opponents. Bobby Brown had given us a wee pep talk before we left the dressing room. I had to laugh when I heard that unmistakeable Fife accent telling everyone, "Ah'm no' gonnae mark anyone," adding, "They can try to mark me." How could we lose? I looked at Denis and I saw a fierce determination in his face. He enjoyed a pre-match joke or quip to help ease the tension and soothe the nerves like the rest of us, but on this occasion, very clearly, he was going out to get a job done.

'Happily, I was involved in our first goal when I fired in a low shot from the right side of the penalty area. Gordon Banks went down and got a hand to it, but couldn't hold the attempt. He spilled it and that was all Denis needed to swoop and put the ball away. Denis's reflexes in the box were like lightning. Make a mistake when this lad was around and you would be punished. He was incredible. Banks must have had that sinking feeling as soon as the ball bounced from his grasp. It came back to Denis at a fair pace, but he didn't even break stride as he walloped it into the net. I still get a thrill all these years later just thinking about that strike.'

Banks, like so many others, had succumbed to the master marksman. Wallace continued, 'Denis might have had another that afternoon but for a truly remarkable save from Banks. Law wriggled clear of the England defence and spotted the English goalkeeper off his line. He deftly lifted the ball up and over Banks with his right foot. It was floating unerringly towards the top corner when the keeper somehow miraculously somersaulted backwards, threw his right paw at the ball and clawed it round the post. It was genius from Denis to swiftly sum up that situation in the first place, but it was equally genius from Banks to thwart him. Two world-class players pitting their wits against each other in a sublime moment of football.'

The goalkeeper remembered the incident vividly. 'Denis was leaping to celebrate what he thought was another goal when I catapulted back and palmed away his shot for a corner. Denis, one of the game's great showmen, dropped to his knees in disbelief. "Brilliant," he cried, adding swiftly, "You bastard!" He called it out in a mixture of appreciation and annoyance. Denis was one of those players who always had a word for you during the heat of battle. It was often a rude one, but delivered with a cheeky grin on that Danny Kaye face of his.'

Wallace added, 'I'm sure Denis actually came close to applauding that save from Banks. You know, everyone got a boost from just being in the same team as Denis. With him around you realised you could take on the world with a reasonable chance of success. He just exuded confidence. As my big pal Tommy Gemmell said, the people who wrote off Scotland with Denis Law in the line-up must have been doolally.'

Bobby Lennox, scorer of the second goal with a crisply-struck right-foot drive from the edge of the box that eluded Banks low to his left to make the scoreline 2-0, said, 'Before the game at training in Hendon, north London, I remember being hugely impressed by Denis. He would have a bit of fun in training, but, other than that, everything he did was carried out with professionalism and precision. It was great to have Denis around – he had so much charisma that it rubbed off on everyone and raised our spirits.'

Banks added, 'The Scots really had themselves stoked up for that match and we knew they were ready to run through brick walls for victory. As far as Scotland were concerned, this was the World Cup Final. Denis was at his most effective and swaggered around the pitch as though he owned it. Twelve minutes from the end, Bobby Lennox, who had been giving George Cohen a lot of problems on their left wing, made it 2-0. Jack Charlton pulled a goal back almost immediately and then I let in a bad goal from Jim McCalliog. I committed the cardinal sin of not guarding my near post properly as I came out to meet him after he had evaded two half-hearted tackles.

'When a goalkeeper comes off his line at an angle, he should have his near post covered so that it forces the attacker towards the far side of the goal. That way the goalkeeper knows almost for certain which way he is going to dive. So, I was taken una-wares when McCalliog shot and beat me at my near side where I had left an inviting gap. Geoff Hurst made it 3-2 and we nearly scrambled an equaliser in one of the most dramatic finishes to an England v. Scotland match.

'There was an amusing – or horrifying, depending on how you look at it – postscript to the match. Our team coach, with a police escort to speed us through the traffic, slowed down at a crossroads about a mile from Wembley where an army of Scot-tish supporters were celebrating their victory at a pub on the corner. They saw the coach, thought it was theirs, and started to do victory jigs and to chant "Scot-land ... Scot-land ..." Suddenly it dawned on them that they were cheering the English team. I have never seen such a quick change of mood. Beer bottles and glasses rained down on our coach as our driver put his foot down and got us away unharmed. Goodness knows what they would have done had Scotland lost the game! It had been a nerve-racking day and after their victory the Scots had the cheek to claim the world championship and their maraud-ing fans tried to take the Wembley surface home with them as a souvenir. Hundreds of them invaded the pitch at the final whistle and started to dig up great lumps of the sacred English turf.'

Debutant Ronnie Simpson, who passed away on 20 April 2004 at the age of 73, was annoyed at the end of the game. A superb photograph figured in most of the national press showing the veteran goalkeeper, minus his false teeth, celebrating with the young Jim McCalliog at the final whistle. He had taken over from Bobby Ferguson, the Kilmarnock goalkeeper who would join West Ham United for £65,000 – a British record fee for a keeper at the time – later that summer, and was determined to keep a clean sheet. Ferguson had failed to convince Bobby Brown, a former Scotland international No. 1, of his worth. Ferguson had played in seven of the previous eight Scotland

Left: The Laughing Cavalier, the enduring image of Denis Law in his Scotland strip. *Harry Goodwin*

Below: England beware! The Scots pose for a team group as they prepare for the match against the Auld Enemy at Hampden on April 11, 1964. The line-up (back row, left to right): Alec Hamilton, Jim Kennedy, John Greig, Campbell Forsyth, Ron Yeats and Billy McNeill. Front: Willie Henderson, John White, Alan Gilzean, Denis Law, Davie Wilson and Jim Baxter. Note there are twelve Scots on display – Yeats was a reserve. Alan Gilzean claimed the only goal of a memorable occasion. *Mirrorpix*

Left: The famous Lawman salute. He's pleased with himself after netting a long-range effort in the 2–2 draw with England at Wembley on April 10, 1965. Denis is about to be congratulated by Pat Crerand (No.4) and Willie Henderson. *Mirrorpix*

Below: Denis the Menace. Law thrived on games against the English and he threatens here with Keith Newton and Jackie Charlton teaming up to repel the dangerman. Willie Wallace looks on. Law fired in an unstoppable header, but England won this amazing confrontation 4–3 at Hampden on April 2, 1966. *Getty Images*

Above: Pick it out. Denis Law, with a cobra-like strike, smashes a rebound past a grounded Gordon Banks to put the Scots on their way to a history-making 3–2 triumph at Wembley on April 15, 1967 – one of the player's finest memories. Skipper Billy Bremner prepares to skip in delight while Martin Peters looks on in despair. It was England's first defeat since they upset Law by winning the World Cup the previous year. *Getty Images*

Below: Out of luck. Denis is just off target at Wembley with a left-foot effort where, as usual, his pace and anticipation have made space in the defence. *Getty Images*

Above: The save of a lifetime. Law's wonderful lob is pawed round the post by Banks to deny the Lawman a typical goal. Even Denis acknowledged the agility of his English rival. George Cohen (No.2) and Bobby Moore (No.6) breathe a sigh of relief.

Below: Headmasters. There was talk of a 'fall-out' between Jim Baxter and Denis Law after the 1967 win at Wembley. Baxter wanted to take the mickey while Law was desperate to widen the winning margin. Both laughed off the suggestion later in life. *Mirrorpix*

Above: At full-stretch. Denis sees the ball plucked off his toe by Gordon Banks in his last match against the English which ended in a 1–0 defeat on May 27, 1972 at Hampden. Denis deserved so much better in his last hurrah against his fiercest foes. *Getty Images.*

Below: High and mighty. Denis made his international return after more than a year's exile for the crucial World Cup qualifier against Czechoslovakia on September 26, 1973 at Hampden. Law knew a triumph would take Scotland through to the finals for the first time in sixteen years – and he won Man of the Match applause after his determined display in the 2–1 victory. Here he powers in a header. *Corbis*

Law triumphant. Denis adopts his famous arm-in-the-air pose as he celebrates Joe Jordan's winner against the Czechs. He was on his way to the World Cup Finals – at last! *Corbis*

Above: The final strike. Law launches a typically acrobatic effort into the Northern Ireland net in the 86th minute after keeper Pat Jennings (not in pic) fails to cut out a corner-kick. David Clements is out of luck in his attempt to block the attempt. It was the thirtieth – and alas – the last of Denis's goals for his country. As usual, it inspired the Scots to a 2–0 victory with Peter Lorimer netting the second a minute from time on May 20, 1972 at Hampden.

Below: Rise and shine. In his one and only appearance in a World Cup Finals tie, Denis strikes a typical energetic pose as takes to the air to fire a header at the Zaire goal in Scotland's way to a 2–0 win in West Germany 1974. *Corbis*

Forever The King. The stylish, strutting merchant of menace as all Scottish fans will remember the one-and-only Denis Law, the hero of a nation. *Mirrorpix*

games and had conceded goals in every game, 12 in total and four against England in a 4-3 defeat at Hampden the previous year.

Brown stuck to his guns about the decision to bring in Simpson, quaintly known as 'Faither' to the rest of his Celtic teammates. The newly-appointed manager said, 'I knew Scotland had a problem in that position. I had witnessed it first-hand on several occasions. I thought it was time for a change and not for one moment did I ever think Ronnie Simpson would let us down. He was a reliable, safe pair of hands. He also had experience of the Wembley pitch after having played there twice for Newcastle United in the early fifties, so the ground would hold no surprises for him. To my mind, he was the most consistent goalkeeper around at the time and it was hardly a risk putting him in against England. I didn't care what age he was; I was only ever interested in ability. Anyway, he must have been doing something right if Jock Stein picked him for Celtic week in, week out.' A month and ten days after that ringing testimony, Ronnie Simpson would pick up a European Cup medal as part of the triumphant Parkhead team against Inter Milan in Lisbon.

The goalkeeper wasn't thinking that far ahead, though, in the jubilant Wembley dressing room afterwards. Tommy Gemmell recalled, 'He was genuinely upset that England had managed to score two goals inside the last six minutes or so. That underlined the perfectionist in our goalie. He didn't want to concede any goals and Denis wanted to score more. Some people are never happy!'

The redoubtable Ranger John Greig led out Scotland that day and said, 'What a memory and what an honour to captain a team with the likes of Denis Law, Jim Baxter and Billy Bremner in it. That game was the highlight of my international career. Every player did their bit – and more – that afternoon. I had positive vibes before the game. Honestly, I was convinced we were going to create an upset. The English football press did us a favour by suggesting that we shouldn't even be allowed to share the same pitch as their lads.

'Comments like that went down like a lead balloon, particularly with a guy like Denis. He, more than anyone else, was determined to stick two fingers up to the opposition. They underestimated us, no doubt about it, and I thought the scoreline flattered them. We enjoyed our celebrations afterwards and my club teammate Ronnie McKinnon and I stayed an extra night in London because Rangers were flying to Bulgaria on the Monday for a European Cup-Winners' Cup-tie against CSKA Sofia. We arranged to meet them at Heathrow Airport.'

The timing was fortunate for Greig because Scotland's triumph over the world champions created a bit of a stir in the capital. The Rangers man was hurriedly invited to appear on the *Eamonn Andrews Show* on Sunday night. They used to open the chat show with the words, 'And now live from London ... the *Eamonn Andrews Show*!' Actually, it was taped on the Sunday afternoon and broadcast in the evening. The Scottish captain, thankfully, hadn't overdone the celebrations the previous evening and sailed through the performance while sharing a couch with American crime fiction writer Mickey Spillane. A young singer also appeared on the hour-long show, a Welsh bloke by the name of Tom Jones.

Afterwards, Greig returned to his London hotel and hooked up with Denis Law. 'After a late breakfast, Denis and I visited a nearby pub after Denis had expressed a desire for a pint of shandy. The barman obviously didn't have a clue who we were. The pub was empty at that time on a Sunday and when the barman heard us speak he immediately recognised our accents and asked us if we were down for the game. "Yes," I replied and added, "but that fellow Law is seriously over-rated." The barman totally agreed with me, but you should have seen his face when I turned and pointed to Denis, who was by now spluttering with indignation, and I said, "I'd like to introduce you to Denis Law."'

Law recalled, 'That was a game that all Scots will fondly remember, especially the sight of Slim Jim Baxter doing his tricks and taking the mickey out of the World Cup winners on the very ground where they had beaten West Germany the year before. Everyone had expected us to be slaughtered, but we weren't because we had no fear of England whatsoever. We knew we had a good team and we knew that if we played the way we knew we could play we would cause an upset. I have played in games when I have not been in the better team, but this time we were the better team and nobody could argue about it.'

CHAPTER THIRTEEN

LAW AND BAXTER

Denis Law wanted to annihilate them. Jim Baxter wanted to humiliate them. It would be fair to say the two Scots weren't quite on the same wavelength on the afternoon of 15 April at Wembley in 1967 when Scotland faced England, the unbeaten world champions.

The story goes that Law was raging at his teammate when he attempted to make fools of Sir Alf Ramsey's men. Here was a Scotland team clicking into place, firing on all cylinders, players brimming with confidence, the ball running straight and true and everybody performing to the maximum of his ability. England were groggy, on the ropes and looking for an escape route. Law wanted to go straight for the jugular; Baxter was quite content to play the juggler.

Tommy Gemmell recalled, 'Yes, there seemed to be a wee bit of animosity between Denis and Jim that day. One of the worst experiences in Denis's career was that 9-3 hammering. It rankled with him and he never wanted to talk about it. You brought up that particular topic at your peril. But you knew he wanted to exact revenge at some point and this was the ideal platform. It could not have been stage-managed better by a Manhattan director. England had played 19 games and had remained unbeaten since winning the World Cup the previous year. They were in Denis's sights, though, and he realised this was the day he had waited for for such a long time.

'I have to admit I indulged myself a little, too. Like Slim Jim, I just couldn't help myself. I remember playing a bit of keep-ball with Billy Bremner and Willie Wallace with little Alan Ball in the middle of our triangle trying desperately to intercept a pass. Billy would stick it to me, I would pass it to Wispy and he knocked it back to Billy. Wee Ballie was going off his head. All I could hear in his squeakily little voice was, "You Scotch bastards … you Scotch bastards" as he ran from player to player. All the time, Denis is standing upfield screaming for us to get the ball to him. And who will ever forget those marvellous pictures of Jim indulging in a bit of keepy-uppy as he sauntered nonchalantly down the left-hand side of our midfield? That image will live with many forever. Meanwhile, Denis has got steam coming out of his ears as he hollers for a pass. Jim would just sling him a deaf 'un. He was enjoying himself too much. The scoreline didn't matter to him, just so long as we scored at least one more than England.

'Aye, I suppose we could have piled them on that day. We were in control and sparking in every department. It was a fabulous team performance and, naturally enough, we took a lot of confidence from Denis's early opening goal. I still laugh when I see that goal. If you view film of it again, have a look at the player getting treatment down at the byline beside the England goal. I had taken a dull one from their left-back Ray Wilson as I sent over a cross from the right. It was painful and I went down like a sack of spuds. On came the trainer and he was working on the leg when Denis put us ahead. He went through his usual arm-in-the-air celebration as the stadium erupted. That goal worked better than any magic sponge that had ever been applied by any trainer. I was up on my feet in jig-time and to join in the celebrations.

'Denis enjoyed the moment, no doubt about it. And you could see he wanted more. He was absolutely desperate to stuff that ball behind Gordon Banks as often as possible. We won, but he didn't quite get his wish of a rout and I suppose anyone now looking through the record books will see a 3-2 scoreline and believe it had been a tight encounter. Really, nothing could be further from the truth. Denis would just have to put up with a historic win at Wembley over the Auld Enemy. Hopefully, that helped get him over the frustration of us not piling on the agony and racking up a more emphatic scoreline.'

There were reports of Denis and Jim exchanging pleasantries in the dressing room afterwards. In 1992 I had ample opportunity to ask Jim Baxter about that memorable afternoon a quarter-of-a-century earlier. A video had been put together of Jim's spectacular playing days and someone requested a bit of publicity to help with the launch. I was sports editor of the *Sunday Mail* at the time and I received a call from a producer asking if I could assist in any way. The cost of advertising the tape would have been exorbitant and would have immediately cut into any cash raised for Jim. A normal practice is to give over a reasonable amount of space in the newspaper and run a competition. 'Win 20 signed Jim Baxter videos', that sort of thing. It works both ways. Jim's video is brought to the attention of the public – and the *Sunday Mail* might even pick up an extra reader or two. Back then, the *Sunday Mail* enjoyed by far the biggest circulation of any newspaper in Scotland, achieving figures of over 900,000 and sometimes close to one million. It was just about saturation coverage of a nation with a population of some five-and-a-half million. For advertising purposes, it is reasoned that one newspaper is read by three people. Rounding up figures, that would mean that three million people would have read that *Sunday Mail*. So, if you were a sports fan, you couldn't have missed the fact that a Jim Baxter video had been launched.

Anyway, I arranged to meet Jim and have a quick chat about how we would go about getting the best for both him and the newspaper. We agreed to meet in a pub next to his flat in Shawlands on the south side of Glasgow. Possibly, we might go for a bite to eat at some point, or get some 'lumpy stuff', as Jim called it. No chance. Jim was in fine form, telling all sorts of stories and recanting memories from the past. Some I might even have been able to publish. We got round to Wembley 1967 and the alleged fall-out with Denis Law.

'What argument?' queried Jim, shrugging his shoulders. 'Me and Denis? We're the best of pals. Och, I've heard all the tales and I accept he wanted to rub their noses in it. But, believe me, Denis and I celebrated big style at the end. I just got carried away in the moment. It was allowed, as far as I was concerned. Our wonderful supporters enjoyed every minute of it. Not a day goes by that someone won't stop me to talk about me playing around with the ball. It was just a bit of fun. They remembered that, but would they have stopped me to talk about the goals if we had scored five or six? Probably not. It was just a wee bit of off-the-cuff stuff that brought the house down. Hell, we were all enjoying ourselves, weren't we? It was a good day to be Scottish. Okay, maybe I wouldn't have done it if I had been in a Scotland team thumped 9-3 by England. Maybe I would have thought about getting more goals.'

Jim, dressed casually in a black T-shirt, navy blue trousers, black slip-on shoes and a dark brown suede jacket, then took a sip of his Bacardi and Coke, let the liquor roll past his tonsils, looked me straight in the eye, smiled and said, 'I doubt it, though.'

Denis Law and Jim Baxter always brought something special and indefinable to the Scotland set-up. They were genuine world-class stars – and they knew it. Law was an admitted fan of the elegant Baxter and has always included him in his all-time list of greats. He would never have hesitated in selecting him for any team. Law is on record as saying the Scottish players who have impressed him most are, in no particular order, Dave Mackay, Billy Bremner, Billy McNeill, Pat Crerand, Ian St John, Davie Wilson, John White, Jimmy Johnstone, Alan Gilzean, Danny McGrain, Bill Brown, Eric Caldow and, of course, Jim Baxter.

Law would say, 'You would want John White in your team along with Bremner, Mackay, Baxter and wee Jimmy Johnstone – five foot nothing with the touch of a butterfly. They would be the first names in and you'd quite happily build your team around them.'

Sadly, Jim Baxter, at only 61 years of age, passed away on 14 April 2001 and Denis Law was among the mourners at the funeral at Glasgow Cathedral six days later. Law said, 'He turned on the class when we beat England in 1967. He was the best player on the park that day. To beat the world champions on their own ground was mainly down to Jim Baxter.'

CHAPTER FOURTEEN

SCREEN GEMS

We should file this chapter under 'You Can Never Have Too Much Of A Good Thing'. I have revisited the DVD of the 3-2 triumph over England in 1967 several times in the course of putting this book together; all in the name of research, you understand. It's amazing what you miss first time around. Or second. Or third. I believe that was the finest all-round performance I have ever witnessed from Denis Law and, of course, there is a landslide of great memories from which to choose.

I decided to go through it on almost a minute-by-minute basis and I've noticed a few things that had previously escaped my attention. For a start, the commentary for ITV was provided by Englishman Hugh Johns and the summary came from former England captain Billy Wright, who won 105 caps for his country. What? No Archie Macpherson? No Arthur Montford? The Scottish viewers were getting served the English viewpoint on the big game and some of the observations during the 90 minutes appeared to be transmitted through gritted teeth. Are you sitting comfortably? Here we go as referee Gerhard Schulenburg puts his whistle to his lips.

Kick-off: Jim McCalliog passes to Denis Law who moves to the left and slips a pass to Billy Bremner. Billy Wright, 'I think England will win, but you should never underestimate the Scots.'

40 secs: Law is already looking in the mood as he skips past challenges from Bobby Moore and Nobby Stiles before being blocked.

55 secs: Ronnie Simpson throws the ball to Jim Baxter for his first touch.

2: Billy Bremner intercepts Alan Ball's pass to Bobby Charlton and releases Law on the left wing. George Cohen boots the ball off Law's shin for a throw-in. Hugh Johns, 'Cohen is one of those players out there who play their football really hard.'

3: Tommy Gemmell takes the ball off the toes of Jimmy Greaves with a solid, well-timed tackle.

3.30: Law and Baxter combine for the first time, but the move comes to nothing.

4: First foul of the afternoon, with John Greig clattering into Geoff Hurst. Johns reminds us, 'There's Geoff Hurst, the man who practically won the World Cup here nine months ago.' It's the first of many references to the fact that England are world champions.

4.30: Baxter floats in a cross from midway inside the English left flank. Law springs to meet it, but is just beaten by the alert Moore.

5: Scotland win the first corner on the right after Gemmell and Lennox combine. Willie Wallace sends the kick straight to Bobby Charlton on the edge of the English box.

8: Gemmell is creating danger with his raiding on the right flank and his flashing cross is inviting. Law launches himself at the ball, but it's just a shade too high.

10: Jack Charlton is injured after a lunging tackle on Lennox.

10.30: Lennox's right-wing corner-kick drops to Law who wildly lashes the ball yards over the bar from inside the box. Johns, 'Law looks downcast. He didn't get his accuracy right from a possible scoring position.'

12: Jack Charlton goes in hard again on Lennox. Both players collapse. Lennox recovers after treatment, but the English centre-half limps off with the help of trainers Harold Shephardson and Les Cocker. Johns, 'That's a tragic sight for English supporters.'

15: Law boots the ball away angrily after the ref awards a foul for a challenge on Cohen.

16: Great tackle from Law on Cohen and he stabs a pass in front of Eddie McCreadie, but his left-wing cross is cleared. Johns, 'That's the fervour of the Scots. They've raised their game, they're playing quicker and that's why there is pressure on England.'

17: Simpson is brought into action as he deals with a vicious effort from Hurst on the edge of the box. Johns, 'The Scottish goalkeeper handled that very well.'

18: Law and Cohen are getting stuck into it, as are Bremner and Ball in midfield. Law brushes off the England right-back to pass to Bremner who slips the ball to Jim McCalliog. He finds Law who sets up Baxter. He slides a pass to Wallace who is foiled with a last-ditch tackle from Ray Wilson.

19: Charlton is still off the field. Johns, 'This is a blow to England.'

19.30: Stiles fouls Law who responds with a pat on the head for his Manchester United teammate. Bremner slips the free-kick to Greig who thunders one well wide of Banks's left-hand post.

20: An amazing miss from Law. Banks takes a short goal-kick to left-back Wilson who is caught in possession by Wallace (or wee Willie Wallace, as Johns calls him throughout the commentary). He tees up Law, racing in at speed, but he thumps the ball into the side netting. He lies on his back, a disconsolate figure. Johns, 'Denis must be wondering how to high heaven he managed to miss that one. It was great play from Wallace and Law has missed an open goal with no-one near him. That's the biggest let-off England are likely to get this afternoon.'

21.30: Desperate to make amends, Law tries an acrobatic scissors kick from a Gemmell cross, but is given offside. Law clearly doesn't agree and argues with the ref.

23: Gemmell cuts in from the right to sizzle a left-foot drive goalwards that is cleared for a right-wing corner by Moore. McCalliog becomes the third different player to take the dead-ball effort. He crosses and there is the remarkable sight of Baxter leaping the highest to fire in a header that is dealt with by Banks.

25: Gemmell is sent spinning by Wilson to earn Scotland another corner. The Scottish right-back is injured and needs treatment as trainer Walter McCrae races to his aid. Johns, 'That was a good, strong and perfectly fair tackle. The referee gives no foul.' Lennox's corner is a poor one and is cleared.

26: Jack Charlton returns to the action and moves up to
the forward line with Stiles brought back to play central
defence alongside Moore.

27: Charlton is back just in time to see Law score the opening
goal. McCreadie rolls a free-kick to Baxter who picks
out Wallace. His first effort is cleared, but comes straight
back to him a yard inside the box. He rearranges his body
shape and thumps in a low drive. Banks can't hold the
ball and Law is onto it in a flash and it's in the net. Johns,
'Law has scored.' There is a pause as it sinks in with the
TV commentator. Then he adds, 'There's the Manchester
United man. (Law has his arm in the air and is heading
back up the pitch.) Wallace is the one who got the shot
in. It bounced out and Denis Law smacked it into the net.'
Law is congratulated by Baxter, Bremner and Greig. There
is a handshake for Wallace and then Gemmell, making a
remarkable recovery from the injury for which he was being
treated only moments before, comes into view with Lennox
and McCalliog joining in. Wright, 'It's been coming, Hugh.
Scotland have been the more impressive side and especially
Law. He has been a real terrier. He has worked and worked
and he got his just reward coming to him there. He was so
quick to put the ball in the net. England are right up against
it now.' Johns, 'The flags are waving and we can hear the
roars from the Scottish fans. There must be about 40,000 in
the stadium and they are really making themselves heard.'

29: Law is still all action as he races at Jimmy Greaves,
sidesteps him, does likewise with Moore and has his shot
blocked by Martin Peters. There is a quick square-up
between the players, but the referee calms things down.
Law looks as though he is ready to go to war with anyone
wearing a white shirt. Johns, 'The Scots are turning on the

133

pressure and they're fighting for every ball. They are not giving England a moment's peace.'

30: Wallace leaves Banks helpless with a rasping 18-yard drive, but it zooms just too high. Johns, 'The man who made the goal for Law very nearly got the second.' There are already cries of 'Easy … Easy' coming from the visiting fans. Banks's goal-kick sails into the Scottish half and Baxter outjumps Jack Charlton to head clear. The Sunderland midfielder, like Law, is clearly in the mood.

31: Not content with using his head, Baxter stops a Hurst cross with his hand. Moore sends in the free-kick and an unmarked Jack Charlton heads over the bar. Simpson remonstrates with his central defenders and Gemmell joins in.

33: There's the strange sight of Law in the right-back position as he gains possession and passes the ball forward to Baxter.

34: Law is downed by Moore deep in enemy territory. Johns, 'No foul, that was a good, hard tackle by England's captain.'

35: Balancing things up, Greig flies into a tackle on Stiles. Johns, 'That was a great challenge by the Scottish skipper.'

36: Jack Charlton is proving to be a threat as he sends in a flying header from a Ball left-wing cross that is excellently held down at the post by Simpson.

37: Now we have Law at left-back as he outjumps Jack Charlton to nod the ball down to McCreadie who is then fouled by Ball. Free-kick. Before it can be taken, Baxter gets treatment in the Scottish penalty area. Johns, 'He looks happy enough. He is just taking the opportunity to have a breather with Scotland winning 1-0.' The camera pans into the crowd while there's a lull in play. Tartan-tammied supporters are singing, 'Scot-land … Scot-land.'

39: The Scots are passing the ball around slickly from back to front. Wright, 'With Jack Charlton a virtual passenger, it needs hard work from England and that's just what they are doing. But the Scottish side is in full song and it's even more of an uphill battle because of this.'

40: Law clashes with Banks and Stiles as he attacks a left-wing cross from Baxter. The English keeper and Law are hurt. Johns, 'England needed Banks and Stiles combining to stop that one. It looks as though Banks has hurt his knee and Law is also lying there.' The ball has been cleared upfield before it works its way to Simpson who kicks it out of touch. Johns, 'That was very sporting of Simpson kicking that one straight into the crowd so the injured players can receive some attention.' Law protests his innocence as Stiles pats him on the head. Both Law and Banks recover.

41: The game restarts with Bobby Charlton unsportingly throwing the ball to teammate Ball. He might have considered giving it back to Simpson.

42: Scotland still look menacing. Johns, 'England are under constant pressure and they are being hurried into making mistakes.'

47: Lennox wins a corner-kick on the left-hand side and passes to McCreadie who launches over an inviting cross that Law, with an acrobatic flick, puts past the upright.

49: A Banks throw to Greaves sees Baxter slide in to challenge. Johns, 'That was a good, strong tackle from Baxter. The Scots boys are fighting for every ball and not allowing the England players to compose themselves. The referee has added on four minutes of injury time, he's looking at his watch and, indeed, there goes the half-time whistle. England have got a lot to do to get back into this game and we'll be showing you it right after the break.' (What, no army of panellists dissecting every pass?)

For reasons of accuracy, we can restart the second-half at the normal kick-off point.

46: England kick off. Johns, 'The English players might be thinking their 19-game unbeaten streak could be coming to an end. Remember, it was a Scottish side back in 1896 who ended a 20-game unbeaten run by England. These players were hoping to equal that record today. However, Law's first-half goal has set England a tremendous task now.'

47: Bremner gives England a fright with a crisp 20-yard shot that zips wide of the upright. Johns, 'Banks was short of reaching that one. The Scottish faces are looking happy.'

48: Lennox accelerates away from Stiles and sends in a low cross from the byline. Banks gets down well to hold on as the figure of Law comes hurtling in behind him. Johns, betraying a flicker of English emotion, yells, 'Well done, Gordon Banks.' Seconds later he observes, 'Scotland are still bossing this game.'

49: Ball skips past Gemmell on the English left, hits the byline and sends over a cross that is nudged goalwards by Jack Charlton. Simpson makes a miraculous save on the goal-line.

Johns, 'Play on says the referee. Simpson pulled it down, but that ball looked over the line from up here. The linesman was down at the corner flag looking right along the line and said, "No goal". Billy, what did you think?' Wright, 'It was very close, but the linesman is in the right place to make the decision. It's a great shame. If Jack had scored it would have been great for him, but, however, that's football.'

52: Wallace has a shot deflected for a corner-kick. A helpful ball-boy hands the ball to Law who thumps it into the roof of the net. The ball is fished out and Wallace's left-wing corner-kick is headed clear by Moore.

53: Law is all over the Wembley pitch as he searches for another opening. Bremner and Ball are still hammering away at each other in midfield. 'Let's forget the ball and get on with the game,' could be their outlook.

55: Baxter races across to take the ball off Cohen and waltzes forward. Johns, 'England are the world champions and they are being teased and taunted by Scotland.'

56: Ball comes in late on Baxter. The Scot is far from impressed.

58: Lennox drives in from the right and wallops a shot into the side net. Law glowers at his colleague. Johns, 'If Lennox had tried for the back post where Law and Bremner were he might have had more success.' A pause, followed by, 'Oh, the referee's given offside.'

59: Stiles barges into Gemmell. There's a bit of verbals before the match official awards a corner-kick. Johns, 'Nobby is saying that is a goal-kick.' Law's shot from the corner is blocked.

61: Johns, 'There are two tired sets of players out there and England look the more tired of the two. Scotland still look the more incisive. They are forcing England into errors.'

62: Ball snaps into a challenge on Baxter that wouldn't look out of place in a wrestling ring. Remarkably, the referee awards England a free-kick to a chorus of jeers from the Scottish support. Baxter and Law look at the match official, shake their heads in unison and get on with the game. Johns, 'Scotland only have themselves to blame for that little bit of gamesmanship.'

63: Peters' left-wing cross finds Jack Charlton smack in front of goal and his header beats Simpson before being cleared off the line by Greig. Johns, 'The Scotland skipper certainly saved his country there.' Wright, 'That was a very close shave. Yes, I thought that one was in. I would like to praise this England side for their second-half display. They have given even more than they did in the first-half. They haven't allowed Scotland to dominate and they have had a couple of chances that might have brought an equaliser. Remember, too, they are facing a Scotland team who are at the top of their form.'

64: Ball has a nasty trip to send McCalliog tumbling. Law is quick to tell the Englishman what he thinks. The ref once again steps between them. Johns, 'Law really takes his football seriously.'

66: McCreadie cuts in from the left to blitz in a ferocious drive that beats the diving Banks, but edges just wide. Johns, 'That wasn't far away from being goal number two.'

67: Scotland are looking for the killer second. Lennox takes a quick corner on the right to McCalliog, but the youngster's shot is blocked for another corner. This time Moore clears.

68: Law sends an overhead kick past the post. Johns, 'If he had left that McCalliog might have had a shot at goal.'

70: Baxter surges forward and, unusually for him, lets fly with a 25-yard effort that thunders over the bar. Johns, 'He's really been in this game has Jim Baxter.'

71: The chant of 'Scot-land … Scot-land' is now ringing round the ground. Johns, 'The chant was "England … England" nine months ago when England won the World Cup. Now it's resounding to "Scotland" with 40,000 Scots making a lot of noise.'

72: Ball loses the plot. He clearly shoves Baxter off the ball and the ref, this time, gets it right by awarding Scotland a free-kick. The Englishman angrily kicks the ball away. Baxter, socks rolled down to his ankles, stands with his hands on his hips with a wry smile. Johns, 'Ball's a fiery little character. He's got plenty of spirit and he really puts everything into his football.' The kick is taken, Ball hares after McCreadie and dumps him on the byline. Johns, 'That's another free-kick. Oh, there's a dramatic gesture from the referee. He's clearly telling Ball, "One more foul and you're off." You can see his mouth moving.' The free-kick is cleared and drops at Ball's feet and the boos from the Scottish fans rattle round Wembley.

73: The visiting support continue to taunt the English. 'Easy … Easy' sweeps round the stadium. Johns, 'There isn't the snap in the England chants there were in the World Cup. England's world champions are being made to struggle by this good, strong, fighting Scottish side.'

75: Johns is beginning to fret. 'We've seen so little of Jimmy Greaves in the goal-poaching, sharp-shooting role the England fans had hoped to see this afternoon.'

77: There's a glimmer of hope as Peters sets up Hurst before Simpson races from his line to block the effort. There's a pause before Johns says, 'What a fine save from Simpson.'

77.30: There's a clash between Law and Stiles. Johns, 'That's a foul by one Manchester United man on another.' Both players are puzzled by the ref's whistle and have a word with each other. Law smiles and then nods when he realises it's a free-kick for Scotland. Wright, 'Those were two players discussing the matter and I'm just glad I'm not down there between them with a microphone.'

78: It's number two for Scotland. Baxter strokes a free-kick in front of the adventurous Gemmell. He thumps in a typical effort from 25 yards that is headed clear by Moore. The ball goes into the air and Gemmell charges after it to outjump Ball, trying to block his run, and nods it down to Lennox. A quick swivel, a right-foot drive and it's past Banks. Law, 12 yards out, gets a good view of the goal. Baxter, Wallace and Bremner are first to congratulate Lennox. Law is next and then McCreadie leaps on top of the pile. Johns, 'The Scottish fans reckon this game is in the bag now. Bobby Lennox scores the second goal for Scotland, his second goal for Scotland in his second game for Scotland. I would now say, Billy, this game has escaped England completely.' Wright, 'That could be the final nail because just before it only a brilliant save from Simpson denied them an equaliser. It will now be a very hard task to pull this game out of the fire.'

80: There's another tussle between Bremner and Ball. Johns, 'Two fiery redheads together.'

81: 'Easy … Easy' is the cry again from the terracing and Johns mishears it and thinks the home fans are chanting for the hosts. Johns, 'The crowd are getting behind England.' Wallace crosses from the left and Banks's timing is immaculate as he plucks the ball off the head of Law.

82: Moore, for the first time all afternoon, finds himself in the Scottish penalty area. He crosses from the left and sees Simpson spring to pat the ball down and then clear from Ball. Johns, 'There's Ball thinking, "How on earth did Simpson save that one?"' Wright, 'You can't take anything away from an enterprising Scotland side, but, remember, England have played most of this game without a fully-fit Jack Charlton. I'm disappointed with one or two of the forwards.' (He doesn't name them.) 'But the defence has done a magnificent job. It's the guys up front who haven't performed.'

83: Law back-heels the ball to Baxter who indulges in a bit of keepy-uppy. (Time does lend enchantment because I have spoken to fans who believe Jim kept the ball in the air for at least a minute. In fact, it's exactly three seconds.) Baxter chips it onto Law's chest, who twists away in an attempt to get in a shot, but is crowded out.

84: Johns gets excited as Ball sends in a low cross from the left. 'There must be one here. YES IT IS! Jack Charlton, brave and limping, is the hero. Can England pull it back? Can they get a surprise draw?' Scotland go right up the park when a long pass from Law releases Lennox who forces a mis-kick from Cohen. Johns, 'Oh, the referee has awarded a corner-kick. I would have thought it was a throw-in.'

86: Law seizes onto an opportunity and lifts a delicate lob over the head of Banks. However, the keeper produces a stunning, athletic one-handed save. Johns, 'What a save from Gordon Banks.' Pause. 'And what a cool bit of play from Denis Law.' Only seconds later Law flashes in a low drive from outside the area that is smothered by the England keeper.

87: This time there is no chance for Banks. Bremner, Lennox and McCalliog combine before the Sheffield Wednesday youngster plays a neat one-two with Wallace. Running clear, McCalliog steadies himself before launching a ferocious drive between Banks and his near post. Law is first to congratulate him. Johns, 'McCalliog has scored on his debut. The entire Scottish team is running to congratulate him. What a way to celebrate your international debut.' Wright, 'The Scotland fans are chanting, "Easy … Easy" now. Their team is 3-1 up and if there had been a chance of England getting back into this game it has been quickly erased by Jim McCalliog.'

88: The eager Stiles bowls over Greaves as he surges forward. Johns, 'The England players are bouncing off each other.' Stiles passes to Moore who clips one into the middle and the unmarked Hurst sends a header sailing past Simpson into the far corner. Johns, 'This commentator's words are getting stuffed down his throat so often it just isn't true. England are, in fact, back in this game again. On my watch there is about one-minute-and-a-half for them to pull off a dramatic draw.' Wright, 'What a game. What a brilliant, entertaining game. It has had everything and I would say the courage of this England team has been second to none. It's the best game I've seen between these two sides for many a year.'

89: Wallace uses his hand before turning and lashing the ball past Banks, but it hammers back off the crossbar to Law. Sportingly, he throws the ball to Moore to take the free-kick. Johns, 'Scotland are wasting as much time as possible.'

90: The game nears its conclusion. Johns, 'The Scottish fans are whistling for the referee to end this game.' Greig hacks a clearance into touch and it's the last action of an extraordinary 90 minutes. Johns, 'There is the final whistle. The world champions have been beaten here at Wembley by a fine, fighting Scottish side. Photographers are now coming onto the pitch. And there's young Jim McCalliog, the youngest player on the pitch. And there's Ronnie Simpson, the oldest man on the pitch. Both Scotsmen playing in their first international and they have acquitted themselves wonderfully well in a fine Scottish side.'

The camera pans around the pitch. Law is seen shaking hands with Wilson as Bobby Charlton walks by. A fan congratulates Wallace and there's another hugging Baxter. 'Scot-land … Scot-land' is the chant. Hugh Johns is unmoved. 'With that, we'll say good afternoon to you with the final score: England 2, Scotland 3.' Both sets of players line up with the band playing 'God Save The Queen'. Even the fans on the pitch seem to stand to attention for a moment or two.

Poring over the action, there are several things to note. For instance, Jimmy Greaves, fabled marksman, didn't have a single shot at goal. The injured Jack Charlton not only scored, but he had another two efforts saved by Ronnie Simpson, had one cleared off the line and yet another header that swept danger-ously over the bar. Denis Law later described his presence as 'nuisance value' and, right enough, he did prove to be difficult to shut down despite his injury. (It was later discovered that a stud had broken through the sole of his boot after his tackle on Bobby Lennox.) Apart from goal-kicks, Simpson used his feet only twice – and one of those occasions was to boot the ball out of play for Law and Banks to get treatment. On every other occasion he threw the ball, mainly to Jim Baxter. Willie Wallace and Lennox switched wings constantly, probably off their own

143

bat rather than a pre-match instruction from manager Bobby Brown. Left-back Eddie McCreadie popped up almost on the right touchline at one stage in the first-half. No wonder England were bewildered! This was Total Football before the Dutch came on the scene to claim it as their own. Full-backs Tommy Gemmell and McCreadie spent more time in the English half than they did in their own. Jim Baxter, not known for his aerial work, won plenty of headers. Ronnie McKinnon hardly gave Geoff Hurst time to turn with the ball at any time. John Greig was a powerhouse throughout. Billy Bremner's energy was immense and Jim McCalliog spent a huge part of the game in midfield leaving Law a lone marksman. It all gelled on the day.

I don't know how many times commentator Hugh Johns mentioned the fact that England were World Cup holders. I stopped counting at 20 after the first 15 minutes or so.

CHAPTER FIFTEEN

LAWLESS SCOTLAND

A trademark flashing header from Denis Law signalled the kick-off to the 1970 World Cup qualifying campaign. Scotland, generous to a fault, gifted the visiting Austrians a goal of a start in only two minutes before surging back to triumph 2-1 in front of 80,856 ecstatic supporters on a chilly evening at Hampden on 6 November 1968. The Scots picked up seven points from a possible eight in their first four games, but realised that the last two ties, against West Germany in Hamburg and then Austria in Vienna, would be the ones that mattered. Cyprus were also in the qualifying group, but offered very little resistance with Scotland scoring 13 goals over the two matches.

Scotland, after missing out on Chile in 1962 and England in 1966, were anxious that they would not be restricted to watching the Mexico finals on television. We were all getting thoroughly sickened by the old joke, 'What do you call a Scotsman at the World Cup Finals? The referee.' How the English chortled. So, no-one predicted the shocking start against a workmanlike Austria, a team totally bereft of big-name stars. August Starek fired in a hit-and-hope long-range effort only moments into the game and a deadly hush fell around Hampden as the wind-assisted swerving effort baffled Ronnie Simpson and thudded into the back of the net.

Help was at hand, though. Law, as he had demonstrated so often in the past, provided the answer. Once again, he was the master in the air and angled a typical header beyond the helpless Garald Fuchsbichler in the seventh minute to calm the nerves of his teammates and the supporters. The tension was palpable as Bobby Brown's side pushed for the winner and it duly arrived in the 75th minute, delivered by captain Billy Bremner. The gutsy little Leeds United midfielder battled in a packed penalty area to force the ball over the line. It was untidy and would never figure in any DVD of the Best 50 World Cup Goals, but it was enough to ensure that the nation enjoyed a winning start and no-one complained.

The following month, on 11 December, Scotland travelled to Nicosia for their first-ever match against Cyprus. The only problem appeared to be the playing surface. The *Daily Record*'s Alex Cameron described it thus, 'It will be nigh on impossible for Scotland to play good football on this pitch. There's precious little grass, there are bumps and lumps everywhere, and we can only hope that they remember to put down some lines to actually let the players know where the pitch starts and where it ends. That would be helpful.'

There was no need to worry, though. Celtic's masterly midfielder Bobby Murdoch, defying the underfoot conditions, strolled through the encounter with commanding ease as the Scots surged to a 5-0 victory with all the goals coming in the first-half. Denis Law was missing through injury, but, on a rare occasion, his country could afford to be without his inspirational presence. Alan Gilzean, wearing the No. 10 shirt vacated by Law, scored the opening goal in three minutes and Murdoch rolled in a second 20 minutes later. Gilzean made it three on the half-hour mark and Colin Stein rattled in two in three minutes before the break. Poor overworked goalkeeper Michalalikis Alkiviadis must have wondered what to expect in the second-half. In fact, he could have taken out an umbrella and sheltered under it as a sudden deluge threatened proceedings. Scotland were satisfied to stop at five.

It had been a walkover against the Cypriots, but Scotland realised they would have to get their working clothes looked out for the next confrontation, the visit of mighty West Germany to Hampden Park on 16 April 1969. Denis Law was urgently required for this one and, thankfully, he was free of the knee injury that had plagued him all season at Manchester United. He lined up in an enterprising frontline alongside Jimmy Johnstone, Alan Gilzean and Bobby Lennox. The West Germans, so unlucky in the 1966 World Cup Final against England at Wembley, were still one of the most formidable football forces in the game. Karl-Heinz Schnellinger, Franz Beckenbauer, Helmut Haller, Gerd Muller, Wolfgang Overath and Sigi Held, all genuine superstars, were in Helmut Schoen's line-up. There was also a gritty little right-back called Berti Vogts, who would come to know Hampden well later in his career as Scotland manager.

West Germany's pedigree in the tournament was breathtaking. They first entered the World Cup in 1954 and, confounding all predictions, defeated Hungary 3-2 in the final. They were fourth in 1958, quarter-finalists four years later and, of course, finalists in England. Even more remarkable was the fact they had never lost a qualifier in the competition. If it had been a breeze against Cyprus, Scotland realised they would have to weather the storm against West Germany. A crowd of 95,951 packed into Scotland's national stadium to witness the spectacle. Curiously, the West Germans had never beaten Scotland, losing two and drawing one of the previous three games. Bobby Brown had a problem to solve before the kick-off. Ronnie Simpson, the Peter Pan of goalkeeping, had come to the end of his glittering career at the age of 38. Birmingham City's Jim Herriot was expected to face Muller and Co, but, unfortunately, injured a hand playing for Birmingham City on the Saturday. An SOS went out for Tommy Lawrence, Liverpool's 14 stone custodian who hadn't played for his country since 1963.

Bobby Brown selected Denis Law alongside Alan Gilzean to give the team an aerial presence. West Germany's centre-half

Willi Schulz was a rarity in that position as he barely came close to six foot. His defensive partner, Beckenbauer, preferred the ball on the ground, where he did his best and most elegant work. Scotland went into the encounter hoping to emulate past successes against group favourites. Spain, in the 1958 World Cup qualifiers, Czechoslovakia (1962) and Italy (1966) had all been beaten in Glasgow. Could the Scots add West Germany to that illustrious list?

West German manager Helmut Schoen had carried out his homework. He identified the menace of Law and Gilzean and pushed left-back Schnellinger, all of six foot two inches, into the middle of the rearguard alongside Schulz and Beckenbauer. Vogts played as a sweeper behind them and wingers Bernhard Dorfel and Sigi Held were instructed to play virtually as full-backs. Scotland, with midfielders Bobby Murdoch and Billy Bremner pushing forward relentlessly, took the game to their opponents. Goalkeeper Horst Wolter saved athletically from Gilzean and then Law. With six minutes of the first-half remaining, referee Jose Gardeazabal, of Spain, awarded West Germany an innocuous free-kick outside the box after Beckenbauer claimed he had been fouled by John Greig. Disaster was only moments away. The supremely-gifted Beckenbauer slid the ball to his Bayern Munich teammate Gerd Muller who appeared to barge into Ronnie McKinnon before turning and lashing a shot beyond the portly Lawrence from 18 yards.

McKinnon protested, but the match official was unmoved. Murdoch recalled, 'Muller would have been nothing but for that backside of his. He made it impossible for defenders to even see the ball. He would back into them, inviting a foul. Ninety-nine times out of 100 he got it, too. If his opponent tried to go through him he would go down theatrically. Muller got away with it throughout his career. And we paid on that occasion. Watch the film of that game – it's a clear foul on McKinnon.'

It was the Celtic maestro who came to Scotland's rescue with the clock ticking down. West Germany had sent on substitute goalkeeper Sepp Maier for Wolter at the interval and he looked composed and assured. Up until the 88th minute, anyway. That was when Bobby Murdoch almost ripped the net from its stanchion with a blistering 25-yard shot that no goalkeeper on earth could have prevented from bulging the rigging. The Scots had held their nerve as they probed throughout a hectic second period. Law and Gilzean continued to threaten a stout and stubborn defence, but it looked to be yet another evening of glorious failure. And then the enchanting Charlie Cooke, a 63rd minute substitute for Bobby Lennox, danced merrily into the spotlight. He weaved in from the right wing before leisurely rolling the ball in front of Murdoch. The Celtic player strode onto it with poise and purpose and shelled a mighty effort into the roof of the net. That's the way it remained. The fans left Hampden Park that night drained totally; satisfied, too, with a rescued point.

Murdoch told me later, 'I knew they wouldn't beat us. I hadn't a clue how long there was to go, but I knew we would get a goal. Charlie's pass was perfection and I just walloped it. We used to train for these situations at Celtic. Jock Stein would get myself and the other midfielders to position ourselves around the 18-yard line and then he would tell the likes of Jimmy Johnstone and full-backs Jim Craig and Tommy Gemmell to cut the ball back to us. We were told to hit it first time. We weren't allowed to tee it up. Big Jock always went on about the element of surprise and not allowing a goalkeeper time to set himself and get ready for the shot. That second or so was absolutely vital. So it proved against West Germany.' He added thoughtfully, 'Mind you a lot of praise must also go to Denis and Gillie. If I remember correctly, they both made great runs to take away defenders before Charlie passed to me.'

It had been an exhausting performance from Denis Law and, sadly, was one of only two international appearances in

1969, the other coming in a 1-1 draw with Northern Ireland at Hampden on 6 May when Colin Stein netted in the 53rd minute to nullify a first-half effort from Eric McMurdie. Alas, it would be almost three full years before the Scottish fans would again witness their hero in their nation's dark blue. Happily, he marked the occasion with a goal in a 2-0 win over Peru in Glasgow. During that barren period, Law would have to overcome the demons of doubt as some ill-informed critics wrote him off. There was still more, a lot more, to come from this man.

Scotland would have to attempt to reach Mexico in 1970 without the inspirational and influential Law. Rangers' rumbustious Colin Stein, a good, old-fashioned centre-forward who relied on brute strength rather than ball-playing skills, was being granted his opportunity on the international stage to show what he could provide at this level. The Ibrox frontman took centre stage in the next World Cup qualifier against the hapless Cypriots at Hampden on 17 May, a week after Scotland had been soundly beaten 4-1 by England at Wembley. On that occasion, Stein was on target with a header after a delightful left-wing run and cross from Eddie Gray but, unfortunately, the English were already two goals ahead with Martin Peters and Geoff Hurst scoring inside the first 20 minutes. Scotland's revival was short-lived with Hurst blasting a penalty-kick past Jim Herriot on the hour mark and Peters claiming the fourth shortly afterwards. It was back to the drawing board once more for Bobby Brown.

Bereft of Law's presence, the Scotland manager didn't have too many options in attack. He pushed Billy Bremner back to wing-half and brought in Charlie Cooke to replace him further forward. He kept faith with the frontline that rarely troubled Gordon Banks at Wembley; Willie Henderson, Colin Stein, Alan Gilzean and Eddie Gray. Stein dismantled a nervy Cypriot rearguard, scoring four goals in a pulverising 39-minute period.

Gray, Leeds United's graceful outside-left, scored the opener in the 15th minute and Celtic captain Billy McNeill added a second five minutes later. Stein lashed in number three in the 28th minute and added three more before the 67th minute. Rangers right-winger Willie Henderson fired in the seventh and Celtic's adventurous full-back Tommy Gemmell brought down the curtain with a thunderous penalty-kick 14 minutes from the end.

There had been a clamour for Stein to take the spot-kick to enable him to emulate Hughie Gallacher's historic five-goal feat in a 7-3 victory over Northern Ireland in Belfast in 1929. Gemmell said, 'There was no way I was going to let Colin Stein take that kick. I was the penalty-taker and I told him that. As everyone knew, I loved the thrill of scoring goals. I was a defender, but I liked to think I could chip in a goal or two throughout a season. It didn't matter that we were already seven goals up in that game. We could have been 70 goals ahead and I would still have taken that penalty-kick. Anyway, a Celtic man allowing a Rangers player to score a goal? That just wasn't on.'

Stein recalled, 'We won the penalty near the end. It was down at the Rangers end, where a lot of the 40,000 crowd were stationed, and they were chanting my name, willing me to take it. I was desperate to give them what they wanted and had the ball in my arms, ready to put it on the spot. But Tommy Gemmell marched up and snatched it away. He was the designated penalty-taker and clearly wasn't happy that I was planning to ignore team orders. I was speechless, just shooting a few daggers in his direction, but nothing I could have said would have changed his mind. He would never have realised it, but Tommy actually did me a favour. With four goals, my confidence must have been bubbling over because I would never normally jump to the front of the queue to take a penalty. The truth is, I was never a dead-ball specialist, whether it was free-kicks or penalties. I preferred to leave them to the experts, apart from a stint at Coventry City when I took it upon myself to volunteer. Big

Tommy tucked the penalty away to make it 8-0 and I had to content myself with the four goals.'

The World Cup crunch was looming; 22 October 1969 at the Volkspark Stadion in Hamburg, where a passionate crowd of 72,000 attended. West Germany went into their last game of the qualifying section with nine points from five games while Scotland had seven from four. Defeat would knock the Scots out of the tournament. A victory would set up Bobby Brown's men nicely for their remaining fixture against Austria in Vienna a fortnight later. Once again, Denis Law was missing. Colin Stein was suffering a lean spell and it looked as though the main striking role would go to Wolves' Hugh Curran, who, like Stein, was fearless, big and powerful. Twenty-four hours before the game he gave an interview to Ken Gallacher, of the *Daily Record*, and left everyone with the impression he wasn't lacking in confidence. Under the headline 'I GO WHERE THE BRAVE GO', he told the newspaper's readers, 'The West Germans won't know what hit them. I know what's expected of me and I can promise the Scottish fans I will give it absolutely everything. This is the most important match I have ever played in and I won't fail. I'll make sure their defence doesn't get a moment's peace. I'll be here, there and everywhere.'

Actually, where Curran was by the time the kick-off arrived was in the stand. A flu bug had bitten and he was out. Colin Stein, with ten goals from his previous six international games, was swiftly reinstated. Brown, realising the menace of West Germany's strikers Gerd Muller and Uwe Seeler, twinned Old Firm duo Billy McNeill and Ronnie McKinnon at the heart of his defence. It was only the second time the Celtic skipper and the Rangers stopper had played alongside each other; the other being a 1-1 draw against England at Hampden in a European Championship qualifier in February 1968.

Jim Herriot continued in goal with the Scots lining up with this starting 11: Herriot; Greig, McNeill, McKinnon, Gemmell;

Bremner, Cormack, Gray; Johnstone, Stein and Gilzean. It was an attacking, adventurous team, but even Brown must have been surprised by his country's dream start. Within three minutes, Scotland were a goal ahead after keeper Sepp Maier failed to hold a low drive from Eddie Gray. Celtic's Jimmy Johnstone was more alert than dozy defender Berti Vogts as he raced in to clip the rebound over the stranded goalkeeper.

The West Germans were clearly astounded. Scotland were elated. Billy Bremner was immense in midfield, patrolling all along the line, harassing the likes of Helmut Haller and Wolfgang Overath, two ball artistes who liked time and space. A bristling Bremner would afford them neither. Johnstone, on the right, and Gray, on the left, were stretching the German defence while Stein and Gilzean kept up the pressure on Willi Schulz and Franz Beckenbauer. For the first half-hour, Herriot was rarely troubled. Gilzean lofted one over the bar as the home side toiled to get a grip. Alas, they snatched an equaliser seven minutes from the interval. The Scottish keeper carelessly allowed a pass back from McNeill to elude him and the Germans took a quick corner-kick. As luck would have it, the ball eventually landed at the feet of the unattended Klaus Fichtel and he sent a rasping drive beyond Herriot.

The second-half was tough and towsy. Johnstone, in particular, had been singled out for some unsavoury tactics from the West Germans, with Vogts the main culprit. The Scots were out of luck when a shot from the tireless Bremner smashed against an upright and bounced to safety. Tommy Gemmell also left Maier scrambling with a lobbed effort from the left that carried just over the crossbar. A goal was in the offing. Sadly, it came for the home outfit on the hour mark. Veteran frontman Seeler nodded a free-kick into the path of Muller and he ruthlessly battered it wide of the unprotected Herriot. Scotland's response was valiant and swift. McKinnon thumped in a cross and Gilzean, escaping Schulz, rose to nod

153

past Maier with poise and precision in the 64th minute. All to no avail, though. With nine minutes to go, Haller picked out tricky outside-right Reinhard Libuda and he streaked through the rearguard before firing past Herriot. Scottish players collapsed where they stood. Worse was to follow with Gemmell being dismissed by Swiss referee Ernst Droz after a kick at Haller in the last minute.

Years later Gemmell told me, 'The bugger deserved it. He had fouled me only moments earlier when I was racing through. I was just about at the edge of the penalty area and was preparing to shoot. It was my favourite distance and I was in full flight. Suddenly, though, I was checked, clipped from behind by Haller. It was a definite foul and the referee, only yards away, waved play on to everyone's astonishment. I just blew a gasket. I sent the German up in the air and I knew what was coming next. I was furious, absolutely raging. It was a terrible end to what had been a real hard-fought match. It was also one of the most frustrating games of my career. We deserved at least a draw in Hamburg and I'm convinced our players would have made an impact in Mexico. For a start, we would have had a fully-fit Denis Law in attack and the Lawman would have made a difference. He would have been in his element. We got two against West Germany, but we could have had more. There were a few occasions when the ball was bouncing around their penalty area crying out for someone with Denis's reflexes and guile to steer it towards the net.'

By the time the game against Austria had come around at the Prater Stadium in Vienna on 5 November, Hugh Curran had sufficiently recovered from his bout of flu. At last, he was ready 'to go where the brave go'. For him, that was up the tunnel in the 54th minute after being substituted. The Wolves forward hardly had a kick and was hooked immediately by Bobby Brown after Austria's second goal from Helmut Reidl, his second of the night after opening the scoring in the 14th minute. Curran would only play four more games for Scotland, scoring one goal, before his international career was plunged into oblivion.

The World Cup Finals of 1970 would go ahead without the presence of the Scots. And Denis Law. There was always West Germany in 1974 to aim at. By then, Law would be 34 years old. Was it too much to hope that he would at last get a chance to play on the world's greatest stage?

CHAPTER SIXTEEN

THE WILDERNESS YEARS

England, Bobby Charlton, Nobby Stiles et al, were preparing for the defence of their World Cup in Mexico in 1970. Scotland, and Denis Law, were nowhere to be seen; the passports put away for at least another four years.

Law played in the 1-1 draw with West Germany at Hampden on 16 April 1969 and then dropped into a World Cup void, only to re-emerge five years later against Zaire in the opening game of Scotland's 1974 finals campaign. After the West German encounter, he played only one of the next 20 international games, a drab 1-1 draw with Northern Ireland in Glasgow on 6 May 1969 when a paltry 7,483 bothered to attend in atrocious, rain-lashed conditions for an encounter that meant zilch apart from pride. That was enough for Law, of course, to look out the boots and drive north to get stripped and ready.

In his absence, Colin Stein (Rangers), Alan Gilzean (Spurs), John O'Hare (Derby County), Jim McCalliog (Sheffield Wednesday) and even journeymen such as Hugh Curran (Wolves) and Aberdeen double-act Davie Robb and Drew Jarvie had shouldered the burden of scoring goals for their country. They weren't too successful. In the 19 outings Law missed, Scotland managed a meagre 21 goals and that included eight in a World Cup qualifier against Cyprus. Take that rout out of the equation and the Scottish fans had only 13 goals to cheer in the other 18 games. The forwards fired blanks on eight occasions. The highest goalscorer during that spell was Stein with six, and four of them came against the Cypriots. Bobby Brown, the boss who had achieved the astonishing 3-2 win over world champions England at Wembley in 1967 on his international managerial debut, paid a heavy price for such a lengthy spell in the wilderness. He lost his job.

Law returned in typical triumphal fashion at Hampden on 26 April 1972 and netted in a 2-0 victory over Peru. The King had been in exile; three years and ten days, to be precise. Those were dark and lonely days for Denis.

Back in season 1969-70, Law turned out only 11 times for Manchester United. He scored two goals. Wilf McGuinness was toiling during his one-year stint as manager of the Old Trafford side after replacing the legendary Sir Matt Busby. Law was up for sale at £60,000, almost half the fee he commanded when he joined United from Torino in 1962. The lack of interest in the player was reflected in an abrasive comment from Rangers boss Willie Waddell. When told about Law's availability, he said, 'The news does not excite me.' Hamilton Accies, managed by Andy Paton, asked to be kept in touch with developments.

David Meek, a well-respected sports journalist who worked for the *Manchester Evening News*, was often invited into the Old Trafford inner sanctum and was obviously trusted, a rare phenomenon for any journalist at a football club. He posed this question in the renowned *Charles Buchan's Football Monthly*, the soccer bible at the time, 'Are we seeing the end of the reign of Denis Law? This is what thousands of Manchester United fans have been asking.'

He continued, 'No player in modern times has been given such adulation from the home fans as Denis Law. The Stretford End, the vocal part of Old Trafford, made Law their king years ago and even though George Best of the long hair has since burst devastatingly on the scene, it's Law who really still sits on the throne.

'For Best is very much the hero of the girls and if you took away the screaming teenage females, Law would still win the loyalty of the boys and youths who make up the bulk of the Stretford End support. Perhaps it is the streak of villainy that ran through Law's early days that appeals to the mob instinct of Stretford Enders. Certainly, Law only has to score a goal to re-awaken the crowd's fanatical passion for this controversial, puzzling Scot.

'Players such as Best and Bobby Charlton are popular, of course, especially when they score. But Charlton, sportsman supreme and classical player, and Best, who looks more like a pop singer than a footballer, have never really commanded the following of Law, at least from the thousands of male young-sters who swell United's attendances to record levels.

'The basic reason, of course, is goals and, in that respect, Law stands head and shoulders above everyone else at Old Trafford. Charlton, for instance, is renowned for his cannonball shot and has scored more goals than any contemporary player at the club. He kicked off this season with a total of 167 league goals, but it has taken him 448 games to score them.

'Compare this return with Best and Law. Best, at the end of last season, had scored 79 times in 213 league appearances, but Law has the incredible tally of 140 goals from 226 games. And in Cup football there just isn't anyone to compare with the Lawman. Three years ago he scored his 31st goal in the FA Cup to go in front of Stan Mortensen, Ronnie Allen and John Atyeo as the top marksman in post-war Cup football.

'Those goals were scored for Huddersfield Town, Manchester City and, of course, Manchester United. Since then, he has scored more goals in a season and beaten Jack Rowley's club record which stood at 28 goals. For United, Law has a goal-a-game average of 34 from 34 ties, a fantastic record. In the European Cup, he has scored 14 goals for United, one more than Dennis Viollet and another record.

'As Law banged in a hat-trick in the first leg against Water-ford, the League of Ireland champions, last season and then scored four in the second leg there was no doubt who was still king at Old Trafford. Overall, though, Law did not have a good 1968-69 season, at least compared with his best years. Yet he still managed to finish as the club's top scorer. Best was leading marksman in the league with 19 goals, Law next on 14. But, whereas Best only scored once in the FA Cup and twice in the European Cup, Law netted seven in the FA Cup and nine in Europe.

'The Law of old we shall never see again. In some respects, that is a good thing. The Scot did little to enhance the club's sporting image with two month-long suspensions and one for six weeks – one for kicking an opponent, one for swearing at the referee and one for fighting with fellow-Scottish international Ian Ure, now a teammate at United! It was his volatile, razor-sharp temperament and it had to be curbed. Law succeeded and has not been in any kind of trouble since his brush with Ure two years ago.

'At the same time, Law has undoubtedly lost some of the fire and deadly reflexes that made him such a supreme striker. He was still getting goals last season, but they tended to come in comparatively easy matches and not, as in the old days, when the chips were down, the game was in deadlock and only master footballers could get a goal.

'Law, of course, has also had a fearful battle with injury. He was plagued for a year with a mysterious knee complaint that put him into hospital for an operation when United were winning the European Cup in May 1968. His fans hoped that after feeling his way back to the top of the goal charts last season, he would really become his old formidable self this winter.

'But it is clearly not going to be easy. After playing in the first three league games this season, he experienced the indignity, along with Charlton, of being dropped – the first time he had been left out of the side in his career, by the way. He came back after one game only to suffer a further injury to his groin. At the time of writing he has made only 10 appearances, scoring two goals, one in the League Cup semi-final against Manchester City.

'Clearly, The King is not going to be allowed to reign by his reputation alone. Wilf McGuinness means business as he hurries along the footsteps of Sir Matt Busby as team boss. Manchester United managed to snap out of their worst-ever start to a season without Law's help and, though there is clearly a place for him in the Old Trafford team, he will have to deliver the goods if he is to stay on the throne his fans love so much.

'This is Denis Law's testing time.'

Washed up? Written off? On the scrapheap at 30? While the news of the player's availability at a knockdown price didn't 'excite' Willie Waddell, others toyed with the idea of taking a look. Blackpool, then fighting relegation in Division Two, were said to be sniffing around. That prospect surely wouldn't excite Denis Law, either. A story spread in 1970 that Law had actually signed for the Bloomfield Road club. Hearts, I was informed, were also showing a genuine interest. I quizzed Denis on this possibility years later. 'Naw, no truth in that,' he said, 'none at all. Aberdeen are my team. If I was going to Scotland it would have been to Aberdeen – no-one else.'

Hearts manager Bobby Seith told journalist Fraser Elder that the Edinburgh team did, in fact, make a move for Law – three years later in 1973. Seith informed my good friend and colleague, in an article published in the *News of the World,* 'Our season was going nowhere after being dumped out of the Scottish Cup. We were eighth in the league and felt we could really revive interest with a big personality signing. The club's biggest deal had been £20,000 to Wolves eight years earlier for George Miller and we knew signing Denis would break all records. The record Scottish deal had been Hibs selling Colin Stein to Rangers for £100,000 in 1968. I had played against Denis during a Cup-tie while I was at Burnley and he was at Huddersfield

Town. I knew he was an exceptional player. Denis considered our initial idea of a loan deal with perhaps a permanent move later, but he said he wanted to end his career at Old Trafford.'

Apparently, Tommy Docherty, by then the Manchester United manager, had granted the go-ahead for Seith to make his move for Law. At the end of the season, the player was shocked to hear the news he was being freed by United. Manchester City took him back to Maine Road after an absence of 12 years. Curiously, and maybe fate was lending a hand, Law did, in fact, end his playing days at Old Trafford. The goal he scored to confirm the relegation of his beloved Manchester United in April 1973 was his last kick of the ball in club football.

It was extremely difficult to believe that before his move across Manchester, some of the Stretford End fans, who had acclaimed him as The King through so many dynamic and dazzling displays over so many years, were beginning to turn on their hero. English international striker Allan Clarke admitted he had idolised Law when he was starting out at Walsall before moving through the ranks at Fulham and Leicester City and ending up at Don Revie's Leeds United. He said, 'It was pathetic to hear some of the United crowd getting on to Denis after all he had done there. If only they'd realised how hard he was trying at half fitness. If he turned or twisted he was obviously in agony. It took a lot of guts even to make an effort to play at First Division level.'

One manager who would have been delighted to have snapped him up was his former United colleague Harry Gregg, the goalkeeping icon who had been appointed manager of Shrewsbury. He recalled, 'Before his departure for Maine Road, I actually attempted to sign him for Shrewsbury Town. A player called Alf Wood held the key. I had moved him from centre-half to centreforward where he scored a club record 42 goals in one season. I'd also gambled, at least in the eyes of the board, on bringing in the unproven Jim Holton to replace Alf at the back. Jim, of course, went on to become a Scotland international and was a team-mate of Denis in the 1974 World Cup Finals in West Germany.

'Back then, though, Alf's exploits in front of goal were attracting considerable attention from other clubs, Liverpool among them. Bill Shankly phoned me and asked me what we wanted for him. I told him £75,000. The following day I had a telegram from Wolves manager Bill McGarry, who was in New York, asking me to do nothing until he returned. Behind the scenes, Ted Fenton, of Millwall, was also chasing Alf and the Shrewsbury board, fearing that their player might be a one-season wonder, decided to sell. I can tell you Bill Shankly was not a happy man when he found out.

'He offered to pay the £75,000 price I had first stated, more than the board had settled on from Millwall, but the Shrewsbury board refused to go back on their word and the deal stood. The transfer did provide me with some money to spend. So I decided I would make some enquiries about Denis. I asked the board how much I had to play with. They told me £20,000. I then enquired as to whether they objected to the money going to a player, as opposed to a club. They gave me carte blanche to spend it as I saw fit. Frank O'Farrell was in charge at Old Trafford and Denis found himself out of the team. I was assured by old friends of Denis that he was not a happy chappie. A circular came around stating that United had players in all positions available for transfer.

'I rang up Frank and we chatted. He spoke about players in the "A" team, "B" team and reserves, but I told him there was nothing there that I wanted. I told Frank I would take Charlton, Law and Best. He replied, "You're very funny." Nothing came of our discussion, but on the Sunday night I phoned Denis. His wife Diana answered and told me to call back because Denis was in the bath. It was a difficult few minutes because this was a call I didn't particularly want to make. I was not Harry Gregg, friend and former teammate; I was Harry Gregg, manager of

Shrewsbury Town. I was going to ask one of the greatest-ever players to don the red shirt to drop out of the top flight and move to the modest surroundings of Gay Meadow. I eventually spoke to Denis and, after a bit of banter, I told him I had £20,000 to spend and I asked him if he fancied a move. Denis replied, "Give me the name of the pub you're in for that must be strong ale!" Unfortunately, that was as close as I got to signing Denis. Within a few days, Frank O'Farrell was gone. Tommy Docherty took over and Denis was back in the team – for the time being, at least.'

Denis Law wasn't quite ready to throw in the towel. He admitted in an interview for *Book of Football* in 1980, 'I trained like a lunatic for almost four months.' He also revealed that Brazilian great Pele's performances in the 1970 World Cup Finals were a source of inspiration. 'I was moping about the house all day feeling sorry for myself. Pele played brilliantly, despite taking a lot of punishment. I realised, like me, he'd been taking it for years, was still going well after some setbacks and I needed to pull myself together.'

An editorial in the *Charles Buchan Football Monthly* magazine in 1972 stated, 'Any doubts Denis Law had about his future, at Old Trafford or anywhere else, he kept to himself. Nagged by injury, he didn't make a song and dance about it. We might have been seeing less of that Law trademark – the raised clenched fist salute to the crowd when he scored. But he was making no excuses. He never looked for a wailing wall. His critics could never accuse him of whining or being a quitter.

'Yet, even for a player who has made the critics eat their words before, Law's comeback this season has been quite fantastic. His game has mellowed. Still razor-sharp at picking up the chances, there is a subtle difference in his style. The old flashing arrogance has been replaced by a quieter, more thoughtful approach. He turns aside any suggestion that he went about his fightback in an "I'll show 'em" mood.

'Instead, he says, "If there was anything to prove it was to myself. You could say that pride comes into it. Apart from anything else, it was far too early for me to talk about going out of the game. The whole thing stemmed from a knee injury in 1968 when they found this bit of cartilage floating about. The next season the leg was a bit weak. People may have thought I was finished, but it all boiled down to fitness. I suppose it was partly in the mind as well as physical. But I made the decision to train right through the close season and it was the best thing that happened for me. United went to the States and they didn't take me. I trained solidly. I trained all the way through the last close season, too, and, mentally, I felt marvellous. My confidence was back."'

Did the transfer-listing by United shake him?

He replied, 'I think I felt a sense of shock about it later on. At the time I was surprised, but business is business in football as in anything else. I went through a bad two-year spell in my career and I suppose I was taking my nerves on the field a bit. I still get nervous before every match. I don't sleep too much on Friday nights. But now, once I'm on the pitch, the nerves vanish. I weigh up situations more these days and realise there is no point dashing in if the end product isn't going to be there.'

Without a trace of bitterness, Law added, 'In a way, it's good to reach the bottom as well as hit the top. During my bad spell I found out who were my friends in football as well as outside.'

Gordon Banks, so often a foe at club and country level, observed at the time, 'Denis has done remarkably well for a player, who, according to some people, was finished two years ago. He is an outstanding striker, one of the fastest movers over a short distance, and is constantly looking for mistakes. If a defender slips up, Denis is the first to go for the ball. He senses danger and he's in there looking for a goal. He's a constant menace and he is just as deadly with his head and feet as ever he was.

'Perhaps he doesn't mix it quite the same as far as bodily contact is concerned, but that takes nothing away from his undoubted skill. He can still strike a ball hard and still get up with the best of them in a crowded penalty area. He doesn't go chasing from man to man like he used to do. He sizes up situations, but you know he will still be right in there if a chance is presented.'

Denis, as ever, had come up with the answers. It was dangerous to write off this man.

CHAPTER SEVENTEEN

RETURN OF THE KING

Denis Law played only six games for Scotland in the years spanning 1967 to 1972. 'It was a thin time for me,' he admitted with masterly understatement. A persistent knee injury, an unexpected collapse in form and a perplexing loss of confidence hindered Law's progress. In all, he sat out 25 international contests during that bleak period.

Tommy Docherty, who had replaced Bobby Brown as Scotland manager, brought the player back for a friendly match against Peru at Hampden on 26 April 1972. Remarkably, Law would play for his country seven times over the next three months and would miss only two games that year – the back-to-back World Cup victories over Denmark in October and November. He was removed from the international scene for the first six matches in 1973 before his astounding and victorious return against Czechoslovakia at Hampden on 26 September. It wasn't easy keeping Denis Law out of the limelight.

Preparing for his fourth game in charge of his country, The Doc had been suitably impressed by Law's club form to not only bring him back from the international wilderness but to also make him captain against Peru. Denis was one of nine Anglo-Scots in the team, with only Celtic goalkeeper Ally Hunter and Hibs right-back John Brownlie making their living in Scotland. The Scots boss was never one to be too bothered about public outcries and those who continually demanded that Home Scots only should be selected were wasting their time in voicing their outdated opinions. Some

Anglos were almost portrayed as traitors for taking their skills outside the nation of their birth. And, just to stir up things even more, Docherty, planning for his first game as a manager at international level, brought in Chesterfield-born Bob Wilson for his debut against Portugal in a European Championship tie at Hampden on 13 October 1971. 'If he's good enough for Arsenal, then he is good enough for Scotland,' was Doc's thoughts.

So, in came Law against the Peruvians, welcomed back to the fold by a crowd of just over 21,000. He was returning as captain, too, the fifth time he had led his country. The other four occasions were split equally in 1963 – a 1-0 loss against the Republic of Ireland and a 6-2 win over Spain in Madrid – and the following year, a 3-2 defeat to Wales in Cardiff and a 3-1 victory over Finland at Hampden. Docherty put out this side: Ally Hunter (Celtic); John Brownlie (Hibs), Eddie Colquhoun (Sheffield United), Bobby Moncur (Newcastle United), Willie Donachie (Manchester City); Willie Morgan (Manchester United), Willie Carr (Coventry City), Asa Hartford (West Brom), Archie Gemmill (Derby County); John O'Hare (Derby County) and Denis Law (Manchester United).

There were suggestions that Law had been selected to add a bit of glamour and sell some tickets for a fixture that was being played at the end of a season and held little appeal. The Doc's response? 'Rubbish.' Law was in on merit. The South Americans had reached the quarter-finals of the World Cup in Mexico two years earlier before losing 4-2 to eventual winners Brazil. In Glasgow, they paraded the likes of Teofilio Cubillas, Hugo Sotil, Juan Munante, Rodolfo Manzo, Jose Velazquez and Percy Rojas. Six years later, the same players were on show again in one of Scotland's darkest days – the 3-1 defeat in their first game of the World Cup Finals in Argentina 1978. Who could ever obliterate from their memory bank Cubillas rifling two long-range rockets behind Alan Rough within six second-half minutes to seal the Scots' fate? Denis Law was there to witness the downfall of his nation, working as a broadcaster with the BBC. He spent more time in Argentina than the Scottish team as he also took in the final, the host nation's 3-1 extra-time victory over Holland.

Back in 1972, though, Law was sharply focused on events on the field and saw the bustling John O'Hare put Scotland ahead shortly after the turnaround when he touched in a free-kick from Willie Morgan. The Manchester United man, revelling in his return, had the final say with a second goal in 65 minutes. Tommy Docherty declared himself 'more than satisfied' and began making preparations for the upcoming Home International encounter against Northern Ireland at Hampden the following month. Scotland won 2-0 and it was memorable for one reason; Denis Law netted his 30th – and final – goal for his country. There was never any doubt about Law playing against the Irish after facing Peru with renewed vigour. The swagger was back; and it was good to see.

Law's good friend George Best had gone AWOL – again! – and Northern Ireland were denied his marvellous skills in Glasgow. However, they still possessed a twin threat up front in Willie Irvine and the crafty Derek Dougan. Docherty, mindful that Scotland would play Wales and England over the next eight days before embarking on a three-match trip to Brazil, wanted to use as many of his squad as possible to keep them tuned up. Into the team against the Irish came Aberdeen goalkeeper Bobby Clark, Celtic pair Billy McNeill and Jimmy Johnstone, Arsenal's elegant midfielder George Graham and Billy Bremner, the Leeds United dynamo taking the captain's armband from Law. The Northern Irish either retreated into defence right from the off or they were forced back by Scottish attacking aggression, but they seemed content to have nine men behind the ball with only Irvine and Dougan foraging for scraps in enemy territory. Denis Law was an admitted fan of goalkeeper

Pat Jennings – 'a man with hands as big as dinner plates' – and the Northern Irish No. 1 was in fine form in Glasgow. It was heading for a scoreless stalemate until Law struck with only four minutes remaining.

As you might expect from Denis Law, it was something special, another defining moment. It was a goal that was a compelling combination of everything Law was renowned for in the game; speed of thought, breathtaking mobility, electric reflexes, athletic prowess and devastating accuracy. The visitors failed to clear a corner-kick. Jennings was out of position, but David Clements, the Northern Ireland defender, was on the goal-line. The ball dropped awkwardly to Law, about hip level. No problem. He launched himself into the air, was virtually horizontal when he caught the ball perfectly and his effort soared high into the net. The arm, once more, was characteristically thrust towards the heavens, the cuff tightly clenched while the Scottish fans saluted the legend. No-one could have thought at the time that they would never again witness the famous Denis Law goal celebration in the dark blue of his country. However, once more Law had reached a milestone in style. That was the end of the Irish resistance and Peter Lorimer, a substitute for Jimmy Johnstone just after the hour mark, slammed in a second.

Next up was Wales for Hampden's third international inside four weeks and once again Tommy Docherty shuffled the pack with Hibs skipper Pat Stanton coming into the defence alongside Celtic's Billy McNeill, Newcastle United's Bobby Moncur and Martin Buchan, the composed Manchester United defender. Tony Green, of Newcastle, took Asa Hartford's midfield berth and there was a starting place for Peter Lorimer. The Doc, for the third successive game, went with the forward line pairing of John O'Hare and Denis Law. Lorimer and Green combined in the 72nd minute to fashion the game's only goal. The Leeds United forward strode forward purposefully to thunder another of his specials behind his Elland Road teammate Gary Sprake. Three games, five goals scored and none conceded. The run came to a halt when Alan Ball squeezed a 28th-minute shot under Bobby Clark to give England a 1-0 win at Hampden three days later. That encounter is covered in more detail in another chapter.

Denis Law and his international teammates were allowed to spend some time with their families during the brief summer interlude, but they were all back in place again by the time the Brazil Independence Cup kicked off in Belo Horizonte on 29 June. A disappointing crowd of only 4,000 bothered to attend at the Estadio Mineiro for the game against Yugoslavia which was a pity because they missed a stirring, rousing confrontation. Law started alongside Celtic's pint-sized predator Lou Macari who would later become a teammate at Manchester United, bought for £200,000 by Tommy Docherty, an obvious admirer of the player. The Doc sprung a surprise by giving Partick Thistle defender Alex Forsyth his first cap. John Hansen, brother of Alan, also made his international debut, coming on for Firhill teammate Forsyth at the start of the second-half. In searing temperatures of 80 degrees, Macari enhanced his growing reputation by turning in a cross from Willie Morgan in the 40th minute. Dusan Bajevic equalised just after the hour, but Macari responded immediately by giving the Scots the advantage again, once more set up by Morgan. It seemed as though Manchester United winger Morgan could do no wrong, but he slipped up in the 77th minute when he missed a penalty-kick. Yugoslavia took full advantage with the leveller from substitute Jure Jerkovic near the end.

Law lasted 76 minutes in uncomfortable conditions before being replaced by Jimmy Bone and would play 78 minutes in the next match, a goalless draw with Czechoslovakia in Porto Alegre watched by a crowd of 15,000. Law, substituted by Colin Stein, had started the match up front alongside Macari and it was a pairing that more than satisfied the manager. 'They dovetail perfectly. They are a good mix, they both put a lot of energy into their game and there are goals in them, too.' The next game was the one in which everyone wanted to be involved; Brazil in the Maracana, the massive grey bowl of a stadium in Rio de Janeiro. A crowd of 130,000 was there to witness the action on 5 July. Scotland were earning good reviews in South America and were undoubtedly making friends with their enterprising, entertaining style of play.

The Brazilians had Jairzinho, who had scored in every round of the 1970 World Cup Finals, leading the attack, abandoning his more orthodox outside-right role, and also gave starts to Roberto Rivelino, Hercules Brito, Clodoaldo, Gerson and Tostao, five of the team that beat Italy 4-1 to claim the trophy in Mexico. Law and Macari were once again the double spearhead with Aberdeen's Bobby Clark preferred to Ally Hunter in goal for the second successive game. Alex Forsyth, Eddie Colquhoun, Martin Buchan and Willie Donachie made up the back four with a midfield of Willie Morgan, Billy Bremner, George Graham and Asa Hartford backing up Law and Macari. Everything was going according to plan, but Jairzinho spoiled the party ten minutes from the end with the game's solitary goal. The Doc was far from despondent. 'We came to put on a show and I think we managed that. I am so proud of the boys, they were a credit to their country. There wasn't a failure in sight and everyone played their part.'

The Brazilian press again marvelled at the Scots and quizzed if Denis Law was really 32 years old such was the impact he had made in the mini-tournament. The South American hacks rated Law as 'a phenomenon' and Docherty as 'a master strategist'. They also acclaimed Partick Thistle full-back Alex Forsyth who, oddly, would only win another seven caps. Like Macari, he had done well enough to be noted by the manager and he was also snapped up for Manchester United once Docherty had quit the international post.

Law had been hugely impressed, too, by the din created throughout by the colourful, drum-beating, samba-dancing fans inside the Maracana, but, although he didn't realise it, that carnival atmosphere would be eclipsed by a Hampden crowd on 26 September the following year.

CHAPTER EIGHTEEN

NINE AND OUT

Dear old Hugh Taylor, chief sportswriter and a splendid colleague for over a decade at the *Daily Record*, wrote in his *Scottish Football Book No. 18* about the 1972 Scotland v. England encounter at Hampden. The doyen of the written word was far from impressed with what had been on show in Denis Law's ninth and last head-to-head with the Auld Enemy. Denis was hailed, but the confrontation of the oldest enemies in world football did little to ignite the imagination of my old journalist friend.

Hugh wrote: 'It was to have been the day of Scottish national rejoicing – the day of triumph over England, our oldest rivals. Hopes had seldom been higher than on the windy afternoon of 27 May 1972. As the 119,325 spectators filed into Hampden they felt disasters in the past were over. They considered the new spirit and confidence of the boys in blue would bring an epic victory.

'With the advent of Tommy Docherty as team manager, there was great enthusiasm. Scotland had beaten Northern Ireland and Wales and needed only a point to win the Home International Championship. England had faltered, losing at their own Wembley to little Ireland. The scent of victory was in the air.

'Alas, for the high hopes. Alas, for British football.

'The international of 1972 between Scotland and England was a disgrace, a blot on football and the season ended in one of the most unpleasant matches between the two countries, with a snarl and a scowl and a bitter clash. Everything went wrong for Scotland – and it was a pity red-shirted Italian referee Sergio Gonella was so lenient. We all knew it would be a tough game – but little did we think it would turn into a battle.

'The teams were: Scotland: Clark (Aberdeen); Brownlie (Hibernian), Donachie (Manchester City); Bremner (Leeds United capt), McNeill (Celtic), Moncur (Newcastle United); Lorimer (Leeds), Gemmill (Derby County), Macari (Celtic), Law (Manchester United) and Hartford (West Bromwich Albion).

'England: Banks (Stoke City); Madeley (Leeds), Hughes (Liverpool); Storey (Arsenal), McFarland (Derby County), Hunter (Leeds), Moore (West Ham capt); Ball (Arsenal), Bell (Manchester City), Chivers (Tottenham Hotspur) and Marsh (Manchester City).

'Hardly had the match begun on a dreadful day for football, with the violent wind starching the flags to the poles, than the martial arts began and high tackles, wild kicks and brutal charges were taken as a matter of course. Who was to blame? Undoubtedly England took a psychological advantage. They knew the Scottish temperament – and its failings. They felt that the menace of husky destroyers like Peter Storey and Norman Hunter would provoke the Scots, fiery bantam cocks, into retaliation. That is what happened. So no-one took credit.

'Scotland started promisingly enough. In the third minute John Brownlie, a magnificent young back, surprised even the redoubtable Gordon Banks with a high, dropping shot from the wing and the Scots claimed the ball was over the line as the keeper grasped it above his head.

'Then the kicking started and the game became disgracefully physical. Roy McFarland fouled the volatile Denis Law – and was then punched on the jaw. Hunter kicked Brownlie, Storey had a swing at Billy Bremner, Alan Ball felled Bremner from behind. And these were merely the principal fouls in a period of violence that had no place on any football field, far less an international arena.

'Three players were cautioned, England's Ball and Scotland's Billy McNeill and Asa Hartford. Matters became so bad that referee Gonella called the two captains together and asked them to calm their men. It made no difference. It took nearly 25 minutes for the Hampden fans to see a real soccer move and that was when Storey kicked a Hartford shot off the line that had been deflected by Bremner and deceived Banks. Scotland were on top, but were cynically stopped by sheer strength and they were spiteful in retaliation, although it was a case almost of boys against men.

'Scotland, however, played neat, constructive football and Banks blocked a Peter Lorimer effort. Then, in almost complete silence, England scored against the run of play – a goal, in the words of sad Tommy Docherty, like something out of *Comic Cuts*. A bad pass from Bremner was intercepted by Ball and he and the massive Martin Chivers combined well deep into the Scotland penalty area. Ball's final prod sent the ball under Bobby Clark's diving body and it rolled slowly over the line, with a posse of blue-clad defenders trying vainly to stop it.

'Still the violence went on and there was a tackle on little Lou Macari which left the Celtic striker with his torn jersey flapping round his neck. Now there was unease in the Scotland defence and Colin Bell, the best player on the field, had bad luck with a superb shot which shaved the outside of the post. Some of the poison drained out of the game in the second-half, with England much less violent, but the polluting effect of their earlier fouls were felt until the end. Play was much better, with England the more organised side. Yet Scotland went near in an exciting spell, with the irrepressible Denis Law and Macari stirring up the action.

'A great tackle by McFarland on Law saved a goal. Macari crossed from the left and a careful Law header was stopped by Emlyn Hughes on the line. Banks hurt a hand as Hartford charged in. Jinky Jimmy Johnstone was brought on for Archie

Gemmill, but it was too late and the Celt, who can be so brilliant, did not sparkle. Fifteen minutes from time manager Docherty made another change, taking off the clever left-back Willie Donachie and bringing on Tony Green.

'This enabled Scotland to build neater play in the midfield, but the strong England defence held out. Sir Alf Ramsey took off Rodney Marsh and substituted Malcolm Macdonald and near the end England almost scored again when Chivers, showing his massive authority, flicked a header just past the Scottish post. Unfortunately, the game ended as unhappily as it began, with the petulant Ball giving a two-fingered gesture to the Scottish fans as he walked off the pitch.

'It wasn't a game to remember and officials of both countries condemned the brutality. Said Sir Alf, "I disliked the physical aspect intensely in the first 20 minutes. I think both teams wanted to win and there was rivalry between the players from the same club on opposite sides and there is a great deal of feeling between them at club level."

'In the end, Scotland were probably unlucky to lose 1-0, but, frankly, neither side distinguished itself. I felt the presence in the England midfield of Storey and Hunter, two players not noted for their reluctance to hammer in physically, was seen by some of the Scots as an invitation to war. Scotland fell into the trap. Unlike the West Germans, who had decisively beaten England and who disdained the savagery of their opponents in Berlin and kept on playing football, the Scots became war-like, retaliating with the old fervour of the "Wha daur meddle wi' me?" clans. That suited England perfectly. So there was little football.

'There were 46 physical fouls recorded during the match – 24 against England and 22 against Scotland. And the sad truth was that Scotland failed where the team manager expected them to be strongest – in midfield. There was no player of inspiration or class to vary the style, to bring imagination and a shrewd long pass, no Eddie Gray, Bobby Murdoch or Charlie Cooke, who would have made a world of a difference.

'This deficiency was all the sadder because Scotland carried a real threat at the front. England's crowding defence gave Lorimer little room for his explosive shooting to count. But Law, who became the hero of Hampden again with a fine display, was near his old electric self and Macari was sharp and energetic, a real find.

'It was, however, the war at Hampden that will be remembered, not the good football. The main aim of too many players seemed to be to hurt an opponent and because there were so many culprits on both sides it was impossible to apportion blame. Once the Scotland v. England international was an exhibition of all that was best in British football, hard but fair and sporting with artists allowed to show their talent. Now it's a battle, with a cluttered midfield and anyone trying to hold the ball ruthlessly chopped down. In the end, Scotland were reduced to pumping high balls into the England penalty area, useless against their tall defenders.

'Hampden 1972 was the worst advertisement British football has ever had.'

Actually, I was in the antiquated rundown Hampden press box that afternoon among the hoi-polloi of British sportswriters – along with a scattering of scribes from all sorts of other publications from around the globe naturally curious to see what all the fuss was about concerning the oldest international fixture in the world. I was 20 years old at the time and had been writing a monthly Scottish football column for about a year for the prestigious *World Soccer* magazine. Their editor, Phillip Rising, telephoned and asked me if I would be interested in covering the event for his monthly mag. Try stopping me!

I wrote my article on the Monday and sent it by registered post to the *World Soccer* offices in London. Remember, these were the days long before the internet where you can send an e-mail round the world at the push of a button. Mobile phones? The *Daily Record* had one walkie-talkie for emergencies and it was known as The Talking Brick. You needed a wheelbarrow to cart this thing around with you.

Anyway, I searched through the rubble of the disaster area that masquerades as a library at home and, remarkably and eventually, found a copy of that particular *World Soccer*. I was intrigued to discover what I had said all those years ago. One paragraph leapt out. 'At the start Roy McFarland kicked Denis Law. Denis Law kicked Roy McFarland. Norman Hunter kicked John Brownlie. Archie Gemmill kicked Alan Ball. Alan Ball kicked Billy Bremner and Peter Storey kicked everybody in a blue shirt.' Alas, that just about sums up the afternoon when Hampden became a hacker's paradise.

Denis Law's farewell to this fixture deserved so much better.

CHAPTER NINETEEN

CZECH MATE

Willie Ormond had a problem. He was plotting for his seventh game in charge of the Scottish international team and the furrows criss-crossing his brow, running in three deep parallel lines, resembled rail tracks. Clearly, this was a worried man. In public, Ormond disguised his fretting with a quick smile and his courteous, likeable ways. He had taken over from Tommy Docherty at the start of 1973, inheriting a team that was on the brink of winning its way to the World Cup Finals in West Germany the following year. Under The Doc, the Scots had triumphed 4-1 over Denmark in Copenhagen on 18 October 1972 with Lou Macari, Jimmy Bone, Joe Harper and Willie Morgan on target. Goals from Kenny Dalglish and Peter Lorimer eased their nation to a 2-0 victory over the Danes a month later at Hampden. It was to be Docherty's last involvement at this level.

Manchester United sacked manager Frank O'Farrell and, within days, on 22 December the garrulous Glaswegian was on his way to Old Trafford as his successor. He went from £7,500-per-year as an international manager to £15,000 per year with a United side that had struggled to find a suitable successor to the legendary Matt Busby, who had retired from the touchline in 1969 to become general manager and then director at the club. The inexperienced Wilf McGuinness moved into the dug-out before being handed his P45 a year later. Busby returned for a season and then Irishman O'Farrell was lured from Leicester City. This was the same manager of whom Denis Law would later say, 'Frank O'Farrell arrived as a stranger and left as a stranger.' Again the choice was hardly inspired and 12 months later it was time to call for The Doc.

Former SFA secretary Ernie Walker sighed, 'It was astonishing. The Doc had come to us professing undying love for Scotland, saying it was the job of his dreams. He was the happiest man in the universe when he got the position. However, it seems that love for Scotland disappeared overnight when Manchester United came calling. That's the way it is, I suppose. One learns to know Tommy.'

However, there was no time for Scotland to wallow in self-pity. There was a World Cup place up for grabs. The SFA assured everyone they would think big before naming Docherty's successor. Celtic's Jock Stein, Liverpool's Bill Shankly and Hibs' Eddie Turnbull were all mentioned, either in a full-time or part-time capacity. So, they opted for Willie Ormond, of St Johnstone. To be fair to the SFA bosses, they had to act fast and Ormond arrived on 5 January 1973 – only 14 days after Docherty had vacated the premises. Supporters were slightly puzzled, possibly even perplexed. Ormond had had reasonable success with unfashionable St Johnstone and could even point to magnificent wins in Europe over West German giants SV Hamburg and Hungary's Vasas Budapest in the UEFA Cup two years beforehand. He also put together a fairly attractive Perth outfit that reached the League Cup Final before a first-minute goal from Bertie Auld took the trophy to Celtic in 1969. Players such as John Connolly, Jim Pearson, Kenny Aird and Henry Hall were lighting up the domestic game and Ormond's stock was high. Ernie Walker said, 'Willie was a great wee guy and it was difficult not to like him. He was perky, good company and liked a drink. Everybody liked Willie Ormond.' Enough of the popularity contests. The nagging question for a sceptical nation remained: was he good enough at international level?

Ormond's take on the appointment was a simple one. He summed up, 'I wouldn't like to say I am a hard man. I would like to think I am fair and I expect the players to be fair with me. I'll respect them as men and I would hope I would get that respect back from them in return. If we can go forward on that basis I will be more than satisfied.'

Five weeks after Ormond accepted the job, England rolled into town to provide the opposition in the SFA Centenary Celebration Match at Hampden. Obviously, no expense was spared by the governing body in their plans for a glamorous occasion. A reasonable crowd of 48,470 turned out on a freezing evening in Glasgow to witness players slipping and sliding their way around a treacherous pitch. The English players seemed to cope a bit better than their Scottish counterparts; they thrashed five goals beyond Bobby Clark without reply. Underlining the arctic antics on a bizarre night, the best goal of the game probably came from Scot Peter Lorimer with a pulverising sliced effort from the edge of his own penalty area. Clark didn't move a muscle as the ball sizzled high into the net. Ormond had every right to groan.

The new Scottish manager was clearly traumatised when he was asked questions about the debacle the following day. Unusually grim-faced, he fixed his inquisitors in his gaze and said, 'If some players think I will accept that sort of performance, irrespective of the ground conditions, they will have another think coming. A few of them didn't do themselves any favours in that game, that's for sure. I would go as far as to say that a few international careers are now in jeopardy.' These were words from a man who was known to be almost shy in most circumstances. He was wounded, though, and it showed. Changes were on the way.

Ormond put out this line-up against England: Bobby Clark (Aberdeen); Alex Forsyth (Partick Thistle), Eddie Colquhoun (Sheffield United), Martin Buchan (Manchester United), Willie Donachie (Manchester City); Peter Lorimer (Leeds United), Billy Bremner (Leeds United), George Graham (Manchester

United), Willie Morgan (Manchester United, sub: Colin Stein, Rangers); Kenny Dalglish (Celtic), Lou Macari (Celtic).

The next game was against Wales in Wrexham on 12 May. Ormond had plenty of time to ponder his changes. This was his selection: Peter McCloy (Rangers); Danny McGrain (Celtic), Jim Holton (Manchester United), Pat Stanton (Hibs), Donachie; Dalglish (sub: Macari), Graham, Davie Hay (Celtic), Morgan; Derek Johnstone (Rangers), Derek Parlane (Rangers, sub: Stein).

No Bobby Clark. No Alex Forsyth. No Eddie Colquhoun. No Martin Buchan. No Peter Lorimer. No Billy Bremner. And, clearly, no messing with Willie Ormond. All he required now was a victory and it was duly delivered when two goals from George Graham gave Scotland a 2-0 win. Ormond looked a lot more at ease in front of the inquisitive TV cameras after this one. 'I thought we played well, but I know we can do better. We were a lot more solid and credit to the players who followed pre-match instructions.'

The storm clouds weren't far away, though. In fact, they were already gathering as Ormond spoke to the press in Wrexham about his optimism for the future. Four days later Northern Ireland arrived at Hampden and left with the points after a well-merited 2-1 triumph. Dalglish scored, but some horrendous goalkeeping from McCloy gifted the visitors the points. It was swiftly back to the drawing board and no-one was unduly surprised when Ormond unceremoniously axed the blundering McCloy and brought in his Celtic rival Ally Hunter for the match against England at Wembley three days afterwards. This was an altogether different Scotland unit from the one that had gone through the comic routines favoured by Mack Sennett, acclaimed producer of the *Keystone Kops*, in Glasgow four months earlier against the same opposition. A typical Martin Peters goal gave the English a narrow win.

Celtic's Davie Hay recalled, 'Willie Ormond wasn't the most demonstrative human being you might ever meet, but he was activated for this one, believe me. The five-goal drubbing in his debut match hurt a proud man like hell. He wanted his revenge and he came close, too. Unfortunately, our defence switched off once and that was enough for them to snatch a slender win. Alan Ball flighted over a free-kick and Martin Peters, as he did so often, ghosted in at the far post to send a header spiralling away from Ally Hunter.'

However, if it hadn't been for a soaring, gravity-defying save from Peter Shilton from a Dalglish howitzer with only five minutes to go, the Scots would have got a deserved draw. Still, there was some hope from this performance. There was the emergence of Hay in midfield, a young Joe Jordan came on for Macari at Wembley, Holton looked reliable and unfussy in the middle of the rearguard and McGrain, picking up only his third cap in the game against England, was poised and assured at right-back. He would go on to represent his country on another 59 occasions and it would have been closer to 100 but for a cruel injury that derailed his progress for two years.

Ormond watched his team draw a blank at Wembley and he winced on 22 June when the forwards again failed to impress in a 1-0 defeat in a friendly against Switzerland in Berne. Eight days later, a Scot was on target, but there was little to celebrate as a flashing header from Derek Johnstone thundered beyond McCloy for the only goal of the game against Brazil at Hampden. Rangers' Derek Parlane was doing well on the domestic front, but he was struggling in the international arena. He played against the Swiss and the South Americans without making any sort of worthwhile impact. His Ibrox teammate Johnstone was now playing in central defence and his goal threat had been removed. In desperation, Ormond turned to his old St Johnstone favourite John Connolly, who had since been transferred to Everton. He pitched him in against Switzerland without success. Connolly only lasted the first-half before being replaced by Joe Jordan. He was never selected again.

So, it was a thoughtful Ormond who sat in his Park Gardens office in Glasgow and pondered his next move. At his home in Musselburgh, East Lothian, he would pour his favourite tipple, gin and lemon, and continue to agonise. It was the same old Scottish failing. There was a distinct lack of firepower, no cutting edge up front, little thrust, no-one who could be relied upon to seize upon the half-chances. Czechoslovakia were due to provide the opposition in one of Scotland's most important international games in history. They would be in Glasgow on the evening of 26 September and the good work done by Tommy Docherty in the double-header against the Danes would simply disintegrate if Ormond didn't come up with a solution to the dilemma. Four games leading up to the visit of the formidable Czechs had seen Scotland score one goal, concede five and lose on each occasion. Where was Superman when you needed him?

He was at Maine Road playing in the sky blue of Manchester City, ironically, after being freed by Tommy Docherty at Manchester United. The Lawman, at 33, was upset and hurt at the way he discovered he was no longer wanted by the Old Trafford side. If you ask him his views today on Docherty you will be greeted with a one-word answer, 'Pass'. But he went to City with an ambition, hunger and desire to show Docherty he had been far too hasty in dumping the professional he had played alongside on his international debut against Wales in Cardiff 15 years earlier in 1958. Hell hath no fury like a Lawman scorned.

Keith MacRae, the former Scotland Under-23 goalkeeper who cost Manchester City £100,000 when he signed from Motherwell in 1973, remembered Law's season at the club. He said, 'Yes, it looked as though Denis had a point to prove to Docherty and every other doubter, for that matter. He was genuinely excited at the prospect of playing for City alongside the likes of Colin Bell, Frannie Lee, Mike Summerbee and Rodney Marsh. There was a lot of flamboyance in the squad. Denis was eager to get started. He proved his fitness and played 22 first-team games and, if memory serves correctly, netted nine goals. Not bad for a guy who was supposed to be over the hill. Injury slowed him down, of course, but he could still do the business in front of goal and that is something you cannot coach into anyone, young or old. We all knew he was desperate to play for Scotland in the World Cup Finals and everyone at the club, even the English players, expressed delight when the news broke that he would be going to West Germany. If anyone deserved to be on that plane it was Denis Law.'

Watched by an SFA contingent in the Wembley stand, Law readily admitted he didn't do himself justice when Manchester City faced Wolves in the English League Cup Final that season. City slumped to a 2-1 defeat and Law said, 'I had taken a knock in the first leg of the semi-final against Plymouth and was out of the team until a week before Wembley and Francis Lee was struggling, too, with knee problems. Still, on paper, our forward line of Summerbee, Bell, Lee and me looked about as exciting and entertaining as any in the country. Bell, however, was the only one fully fit. We played as awful a game as I have ever played in that arena with 100,000 fans watching. It was a big game and a big day, but we let our supporters down completely. It was mainly because we weren't fit and you can't play effectively at Wembley if you're not fit. Few get away with it and we were found out very quickly.'

Any hopes Law had of representing his nation on the biggest stage of all were in jeopardy. Ron Saunders had been brought in to replace Johnny Hart, the man who had persuaded Law to join City in the summer. Hart's health had suffered and he quit the club in November with Saunders moving in. The new manager's sergeant-major approach to the game almost caused a revolt among the Maine Road players. Under Hart, they had been encouraged to play with flair. Saunders had his own ideas and they weren't quite in unison with those of Hart.

These were testing times for Law. Mike Summerbee, who

played eight internationals for England, recalled, 'I don't mind admitting Denis Law had always been a particular hero of mine. I first met him at a party given by former City boss Malcolm Allison and I had just joined from Swindon Town. Denis was there with the likes of George Best and Paddy Crerand and we ended up having a chat in the kitchen, of all places. I liked him a lot. But it was difficult for us all under Ron Saunders. I remember going to training one day and there was Denis acting as a ball-boy behind one of the goals while some of the youngsters had shooting practice. Mind you, he was in good company because Saunders had also ordered Rodney Marsh and Frannie Lee to help out. Ludicrous! Denis Law a ball-boy? That was the mentality of Saunders.'

George Best, a good friend and business partner of Summerbee, was aware of the situation at Maine Road. Best revealed, 'It is always going to be difficult for a manager coming in to a club where there is a nucleus of players who have been there for a long time, have achieved much and are local heroes, but are approaching the end of their careers. However, there are ways and means of dealing with these situations and Ron got off on the wrong foot. He immediately began to refer to Denis Law as "The Old Man" and Francis Lee as "Fatty". Saunders was never material for the Diplomatic Corps, that's for sure.'

Summerbee looked back at the League Cup Final defeat against Wolves and said, 'It was my last game at Wembley and I don't recall it with any fondness. What I do remember above all, though, is sitting on the coach next to Denis as we left the stadium and seeing how much losing had hurt him. Denis was one of the great players of my era, of any era in football, as a matter of fact. I remember saying to him on the coach that at least I could tell my grandchildren I had played alongside Denis Law in a Cup Final. It was a corny line and it didn't cheer him up, but I meant it all the same.'

After Wembley, City lost to Leeds United in a league game

and Law was dropped. A few of his big-name colleagues suffered the same fate. Law was playing for the reserves, a situation, if it continued, that would most assuredly have made certain he would not be representing Scotland in any fixture, never mind the World Cup. Worse still, Law was to discover that, behind his back, Saunders had agreed to sell him to Fourth Division Bradford City. Law admitted, 'I would have retired there and then, but the finals in West Germany were only a few weeks away and I was determined to win back my place in the City first team and at least give myself the chance of going to my first World Cup. I was insulted when Saunders tried to sell me to Bradford. There I was, preparing for a World Cup, and he was getting ready to sell me to a club in the lowest division in the country. I lost all respect for him.'

Law informed Saunders he wasn't going anywhere and set his sights on becoming as fit as possible. An SFA official was on hand to watch his return to the top side at the start of April against Queens Park Rangers. As usual, Law gave it his best shot, but the team collapsed to a miserable 3-0 thrashing. The following day Saunders was sacked after only five months in charge with former City captain Tony Book taking over, the third manager at Maine Road in one season. Law, happily, must have done enough in the landslide defeat against the London side to merit a positive mention in the ear of Willie Ormond. In the last league game of the season, his neat back-heel would confirm Manchester United's descent into the Second Division. It beggars belief that goal was to be Law's last kick of the ball at club level. There were only eight minutes remaining when Law, displaying those lightning reflexes of yesteryear, reacted quicker than the United defence to flick a right-wing cross beyond a helpless Alex Stepney. United fans swarmed onto the pitch and, amid the bedlam, Book signalled for Law, who refused to celebrate the strike, to come off. Before he could do that, though, referee David Smith called a halt to proceedings and the English League held an emergency meeting and decided to let the scoreline remain and award the points to City.

Before that, though, was the little matter of the death-or-glory encounter with Czechoslovakia and, against a welter of expectations and predictions, Denis Law had been named in Willie Ormond's squad. Not only that, he was in the starting line-up. The crowd for the game had to be restricted to 100,000 on the instructions of the police authorities. They could have quadrupled that attendance such was the overwhelming demand to witness the spectacle. Ernie Walker recalled, 'The fans turned out in their thousands to buy tickets. There was a huge snake-like line outside Hampden Park as the supporters queued patiently. I'm sure a few of them had been there for days.'

Sandy Jardine, the assured Rangers full-back, remembered, 'The Czechs had been held to a surprise 1-1 draw with Denmark in Copenhagen and that meant we went into the game knowing a victory would see us qualify. Looking at the section, I think a lot of people thought Scotland would be second favourites. The Danes, at the time, weren't a European force, but Czechoslovakia's pedigree was obvious to all. They were a very good team with some exceptional players.'

Peter Lorimer, the Leeds United heavy hitter, had to sit out the action through suspension following his ordering-off against Denmark in the previous game. However, he added, 'We were a confident bunch of guys going into that game. We had a great squad with some very good players. I wasn't involved, but such was the depth and quality of the squad that I wasn't missed. There was no guarantee I would have started the game, anyway, even if I had been available.'

John Blackley, a sweeper who relied upon anticipation rather than pace, laughed as he recalled Scotland's preparations for the match. He said, 'The build-up to the occasion was obviously quite tense. We trained on the Wednesday morning of the game.

We had a kick about and a few laps as we went through our normal routines. We finished our training session and there was the shout of "Last man in the van." That normally triggered a sprint from the players to pile into the vehicle. We all started to run when we heard a cry from Wee Billy Bremner, "Hey, whoa there. What about set-pieces? We haven't done any work on dead balls. Come on, lads, get back here and let's go through a few of them." Willie Ormond agreed. "Right enough, Billy," he said. "Let's get back to the training ground, lads." The players piled back onto the pitch. Tommy Hutchison took a corner from the left, swung in at the near post and Big Jim Holton got his head on it to send the ball hurtling into the net. That was enough for Wee Willie. He shouted, "Right lads, last in the van." And that was that. One corner-kick! That was our build-up to the night. Incredible.'

Midfield enforcer Davie Hay has vivid memories of the evening of 26 September. He said, 'Willie Ormond's pre-match talk in the Hampden dressing room to the assembled players was succinct and to the point. "Go out there and become legends. Don't let your country down. Don't let yourselves down. Go on and get the job done." Wee Willie didn't waste any time with mumbo jumbo or the like. We all knew what was expected. I recall the bedlam that was already reverberating around the place. Thump, thump, thump. We could hear the supporters banging their feet above us almost in unison, a rhythmic and hypnotic call to arms. It was tribal-like and I could see it was getting through to my teammates, including my great hero Denis Law, who, at 33 years old, must have seen and heard it all before.

'We all made the usual noises. "Let's get in about them." "This is our night." "We'll show them." All that sort of stuff. Denis threw in a couple, as well. It was impossible not to be sucked into this intoxicating mixture of anticipation and expectation. The atmosphere before kick-off was quite awesome and the shrieks and the chants from the frenzied crowd were reaching an ear-splitting crescendo. Players go through all sorts of routines in the dressing room. Some would be fidgeting with their tie-ups. Others would be footering with their laces. Some checked their studs for the umpteenth time. Through it all, though, was a remarkable degree of concentration from each and every one of us. This was our destiny. Then the referee, a Norwegian bloke called Henry Oberg, popped his head round the door and told us it was time to go. Chests out, teeth gritted, jaws jutting, muscles flexed. We walked out of the dressing room and into the tunnel. "Scot-land ... Scot-land" was the cry that filled the stadium.

'I defy anyone to say that sort of enthralling atmosphere doesn't get the adrenalin going. It was awesome. The best I had ever sampled was the night back in 1970 when Celtic beat Leeds United in the European Cup semi-final second leg at the national stadium. There were 136,505 at Hampden on that occasion. But the clamour created by the Tartan Army three years later was simply deafening. It was amazingly uplifting; pure, gorgeous, orchestrated mayhem. We were a mere 90 minutes away from reaching the World Cup Finals. Astonishingly, the last time we achieved it in Sweden in 1958 I was still at St James's Primary School in Paisley.'

Denis Law might have seen the date of the game as a good omen. 'Remarkably, it was 12 years to the day that I had scored twice against Czechoslovakia in the World Cup-tie at Hampden that forced the play-off in Brussels. Unfortunately, we lost that match and I was beginning to wonder if I was fated not to appear in the finals of this competition.'

After much deliberating and soul-searching, Ormond went with this line-up: Hunter (Celtic); Jardine (Rangers), Holton (Manchester United), Connelly (Celtic), McGrain (Celtic); Morgan (Manchester United), Bremner (Leeds United, captain), Hay (Celtic), Hutchison (Coventry City); Dalglish (Celtic) and Law (Manchester City).

Obviously, the first goal was going to be crucial and, sadly for Ally Hunter, the Scottish goalkeeper, it arrived in the 34th minute and it was a personal calamity. Zdenek Nehoda cut inside from the right and lashed what looked like a happy-go-lucky effort at goal. It wasn't particularly fiercely struck and appeared to even lack the oomph to reach its target. Hunter moved to his right to deal with the threat. Alarmingly, the keeper seemed to lose the flight of the ball and it managed to elude his hands and ended up in the far corner.

Hunter said, 'Everything was going perfectly well up until then and they had hardly threatened. It looked only a matter of time before we scored. The goal was a disaster for me. I don't know if the occasion got to me or maybe I didn't concentrate properly when Nehoda let fly. Nevertheless, that was us one down and the place just went silent. I felt sick; really sick.'

Hunter's battle to beat his jitters would have been helped along the way just before the interval. Law forced a corner-kick on the left and Tommy Hutchison raced over to take it before the referee had the chance to blow for half-time. The Scots piled forward and Jim Holton joined them. The Coventry City winger threw in a cross to the near post and Holton, utterly fearless, leapt determinedly to get his head to the ball. Goalkeeper Ivo Viktor was caught in no-man's-land and the Manchester United defender's effort zoomed over a helpless defender on the goal-line. It would be only right and proper to state Scotland had worked on that particular manoeuvre on the training ground. Well, at least once!

It was still stalemated at 1-1 after the hour mark when Ormond made a brave and momentous decision. He sent out Joe Jordan to warm up. The fans must have wondered who was going to make way. It was a straight choice between Denis Law and Kenny Dalglish. The Scottish manager showed enormous faith in Law, a decade older than the Celtic player, kept him on and replaced the younger man. Ormond explained his thinking afterwards, 'I saw Denis was giving them problems when high balls dropped into their box. They knew all about his ability with his head and they were blocking him as he tried to make his runs. Willie Morgan and Tommy Hutchison were delivering good balls into the danger areas, but the Czechs were double-banking on Denis. I was very impressed that he never looked like chucking it. He just kept coming back for more. He was everywhere that night, but he needed support in the air. That's why I sent on Joe Jordan. That doubled our threat in that area.'

The gamble, if, in fact, it was that, paid off handsomely. Jordan's first act was to bullet a header from a Morgan cross just over Viktor's crossbar. He had put down a very positive marker. The Leeds United man had been on the pitch barely 20 minutes when he just about brought the house down in the 75th minute. Skipper Billy Bremner informed Davie Hay he would be forsaking the defensive duties of his midfield beat to push forward. 'It made sense,' said the Celtic player. 'Billy was always a threat up front and had scored some invaluable goals for his club. It curtailed my game, but it was for the good of the team and, naturally, I accepted it.'

It worked in one glorious moment when Bremner, on the right-hand side of the penalty box, twisted and turned to get into a shooting position and fired low past the sprawling Viktor. The crowd rose as one to hail a goal. Their joy was stifled in an instant as the ball clattered against the bottom of the keeper's right-hand upright, ran along the face of the goal and was hastily booted away by a frantic Czech defender. His clearance went straight to Morgan, who jinked one way, went another and sent in a cross off the outside of his boot. Jordan launched himself forward, made perfect contact with his head and the ball was in the net before Viktor, a brave and gallant goalkeeper, could blink. Law, smack in front of goal, punched the air. Jordan admitted, 'I was confident we would get a goal when I came on. I would even go as far as to say I believed I would score it.'

Law, in fact, could also have got on the scoresheet in that frantic second-half. Hay recalled, 'We broke forward at one stage with the Czechs caught up the field. Denis had the ball at his feet and he was zeroing in on goal. I was running alongside him shouting for a pass. I could have saved my breath; there was no way, absolutely no way, Denis was passing the ball to me. I could have been Pele and he still wouldn't have parted with the ball. He probably saw me out of the corner of his eye and thought I would have missed, anyway. On he went, but, unfortunately, their keeper Viktor raced from his goal and managed to block the effort. Credit to their goalie, it was a good, well-timed stop. But how marvellous would it have been for Denis to score on that fabulous night?'

Afterwards, Law was singled out for special praise in the media along with goal hero Jordan and the hard-working Hutchison. One report claimed, 'Denis Law rolled back the years. This was the Denis The Menace we all know and love. The Czechs must have been delighted to see the back of him after this non-stop, energetic display. He didn't stop for a breather and showed, once again, that he is one of the best forwards Scotland has ever produced.'

Billy Bremner said, 'I immediately thought about the boss, Willie Ormond, when the referee blew for full-time. I believed he deserved to share our glory. My first reaction was to go and get him out of the tunnel. Do you know he didn't want to come onto the pitch? He said, "It's the players' night, go and enjoy yourself." I told him, "It's your night, too, now get out there." I felt he had done as much as anyone to get us to the World Cup Finals.' Photographs in the newspapers the following day showed Law, who had by that time swapped his Scotland shirt for a Czechoslovakian one, and Bremner hoisting the unassuming Ormond on their shoulders. The Scotland manager looked ecstatic even if a trifle embarrassed.

So, Scotland were out of the 16-year wilderness that had seen them fail so often when hopes were high. There was a dreadful inconsistency about a team that could achieve some spectacular results against top opposition and fail miserably when confronted by mediocre and average outfits. No matter. West Germany was now on the horizon. There was one fixture left to be fulfilled, the meaningless return against Czechoslovakia in Bratislava on 17 October. Only 15,000 spectators bothered to turn out.

Skipper Billy Bremner had been involved in some spiteful skirmishes with Czech opponents in Glasgow and there was the underlying threat of some retribution coming his way. Wisely, Willie Ormond left out the Leeds midfielder for this one and gave the captaincy to Davie Hay. He went with this side: Harvey (Leeds United); Jardine (Rangers), Forsyth (Rangers), Blackley (Hibs), McGrain (Celtic); Morgan (Manchester United), Dalglish (Celtic), Davie Hay (Celtic), Tommy Hutchison (Coventry City); Denis Law (Manchester City) and Joe Jordan (Leeds United). Donald Ford replaced Law in the second-half.

The game was irrelevant as was Nehoda's penalty-kick that proved to be the only goal of a fairly drab encounter. A report at the time read, 'To describe the game as tedious is to be generous. Scotland had every incentive to avoid unnecessary bookings and their tactics seemed no more threatening than to retain possession. This they achieved without alarm until the 18th minute, when Nehoda carried the ball past Tom Forsyth, who challenged untidily and handled into the bargain. Having manufactured the penalty, Nehoda was given the privilege of scoring from it. The Scots showed no great enthusiasm to make good the deficit; the Czechs even less to increase it or exact gratuitous revenge on their opponents. After an hour, Ormond took off Law and awarded a first cap to Hearts' Donald Ford, Scotland's leading league scorer. Ford came nearest to squaring the issue. In the last minute his shot from a tight angle cannoned to safety off the head of Viktor. At the end, a storm of whistling enveloped the stadium.'

So, it was a beaten, but ultimately successful, Scotland side that left the pitch in Bratislava. Later they were to discover that Poland, against the odds, had drawn 1-1 with England at Wembley and knocked them out of the tournament. Scotland would be Great Britain's only representatives in the World Cup Finals in 1974. They were smack in the spotlight; they were the main attraction.

It was the perfect stage for a guy called Denis Law.

CHAPTER TWENTY

FOR THE RECORD

Sadly, I missed that glorious evening at Hampden on 26 September 1973. I was working on the *Daily Record* sports desk as a sub-editor and, after getting me tickets for the Scotland v. Czechoslovakia game, chief sports editor Alex Cameron – known to all as Chiefy – informed me that there was no chance of me being anywhere near Mount Florida on that date. My desperate pleas fell on deaf ears. I would be very much on call. He thought the tickets were for someone else and, as it turned out, he was proved correct when I passed them on to a pal on the features desk. I can't remember if he paid for them or not, but I'm sure he had a great night at our national stadium. At my expense.

My shift at the country's biggest-selling newspaper normally started at 3 p.m. I rolled in as plans were unfolding for the match that evening. As usual, the *Record* would be sending three sports reporters to the game, the aforementioned Chiefy, Hugh Taylor and Ken Gallacher. That was the norm for such an occasion. Chiefy would provide a 'think' piece – normally under the banner 'CAMERON COMMENT' – Hughie would provide the match report, delivered in his usual colourful and succinct style, while Ken would hoover up the quotes and take care of the back page article. Four photographers were heading for Hampden, Eric Craig, Bob Campbell, Bert Paterson and Robert Hotchkiss.

It's fascinating to look at that newspaper today. In fact, it's fairly bewildering. On the front page there is a six-column photograph of a clearly delighted Old Firm double-act of

Sandy Jardine, sporting some interesting headgear, and Danny McGrain. The headline is in 144 point thin face lower case wob (white on black) stating: 'We did it!' I know the exact point size because I wrote the headline. There is a cross reference running under the picture: World Cup Heroes – PAGES 34 and 35. Jardine and McGrain had to share their joy with a wing column news story, headlined: 'Chrysler storm: But talks end in deadlock.' A strike appeared to be just around the corner.

Here's how Ken Gallacher wrote the caption to the page one photograph:

> Sandy Jardine and Danny McGrain sum up the joy of millions after Scotland qualified for the Finals of the World Cup last night . . . for the first time in 16 years.
>
> The dream became reality at Hampden when Scotland beat Czechoslovakia 2-1 in front of a sell-out 100,000 crowd.
>
> McGrain and Jardine – wearing a tammy handed to him by one of the fans – swapped jerseys with their opponents after the final whistle.
>
> The fans had massed on the terracing as the triumphant players went on a madcap lap of delight.
>
> Now the boys who made Scotland one of the world's best 16 teams will share in a fantastic £250,000 pay-out in sponsored deals.
>
> But last night all that mattered was that Scotland won.

Hugh Taylor's match report was contained to page 35. The headline across the spread read: NOW LOOK OUT, HERE COME SCOTLAND.

Here's Hughie's prose:

> THEY wouldn't leave . . . they couldn't leave. They had to stay on and on at Hampden and make our grim old fortress of a stadium a gay, wonderful, colourful arena of noise and waving standards.

Oh, that magnificent Scottish crowd, the greatest in the world paying tribute to the most courageous Scottish side I have seen.

A fantastic, emotional night – our greatest soccer night of a decade.

For Scotland are through at last to the finals of the World Cup in Munich after a cliff-hanging palpitating battle, a game in which hopes soared and plummeted.

AND SMILING THROUGH IN THE END CAME SCOTTISH GRIT, SCOTTISH GUTS AND SCOTTISH SKILL.

I'll never forget this night, a night which ended with Denis Law lying face down on the turf having given his all . . .

Billy Bremner dashing into the tunnel to bring on manager Willie Ormond for a lap of honour in front of the adoring 100,000 who had shown no club favour, had bellowed non-stop from start to finish for Scotland.

Under the new bright floodlights Bremner's Scotland provided us with an epic.

It all started predictably, Scotland all out for the vital goal. The white-shirted Czechs not a bit dismayed by the tremendous Hampden Roar, ruthless indeed. The shocking Norwegian ref Henry Oberg allowing one brutal foul to follow another. And by half-time the crime count was Czechoslovakia 20, Scotland 8.

But the Scots refused to be intimidated.

Viktor was heroic in the Czech goal. He made fantastic saves. And the Scots were refused what looked like a blatant penalty-kick when Tommy Hutchison, the mesmerising, weaving wizard of the game, was pulled down in the area.

Then tragedy! In 33 minutes the Czechs broke away. Nehoda flashed in a 35-yard shot from an acute angle on the right.

It was a nightmare for Alistair Hunter. He touched the ball, but it slipped past his groping fingers into the net.

Were the fans dismayed? Were the players? Not on your life. Bremner, that awe-inspiring skipper, put new life into his troops.

And in 41 minutes Jim Holton endeared himself forever to the Scottish fans by equalising.

The giant centre-half towered over everyone in the Czech penalty area to head a corner into the net. And so to an even more palpitating second-half.

Tiring as they were, the Scots pressed on. There was a cheer when Kenny Dalglish, who had played his heart out, came off and Joe Jordan took his place.

BUT THEN CAME THE HAMPDEN ROAR OF THE CENTURY.

Audacious Willie Morgan got the ball out on the right, crossed and with a diving header that will be remembered for all time, tall Joe Jordan threw himself at the ball to give us the goal that will take us to Germany.

It all came right. The dream came true. Scotland won and the Czechs can score 100 goals in Bratislava if they like.

They were ruthless, it's true. But, still, they played some splendid football. And Scotland take credit for the way they played.

Our heroes? What a discovery in Tom Hutchison. What a captain in Bremner, whose heart must weigh a ton. What an inspiration by Denis Law, whose leaps in the first-half especially, caused panic in the Czech defence.

And that was that. Twenty-two short, sharp paragraphs. What would such an occasion earn today? A Norwegian forest would be under threat. There would be a 16-page pull-out, for a start. The entire front page would be taken over. Strikes at Chrysler? Find another spot in the paper. The match report would be spread over at least two advert-free pages and quotes pieces would take up another spread. Back in 1973, things were different, drastically so.

Beside Hugh Taylor's report there was Alex Cameron's piece: CAMERON COMMENT. It read:

THERE are 12 good reasons why Hampden should stay as Scotland's national stadium.

And they all wore dark blue jerseys on a memorable night at Glasgow's Mount Florida.

As manager Willie Ormond was hoisted on to the muscly shoulders in the joyous, back-slapping moments of the greatest victory in our soccer history, the full shame of even thinking that Hampden should go became unbearable.

The goals by Jim Holton and Joe Jordan will be seen by millions around the world in TV repeats in the next 24 hours.

And so will the great crescendo of encouragement given to the Scots by 100,000 of the most partisan people you could find anywhere.

They exalted this Scottish team to a state of inspiration. They bawled them into renewed effort when the score stood at 1-0 for the Czechs and then one-all.

THE HERO WAS DENIS LAW.

Oh yes, he missed a chance to score the goal of a lifetime a few minutes from the end. But it was he more than any other player who dictated and taunted the crunchers from Czechoslovakia.

The high-class skill came from new boy Tom Hutchison, who surely had the best international debut ever by any Scot.

The Czechs wanted a brawl. At one point it looked as though they would get it. The Norwegian referee had little control and it was no thanks to him that mayhem didn't break out.

It will be wrong to say the return match in Bratislava on 17 October means nothing. Totally wrong.

Scotland must work to find a side which will do more than just participate at Munich.

There is no reason why Willie Ormond can't take a team fit to win. And who is to say that even 33-year-old Law will not be there to help?

This could be the beginning of a genuinely new era in our ailing soccer game. It was these truly heroic players who administered this much-needed tonic.

Don't think the Czechs were a walkover. They were technically very good and would have gone to any lengths to win.

Afterwards, however, when they knew they had lost, they were sporting in their praise of a better side.

Yes, we must keep Hampden . . . for we now have the makings of a team to match the best.

The entire evening wrapped up in 17 paragraphs. By the way, Hampden's future was under threat because it was obvious the old ground needed a radical makeover. Money was tight and there were suggestions that Rangers would be happy to hire out Ibrox Stadium to the SFA for future games. Happily, the matches remained at Scotland's spiritual international home at Hampden.

Still on page 35, there was a sidebar piece under the simple, straightforward headline: THOSE GOALS.

THE goals that carried Scotland through to Munich came from two players who didn't join the international squad until last season.

The first was from centre-half Jim Holton, an unknown with Shrewsbury eight months ago. He said afterwards: "I felt great when the ball went in.

"I had started to come up for any deadball situations because we could see that they were struggling a bit in the air.

"We thought that we would be able to get a goal in the air . . . and that's how it worked out."

And Joe Jordan, the 21-year-old striker from Leeds, said: "I was ordered to play up alongside Denis Law and to look for the ball in the air. I had one header before the goal came, but I mistimed it. Then I had the goal header and I got it just right. It was fantastic.

"After the goal I got just one more header which slipped past the post. So, really, I got three headers and one of them was THE one.

"I feel great . . ."

Six quotes wrapped up in seven paragraphs. Ken Gallacher's back page piece was condensed into six paragraphs. Under the headline: ORMOND'S NIGHT OF GLORY, it read:

HAMPDEN PARK belonged to Willie Ormond last night as the Scotland manager saw his team crash through to the Finals of the World Cup.

For Ormond it was the night of nights and one when he admitted: "The last 10 minutes were the longest of my life. I'd never want to go through that again.

"Still, I always felt that we would win. Even when we were a goal down I knew that we had the ability to go on and win. And the lads were magnificent.

"So were the fans. It was Wembley all over again and that's what we wanted."

The 100,000 fans who were at the game stayed behind to cheer Ormond and his players on a lap of honour.

One of the Hampden heroes, Coventry City star Tom Hutchison was taken to hospital after the game for an x-ray on a badly bruised leg, but Ormond stressed it was just a precaution.

There you have it. Nine paragraphs of quotes in all on one of the biggest nights in Scottish football history.

Back in 1973, four photographs were used. As well as Sandy Jardine and Danny McGrain on the front page, there was one on the back page of Willie Ormond being lifted shoulder-high by Billy Bremner and Davie Hay with Tommy Hutchison, McGrain and Willie Morgan also in the shot. On page 35 there was the image of Jim Holton leaping high above the Czech defence – and Denis Law – to score his headed equaliser. On page 34, there was a snap of Joe Jordan flying through the air to score the winner. The ubiquitous Law is in that picture, too.

Ah, the good old days.

CHAPTER TWENTY-ONE

THE FINAL FAREWELL

No-one ever expected Denis Law to go quietly; that was never in the script. He kicked his last ball in competitive action at the age of 34 in the 2-0 victory over Zaire in Dortmund, West Germany, in front of 30,000 fans on 14 June 1974. It was, alas, his solitary appearance in the World Cup Finals. At least, looking on the bright side, he was afforded the luxury of performing on the most glittering stage global football had to offer and that was something even his great hero Alfredo di Stefano never managed to achieve. Nor his good pal George Best, for that matter.

Before the 1974 World Cup Finals, there were rumours that Law had decided to hang up his boots at club level. However, Law has always been adamant that was not the case. In fact, he has insisted he had every intention of playing on and had a meeting with the Manchester City manager Tony Book after the West German tournament. Book, we're informed, had told Law he was looking to the future. His plan was to play Law only in home reserve games to keep him fit if he was suddenly required for first team football. The idea did not sit well with Law. He had no intention of playing in the reserves and pointed out, 'That is where players start their careers, not end them.' After much deliberation, Law would announce his retirement on August Bank Holiday Monday. Putting it simply, he admitted, 'I wanted to go out at the top.'

Law's version of events will no doubt be accurate. If he had made up his mind to quit at the end of the season, there is no way he could have kept it secret. The grapevine in football is a lively one. There is little doubt that the news would have reached Willie Ormond. Equally without question is the fact the manager would not have included a player in his squad for the biggest football tournament on the planet who had already thought it was time to give up the game. There was a clamour from many to go with the youthful strike partnership of Kenny Dalglish and Joe Jordan, both emerging as genuine international material. Lou Macari had his supporters, too. Ormond refused to be swayed by certain members of the public and press. Denis Law was in. He was going to West Germany, 16 years after taking his international bow against Wales in Cardiff. The average age of the squad was 25-and-a-half years. Denis was the oldest and Kilmarnock's Jim Stewart, one of the back-up goalkeepers, was the youngest at 20, 14 years his junior.

The 22 players who got the nod from Ormond were: Goalkeepers: David Harvey (Leeds United), Thomson Allan (Hibs), Jim Stewart (Kilmarnock); Defenders: Sandy Jardine (Rangers), Danny McGrain (Celtic), Jim Holton (Manchester United), John Blackley (Hibs), Martin Buchan (Manchester United), Willie Donachie (Manchester City), Gordon McQueen (Leeds United), Erich Schaedler (Hibs); Midfielders: Billy Bremner (Leeds United), Davie Hay (Celtic), Peter Cormack (Liverpool); Forwards: Jimmy Johnstone (Celtic), Kenny Dalglish (Celtic), Joe Jordan (Leeds United), Donald Ford (Hearts), Peter Lorimer (Leeds United), Willie Morgan (Manchester United), Tommy Hutchison (Coventry City) and, of course, Denis Law (Manchester City).

Intriguingly, there was a startling contrast between the team that started the World Cup campaign and the team that kicked off the finals, with under two years separating the games. The line-up in the 4-1 triumph over Denmark in Copenhagen on 18 October 1972 was: Bobby Clark (Aberdeen); John Brownlie (Hibs), Eddie Colquhoun (Sheffield United), Martin Buchan

(Manchester United), Alex Forsyth (Partick Thistle); Peter Lorimer (Leeds United), Billy Bremner (Leeds United), George Graham (Arsenal), Willie Morgan (Manchester United); Lou Macari (Celtic, sub: Kenny Dalglish, Celtic) and Jimmy Bone (Norwich City, sub: Joe Harper, Aberdeen). Thirteen players used by Tommy Docherty and only five boarded the plane for West Germany – Buchan, Bremner, Lorimer, Morgan and Dalglish.

Davie Hay, one of the main performers of the 1974 World Cup despite only having three games to display his talent, recalled, 'Willie Ormond was a smashing wee guy, very much his own man. Some people accused him of being sentimental in naming Denis Law in his squad. I rarely saw Willie hit the roof, but if you made that suggestion in his company you could expect an ear-bashing. Nothing could be further from the truth. Denis was in on merit. He wasn't just there as a talisman, there was no chance of that. You just had to ask the players. We all knew what Denis could still do in the game. Okay, he may not have thrown himself around the way he had done in the past, but his reactions were still astonishing. Everyone witnessed that ability during his performance against Czechoslovakia in the crucial game in Glasgow and we saw it in training every day. I can tell you this – Denis would not have thanked anyone for taking him to West Germany for anything other than football reasons.

'He was the consummate professional, a bit of a perfectionist and everyone realised he was going into the tournament with the same outlook he would have had as a teenager. His enthusiasm never waned, not once. Willie Ormond was a manager who listened to his players, but, in the end, we played the way he wanted. We were allowed to change things on the field as the game developed and our skipper Billy Bremner exercised that right every now and again. But this was Ormond's squad. One thing that always impressed me about our manager was the fact he could spot a player. He had a marvellous knowledge of football and saw things in some performers that others might have missed.'

Law, in his excellent autobiography *The King*, put it this way, 'When I heard I had been named in the squad, I thought, "Whoops, that'll do for me." It certainly came as a bit of a shock at the age of 34, but Willie had ignored the press and gone with the fact that I was doing reasonably well up front and had the experience. To my mind, it was one of those selections where the player might be able to contribute something valuable in part of the game, maybe not the whole game, but somewhere along the line.'

The Scots set up base at Erbismuhle in the Taunus mountains near Frankfurt. Security in the finals was intense. Peter Lorimer recalled, 'After the massacre of the Israeli athletes in the Munich Olympics only two years beforehand, the German authorities were determined there would be no hint of a repeat. There were security people all over the place.' SFA assistant secretary Ernie Walker recalled, 'It was like playing the World Cup in a war zone.' Reserve goalkeeper Thomson Allan noted, 'If you went to the toilet a security guard went with you.' A photograph appeared in the national press of Danny McGrain happily posing with six policemen, one holding a machine gun. The uncertain climate wasn't helped by an observer at the BBC in London who broadcast, 'Trouble could come from the Arabs, the German Bader Meinhof anarchists or the invading horde of Scots fans.'

Scotland were going into the unknown to play Zaire. There was very little knowledge of their players, their style of play, their strengths, their weaknesses, their overall tactics. What was known was that they had overcome Cameroon in the play-offs to become the only African nation in West Germany that summer. They were coached by Blagoje Vidinic, a former Yugoslavia international goalkeeper. It could be assumed, then, that they would be well drilled, at least, and their fitness levels wouldn't be brought into question.

Willie Ormond travelled to watch Zaire in action in Egypt in the African Nations' Cup. One member of the travelling press corps admitted, 'Willie watched them for about 15 minutes or so. He then turned to several members of the press who had made the trip with him. He casually announced, "This lot cannae play, let's go for a wee wet." That was his euphemistic term for a drink.'

If that was the case, then it was a blunder of monumental proportions. If Ormond had hung around he would have seen Zaire beat Zambia 2-0 to win the trophy in Cairo. Four years later, Ally MacLeod refused to watch Peru live and preferred to rely on videos of recent internationals. By his own admission, he thought they were 'told old and too slow'. The history books now show that the South Americans decimated Scotland 3-1 in the opening group game of the 1978 World Cup Finals in Argentina and the dream was over before it had barely started. Will we never learn?

The draw for the group had been far from kind to the Scots. For the first time, goal difference would come into play and, as expected, Zaire would be crucial to Scotland, as well as Yugoslavia and holders Brazil, making progress to the next stage. Willie Ormond's team had to play them first and that would allow the qualifying rivals a chance to see what to expect from the mysterious Africans. Their veil of anonymity would be stripped away, their secrets exposed and the Slavs and Brazilians could plot how to produce goal deluges against them. There is absolutely no doubt the ballot handicapped the Scots.

John Blackley, Hibs' smooth-operating sweeper, was chosen ahead of Martin Buchan for the Zaire fixture. He said, 'The tension before that game was as intense as anything I have ever experienced. It was practically tangible. It was unreal and we all sensed it. This, after all, was a massive game for Scotland, a nation that had never triumphed in a World Cup Finals before. We realised, though, we had to win this one. A draw would have been unacceptable.'

Billy Bremner, the confident skipper, said, 'We won't make the mistake of underestimating Zaire because we have been caught that way before. We won't relax, either, because goals are important all the time. It's only against the English that we like to show our superiority in terms of flashiness. Against the Africans we will play the British way, hustling and bustling. One thing you can count on is the fact we are afraid of no-one.'

Denis Law, wearing the No. 19 shirt for the first and last time in his career, trotted onto the immaculate playing surface of the Westfalen Stadium to play against the Africans, memorably nicknamed the Leopards, which was emblazoned across their lemon shirts. If Denis was supposed to be intimidated, he didn't show it. You can only wonder at what was going through his mind at the time. He must have known this would be his last international competition, literally his last kick of the ball at this level. All sorts of things must have been bombarding his brain, but, as usual, it didn't prevent him from going about his business with a fair degree of verve and gusto and his usual professionalism. The famous long sleeves had vanished with Law favouring short sleeves as temperatures soared in Dortmund.

Ormond went with this line-up: Harvey; Jardine, Holton, Blackley, McGrain; Lorimer, Bremner (captain), Hay; Jordan, Dalglish and Law. Hutchison would replace Dalglish in the second-half.

Referee Gerhard Schulenburg, the match official who took charge of Scotland's historic triumph at Wembley in 1967, put the whistle to his lips, the shrill sound signalling the 7.30 p.m. kick-off and, 90 minutes of football later, he blew the same whistle to bring down the curtain on the extraordinary career of a genuine legend. Despite the sweltering conditions, Law, who, by his own admission, had a relatively successful season with Manchester City, set about playing with a combination of contained energy and cunning. Zaire, rewarded with cash bonuses, houses and cars by their grateful government for qualifying, clearly weren't there to make up the numbers. Their back four must have had an average height of six foot-plus and, although they lacked nous at this level, they were solid, powerful and surprisingly mobile.

Reports at the time, and video evidence backs it up, tell of the Scots being a little hesitant and slightly tentative at the start, not knowing quite what to expect from their opponents. One observer pointed out, 'Scotland received the first shock. The Africans were a lot nippier than expected. Efforts to soften up Zaire were not appreciated by the watching West Germans fans. Immediately, Scotland had not endeared themselves to the neutrals. Jordan went in heavily on their acrobatic keeper, Kazadi. The goalkeeper recovered from one early collision to save from Law. But it was Zaire who could, and really should, have scored first. The Scottish defence fell asleep as their opponents ambled forward. Danger suddenly threatened when Kakoko slipped inside Jardine. He was left with a clear shot at goal, but, thankfully for the Scots, he missed completely with a rushed swing of his left foot. He still had time to regain his composure and this time squeeze a shot under Harvey that struck the outside of the post and flashed into the safety of the side-netting. It could have been so easily 1-0 to the underdogs.'

The mantle of being favourites never did sit comfortably on Scotland. It was the wake-up call Willie Ormond's side required, though. The report continued, 'Scotland's superior strength began to tell. The obvious tactic of projecting high crosses towards Jordan and Law increasingly menaced Kazadi. The opening goal came in the 26th minute and was worth the wait. Jordan, at the far post, headed back Hay's left-wing cross for Lorimer to fire a ferocious right-foot volley past their keeper. It was a well-worked goal delivered with the combination of precision and Lorimer's frightening prowess for striking the ball unerringly first time from range.'

The report went on, 'Scotland's fortunes seemed yet rosier six minutes later when they scored again, this time with a goal of less quality, but no-one was complaining. It was comic cuts stuff from the defence and Kazadi. Bremner clipped in an inviting right-wing free-kick and Jordan timed his run forward to absolute perfection. The Zaire back lot stood transfixed as the action unfolded around them. They were rooted to the spot. Jordan looked miles offside when he made contact with his head, but, in fact, it was a legitimate effort. He glanced the ball forward, but there was little power in the header. Kazadi's attempt to hold the ball as it came to him were that of someone who might have wandered onto the football pitch for the first time in his life. He fumbled the header and the ball barely made it over the line. Jordan and Law celebrated as though it was the World Cup winner. They could so easily have been cringing in embarrassment.

'Zaire, though, were far from crestfallen. Before the break Kidumi clobbered Bremner and became the latest in a growing list of players cautioned for their dislike of the Scottish captain. Kidumi then collected N'daye's pass in front of Harvey, only to dally and allow the keeper to block. In the second-half, Scotland ground forward in the hope or expectation that the Africans would tire. They did not. Kazadi and Lobilo, their able centre-half, repelled all assaults. When Jordan felled Kilasu he found himself threatened with an angry black circle. Mayanga nearly punished the Scots, climaxing a diagonal run with a 20-yard drive that Harvey turned aside. The floodlights were then extinguished, providing everyone with a four-minute breather. For a while it continued as if by candlelight, but as Zaire substituted Mayanga for a fresh forward, Kembo, the lights were restored to full power.

'It was as if the darkness had fallen from the Africans' eyes. For the last 20 minutes they carried the game to Scotland, much to the delight of the neutrals in the crowd, desperate to witness a shock result. Bremner, foolishly, seemed content on Scotland preserving, rather than seeking to increase, their lead. Long before the end he was urging caution among the players, looking to slow down the pace. Zaire brought on a fresh forward and Scotland gave the long legs of Hutchison a run out. Dalglish made way. Chances fell at both ends. Lorimer's piledriver was turned onto the bar by Kazadi, but then N'daye screwed wide with one chance and obliged Harvey to touch over a second. The final score might have been 6-3 for Scotland. They had managed their first win in the World Cup Finals. Zaire had been beaten, but not slaughtered and that might prove painful.'

Prophetic words, indeed. Davie Hay looked back more in dismay than anger and said, 'There was the remarkable sight of Denis Law racing deep into his own half after the turnaround to take the ball off Billy Bremner, who was indulging in a bit of keepy-uppy. The Lawman, displaying all his experience, instinctively realised that we would need more goals. Unfortunately, that urgency didn't get through to all of us. We took our foot off the gas, no doubt about it. Possibly we also had an eye on our next game that was coming up four days later against Brazil in Frankfurt. It's all conjecture now. We had gone into the match against Zaire with one thought on our mind – to win. A draw was no use and a defeat was unthinkable. I'm not making excuses, but it was bloody hot out there that evening. We had a wee kickabout before the game and the sweat was rolling off all of us. That makes Denis's action all the more laudable and praiseworthy. He was the oldest man in our squad and he still had the appetite to try to get us moving forward. He demanded that we attack. I suppose you could say he ended his career the same way he started – on the front foot.'

Willie Ormond hinted at changes for the match against Brazil and was convinced Scotland could beat the South Americans for the first time in history. 'Why not?' he asked the press corps. 'I happen to believe we can be successful in this one. My players believe in each other, individually and collectively. We're confident.'

Denis Law was desperate to be involved and, certainly, he had done enough against Zaire to show he wouldn't be out of place on a pitch alongside Jairzinho, Rivelino etc. Yet when Ormond finally unveiled his starting 11, Denis's name was missing and in came his Manchester United pal Willie Morgan. The only other change was Martin Buchan taking over from John Blackley alongside his Old Trafford colleague Jim Holton in central defence.

Law admitted, 'I was extremely disappointed not to get a 56th cap against Brazil. I didn't think my exclusion was merited as I felt I had played well enough against the Africans to keep my place or, at least, to play part of the Brazil game. But I accepted the decision even though I would have loved to have played against the world champions.'

Davie Hay said, 'You had to feel for Denis. It was obvious he was coming to the end of his career and who wouldn't have wanted to go out after a match against the reigning World Cup holders? Denis was always style personified, a flamboyant personality who captured everyone's imagination. Personally, I thought he was one of our best players against Zaire. As I said, he realised the importance of running up a big score against them. It would have been interesting to see how he fared against Brazil. They had a giant centre-back called Luis Pereira and he was one of the hardest defenders I have ever faced. He clattered into everything in sight and got away with it. Maybe it's a Brazilian thing. Possibly the referees are brainwashed into believing they are all about slick passing and so on. Believe me, that lot back in 1974 could put the welly in with the best of them.

'Denis would have loved it! He had come up against those sort of centre-backs all his life and was rarely found wanting. Anyone looking at his slight frame and thinking they were going to coast through a game soon found out differently to their cost. Denis was frightened of no-one. Luis Pereira would have had his work cut out for him if Denis had got the nod. He didn't and I have to say he was the perfect professional when it came to accepting the manager's decision, although inside he must have been more than a little upset. He never betrayed those feelings, I can tell you that. Not once, not even privately. To me, that is the sign of a real man. He would have known his international boots were getting hung up following this tournament. After Zaire, there were two more games, at least, to go. He would have been desperate to be involved; that had been his style from day one. He was a terrible spectator. If he wasn't playing he was, mainly, not interested. There was a lot of dignity involved at the time.'

Scotland's preparations were disrupted when it was discovered that someone had alerted local police that a bomb had been planted at the team's base. The West German authorities took the threat very seriously. It was said to be from the IRA and, apparently, two unnamed Protestants in the squad had been targeted. Sandy Jardine later revealed, 'It was me and Willie Ormond.' It turned out to be a hoax and Tommy Hutchison can afford a smile at the memory when he looks back. 'There was Wee Jimmy Johnstone leaving our HQ to get on the coach and he was holding up his bag, covering his face while shouting, "I'm Jimmy Johnstone and I play for Celtic!" Obviously, he believed no-one from the Irish Republican Army would harm a Celtic player.' Davie Hay added, 'Yes, the players knew the two guys in question were Sandy Jardine and Willie Ormond. I just made sure I wasn't sitting beside Sandy at any time when we were having meals!'

Law missed the game against Brazil in the Wald Stadion,

Frankfurt, on 18 June. It ended scoreless and the nearest to a goal from either country came midway through the second-half when goalkeeper Emerson Leao pushed out a close-range header from Joe Jordan straight to Billy Bremner. Before the skipper could react, the ball struck him on the shin and, luckily for the three-times World Cup winners, bounced wide of the upright. It was the sort of opportunity that Law had snapped up on countless occasions. Leao was also forced to make two splendid saves as the Brazilian drums were drowned out by the singing, chanting members of the boisterous Tartan Army, some 12,000 in the ground. Hay, enjoying the game of his life, stormed forward in the second period to unleash a 25-yard drive of awesome power. Leao took no chances as he nudged it over the bar. He did likewise again when Peter Lorimer sent in a typically thunderous free-kick. And that was that; Scotland sitting on three points, the Brazilians on two after two successive goalless draws. Lorimer reflected, 'They didn't play like Brazil at all. This lot were brutal.'

Both teams had been told Yugoslavia were leading Zaire 6-0 at the interval. They would add another three in the second-half. It left a huge question mark over Scotland's continued interest in the competition. Brazil believed a three-goal winning margin over the African nation would see them qualify for the next stage. Scotland realised they had to beat an impressive Yugoslavia. Davie Hay said, 'We were all stunned to hear the Slavs had won by such a margin. We thought they would win, but not by nine. No team should lose to that extent in the World Cup Finals. A steward's enquiry might have been demanded. We checked with the Scottish reporters and they confirmed that it had taken eight minutes for the Slavs to score first and then they added five in just over 20 minutes. We also wondered why the Yugoslav coach of the Africans took off his No. 1 goalkeeper Kazadi after he had conceded the third and replaced him with the inexperienced Tubilandu. It looked to us like an invite for the Slavs to pile on the goals. Skulduggery? Who knows? At the end of the day we realised what we had to do and that was to beat Yugoslavia. It was impossible to believe the Brazilians wouldn't beat Zaire. There was no way they would drop points in that fixture, but could they score three and not concede any? We had to hope.'

The Brazilian press were very kind to Scotland while making scathing comments about their own country, bereft of the talents of the incomparable Pele, who had retired from the international scene after the memorable 1970 World Cup Finals. Only Roberto Rivelino, Jairzinho and Wilson Piazza remained from that successful team. The South American reporters labelled Bremner 'a small giant'. Hay was 'one of the best midfield players in the world'. Scotland returned to Frankfurt four days later to take on Miljan Miljanic's team. It was almost a home game for Miljanic's men with some 40,000 Yugoslavs working and living in the city. A crowd of 54,000 was in place in time for kick-off. Willie Ormond went with the side that had drawn against Brazil; there was still no place for Denis Law.

And there would be no place for Scotland in the next round. The game ended 1-1 while, agonisingly, the Brazilians were wrapping up a 3-0 victory over Zaire with an extremely fortuitous third goal, gifted to them by the blundering Kazadi. Joe Jordan's heading ability had been noticed in the previous games and Slav strongman Josip Katalinski rarely left his side. Branko Oblak and Vladislav Bogicevic were never far away, either. Neither David Harvey nor Enver Maric, the respective goalkeepers, had too much to do in sweltering conditions. The game was being dictated by the opposing defences and midfields. Once again, Bremner and Hay were the pick of the bunch as Scotland tried to break down their stubborn opponents. The Scots were caught out in the 81st minute when substitute Stanislav Karasi, on the pitch only nine minutes after replacing Dusan Bajevic, launched himself at a cross from the ever-dangerous Dragan Dzajic and Harvey, totally exposed, was beaten for the first – and last – time in the finals. Scotland's own substitute Tommy Hutchison, on for Kenny Dalglish in the 65th minute, also made an impact. A minute remained when he twisted and turned on the left wing before hammering over a low cross. Peter Lorimer swung at it and missed. The ball dropped perfectly for Jordan, for once free of his markers, and the Leeds United striker fired in at the far post.

All eyes were now on Gelsenkirchen. The Scottish players discovered their fate when the huge electronic scoreboards at the Wald Stadion flashed up: BRAZIL 3 ZAIRE 0. The adventure was over. Brazil were 1-0 ahead at half-time with a goal from Jairzinho and had doubled their advantage in the 66th minute with a sizzling effort from moustachioed midfielder Rivelino. Would it be enough? The South Americans were aware they required a third to make absolutely certain of a place in the second phase. Valdomiro mis-hit a cross from the right wing. It was straight at Kazadi and looked an easy save. Somehow the clumsy custodian flapped hopelessly at the ball as it squeezed past him at his near post and squirmed over the line. Brazil were through; Scotland were out.

The final Group Two table read: Yugoslavia Played 3, Won 1, D 2. Goals For: 10. Goals against: 1. Brazil's stats showed they had won one and drawn two while scoring three and conceding none. Scotland were third with one win and two draws with three goals scored and one conceded. All three nations had amassed four points. Zaire were anchored at the bottom without a win, three defeats and 14 goals lost while failing to register even one. It was of little consolation that Scotland, who had earned universal sympathy, had become the first country in history to be knocked out of the World Cup on goal difference. In fact, they were the only country not to lose a game in those finals. Even eventual winners

West Germany were defeated when they went down 1-0 in a Group One game against East Germany. Yugoslavia weren't far behind Scotland in seeking their passports to return home. They were in a four-nation Group B in the next stage and lost all three games: 2-0 to West Germany, 2-1 to Poland and 2-1 to Sweden, their only victory in the tournament being the mind-boggling nine-goal rout of Zaire. Brazil? They had seen their worldwide appeal to neutral football fans swept into the Rhine with a series of thuggish displays that eventually saw their coarse and merciless centre-half Luis Pereira dismissed after an assault on Holland's Johan Neeskens. Goals from Neeskens and Johan Cruyff secured a 2-0 triumph for the Dutch. An unloved Brazil played Poland in the third-placed play-off and lost 1-0; Grzegorz Lato scoring in the 76th minute of a miserable encounter.

Even the great Pele had to admit he wasn't impressed by his nation – and he went on record as saying how sorry he was for Scotland. He observed, 'Brazil were lucky. Scotland played very well against them and were truly galvanised by the tireless Bremner. The Scots went home with four points, one more than Argentina achieved in their Group Four games where they beat Haiti, drew with Italy and lost to Poland. That's what they call the luck of the draw.'

Danny Blanchflower, the Northern Ireland international legend who had been kicked up and down Hampden Park by a youthful and over-exuberant Law in only his second international in 1958, sympathised with the player. He lamented, 'Denis Law was unlucky that none of the Scottish sides of his best days got far in the World Cup and he wasn't seen around the world too much. He deserved far more recognition than he received.'

The carnival was over and, cruelly, Denis Law had been denied the opportunity to say farewell to football. That was sad. He completed his 55-game Scotland international career as a winner. He was triumphant on his debut against Wales in 1958 and, 16 years later, he was a victor again against Zaire in 1974.

There is a huge difference between style and class. You can buy style. Denis Law travelled first class all the way.

CHAPTER TWENTY-TWO

FROM WORLD CUP TO WORLD SERVICE

Denis Law hated watching football. By his own admission, he was a dreadful spectator. Surprising, then, that after hanging up his boots following the World Cup-tie against Zaire in West Germany in 1974, his next gainful piece of employment would be ... watching football. Or commentating on and analysing it, to be more precise. Law's new choice of work surprised many who knew him, including his former Manchester United team-mate Bobby Charlton.

He pointed out, 'One aspect of Denis that I could never understand was that he refused to be involved the moment he wasn't playing in a match. If he was injured and had to leave the field, he would shower and go home immediately, perhaps with the outcome of the match far from decided. It was the same when substitutes were introduced; if Denis was replaced, that was the end of his afternoon. He wasn't making any statement of anger or resentment. He was just saying that his work and interest were over. He would rather be back home. This lack of involvement if he was not on the pitch was true for even the biggest of games. When United played in the European Cup Final in 1968, Denis was in hospital having a cartilage operation. He claims to have had a few beers – and fallen asleep.'

But Denis received a wake-up call shortly after his momentous decision on the August Bank Holiday Monday in 1974 to tell Manchester City he was calling it a day. 'I have to admit for the first few months after hanging up my boots things were not good,' he said. 'I was only 34, I was out of work, I had no nest egg, I hadn't a trade or a profession and I was struggling to adjust to life without a football club.'

After almost two decades of making a living as a professional footballer, Denis Law found himself in 'the real world', as he called it. There is little doubt if he had been thinking commercially instead of personally, he would have found another club. Law was hardly fit only for football's knacker's yard. He had just finished his club season in the English top flight and had been involved in the World Cup Finals. He wouldn't have found it difficult to land a two-year contract with a team in either Scotland or England. His name alone would have added to attendance figures everywhere. Before Tommy Docherty's somewhat brutal intervention, Denis would have been forgiven for believing there might have been a role for him somewhere on the staff at Manchester United. Although he has often said he never had any intention of becoming a manager, he has also admitted he would have loved to have coached youngsters, preferably at Old Trafford. Pride prevented him from even attempting to earn the all-important and necessary Football League coaching badge. It was a required document back then to continue to work in football and former players took the well-worn path to Lilleshall to sit exams.

That, of course, seemed preposterous to an admittedly head-strong personality such as Law, with his wealth of experience in the game on all fronts; domestic, European and worldwide. He was in good company. Matt Busby, Jock Stein and Bill Shankly were three managers who had done quite well without their badges. They had come through a different era before a scrap of paper informed everyone that they were, in fact, 'fit and proper' people to manage or coach a football team. Law would later admit it was a mistake on his part not to take the course.

Law, father of five, would continue to work. 'I knew I had

to pull myself together. I had a family to feed.' A friend, a Manchester United supporter, owned a carpet company and offered Law employment. He accepted and suddenly the reality of selling carpets for a living overtook the fantasy life of being a footballer who had earned around £200 per week at Manchester City a few months beforehand. There would be no more of the camaraderie of the dressing room. There would be no more naps in the afternoon following training. There would be no more roars from adoring fans. There would be no more spectacular goals. No more trademark salute, arm in the air, grin on the face. All gone. Instead, the alarm clock would ring at seven in the morning and usher in another ordinary working day for Law. It must have been a difficult transformation for a genuine soccer legend to undertake, but Law, with typical Aberdonian grit, made the leap across the cultural chasm. 'Eventually, I began to enjoy it,' he admitted. Unfortunately, the carpet company went bankrupt after a year. Law received some redundancy, but then, in 1975, he received the call he described as 'the lifesaver'.

The BBC contacted Law and enquired if he would consider summarising football matches for radio. At first, Law did not want to take up the offer. As other observers have stated elsewhere, Law is quite shy by nature. Hard to believe when you recall that strutting matador on football fields in his heyday, but true, nevertheless. 'I was fast learning that sometimes you have to do things you don't particularly want to do.' Fortunately, Law enjoyed his radio work and paid compliments to BBC reporters Peter Jones and Alan Parry who were 'as good as gold' and helped him settle in. Law discovered very quickly that commenting on football games for the World Service didn't just start at kick-off and end at the final whistle. Originally, he believed he merely had to turn up, go through the motions, lend his experience to the event and go home. However, he saw his new work mates compiling vast dossiers on teams, players, managers and even referees before matches. They were well prepared; Denis, as he did during his playing days, was happy to do the business 'off the cuff'. That changed. He realised he would have to find out more about players, even those he had performed alongside not that long ago. He said, 'It sounds an easy job when you are sitting in front of your radio listening to commentary, but it's not, I can assure you.'

Law decided to 'make a fist of it' and ironed out the early wrinkles to become an expert summariser. He admitted he was excited at the thought of people around the globe listening to him. Back then, the BBC did not pay fortunes, but it always looked good on an individual's CV that they had worked for such a national institution. To bolster his weekly pay packet, Law accepted a job offer from his former Manchester City teammate Francis Lee, who owned a paper manufacturing company. 'Two wages are better than one,' reasoned Law and the role was very much like the one he had come to enjoy at the carpet business. By now, Law was actually enjoying his radio work with the World Service and recalled them taking him to some marvellous places dotted around the planet. One of the most memorable for Law, after three years' radio work, was the 1978 World Cup Finals in Argentina. Scotland were in South America, of course, while England remained at home. Doors opened for Denis Law, as you would expect. A lot of footballers have a deep distrust, real or imagined, of the press. Some journalists earn trust, but others, looking for a sensational story, are kept at arm's length. Law was welcomed warmly, others were watched warily. There is no doubt that Denis worked hard at his new role.

While I was doing research for this book, I came across a photograph of Law sitting in an empty bath writing on a sheaf of notes. What was all this about? The caption didn't really shed too much light on the matter. It stated, 'This is the earliest early bath ever.' Puzzled, I decided to dig a bit deeper for an explanation. Law's hairstyle pinpointed the picture being taken around the late seventies. Could it have been one from the 1978 World Cup Finals? My good friend Fraser Elder was also in Argentina covering the Scotland games, so I asked him if he had a clue about this curious snap. 'Oh, I remember it well,' said Fraser, helpfully. 'Communications from Argentina to Britain were hellish. It was just about impossible to get telephone calls through. Everything seemed so primitive over there and all sorts of obstacles were put in your way in attempting to send communiqués. Denis and I found the best point to send and receive information was in this particular bathroom in our hotel. For whatever reason, the reception was best in there. We would wire our copy to the Beeb or get calls out from this vantage point. Please don't ask me to go into technical details, but it entailed dismantling a telephone before we could hook up and go about our business. Denis found it easier to contact Glasgow than London to deliver his daily update. Somehow, he was able to get through and get stuff taped that would be relayed to listeners. So, you had the sight of Denis sitting in the bath while I was perched on the loo. Hardly textbook stuff, but it got the job done. Maybe I shouldn't use that particular expression in this case!'

So, Denis Law, in trying circumstances in Argentina, was, as ever, going about his work for the World Service listeners in a truly professional manner. He reminisced, 'The 1978 tournament was definitely one of the best World Cups and I thoroughly enjoyed watching the matches.' Not so enjoyable was witnessing Scotland losing 3-1 to Peru and drawing 1-1 with Iran. 'Ally MacLeod picked the wrong teams for the first two games, then suddenly found the correct formula against Holland.' Alas, once again, too little too late for the Scots with a global audience looking on. Law's next World Cup was 1982 in Spain for Granada Television, then he was 'transferred' back to the BBC for the 1986 competition in Mexico. He worked for

ITV at the following two World Cups, Italy (1990) and USA (1994). As he had done as a player two decades earlier, Law went out at the top. The tournament in America was his last before he hung up his microphone.

Radio work had changed rather dramatically since his early days at the World Service in 1975. The growth in the media industry had expanded beyond belief in a relatively short space of time. SKY piled money into football and suddenly there appeared to be live games every night of the week. The BBC, ITV and other channels had to keep up with the lavish spending of their satellite rivals. Previously, they had been content to tape games and broadcast them on a Saturday night. It was the same story for Wednesday night fixtures. There would be the rare live match, an international, a Cup Final or a big European tie, but, in the main, it was all stuff edited in the studio. The demands on Denis Law now meant he was spending too much time on the road and away from the family, arriving home late as games were being played at all sorts of kick-off times up and down the country. It wasn't merely a Saturday and Wednesday outing any more. Law said, 'To be honest, I just got fed up with all the travelling.'

Law admitted his lasting regret is quitting the playing side too early – 'you're a long time retired' – and not taking the coaching course that would have kept him in the world of football in some sort of capacity. 'I'm sure I would have had something to offer.'

Undoubtedly, the sport would have been all the richer for his presence.

CHAPTER TWENTY-THREE

DENIS LAW AT SIXTY

With all the ease of a very fit teenager, Denis Law nonchalantly swings his feet up on the bench in front of him. He's wearing a blue button-down shirt, open at the neck, a dark grey suit and black loafers. He looks relaxed and fairly happy with life. In a couple of days' time he will be celebrating a landmark birthday. I interviewed him as 24 February 2000 dawned. Here is the discussion in full as it appeared in the *Daily Express* on that date.

Denis Law, Scotland's favourite footballing son, celebrates his 60th birthday today. It's an anniversary the shock-haired legend admits took him by surprise. 'Sixty,' he laughs, 'I just can't believe it.

'My God, I'm ancient. That really is old, man. When I was growing up I thought people at that age were right out of it. Thankfully, I'm feeling good. There's the usual aches and pains, but I get around okay. I just wish I could pull on the boots again – maybe I was born a couple of decades too early.'

Law looks at players who wouldn't have been fit to lace his boots in today's game earning fortunes, but he stresses he has absolutely no regrets.

'None whatsoever,' he says emphatically. 'The boys today must believe their birthdays have all come at once. Back in my day, though, there were comparisons with Stanley Matthews and Tom Finney. They had earned around £14 to £15 and I was picking up something like £100-per-week with Manchester United in the Sixties, so I suppose everything is relevant. But I've got absolutely no complaints about the way things went for me in my career on that front.'

Law ponders only for a moment when he is asked his abiding memory of a glittering career. His reply is more than just a little surprising. 'I was 18 at the time and walking down the street in Huddersfield,' he replied. 'The guy was selling the local paper, the Huddersfield Examiner, if I remember correctly. He told me that I'd been chosen to play for Scotland. I could hardly believe it. Honestly, it almost took my breath away. As far as I am concerned, there is no higher honour than being picked to play for your country. It would be fair to say I was absolutely overjoyed.

'And, of course, the highlight of my international career has got to be the 1967 win over England at Wembley. Beating the world champions on their own midden, as it were, was just wonderful. We had to suffer for a year with the English going on endlessly about being World Cup winners. We had to do something about it, hadn't we? We played some outstanding football that afternoon.

'I got the first goal after Gordon Banks spilled a low shot from Willie Wallace. I followed in Willie's effort and was in the right place at the right time to net from the rebound. It's history now that we won 3-2. I still get a warm glow when I think of that day. Brilliant!'

How much would a player of Law's remarkable penalty-box prowess be worth in today's market, does he think? 'Behave yourself, I'm not answering that question,' he chuckles. 'I cost Manchester United £115,000 when they signed me from Torino back in 1962. That might act as some sort of guideline.'

Law looks back with fondness on his glory days at Old Trafford alongside George Best, Bobby Charlton and his good pal Pat Crerand. 'Smashing times,' beams Law. 'That team had a mixture of everything. We had guile, class, goalscorers and people who could have a little nibble every now and again.

Occasionally, Nobby Stiles would put in a little bit of stick, but only if it was required, of course. To have a championship-winning team you must have a mixture of all that.

'The 1967 title win gave us more joy than any other. We had to play West Ham away from home in the run-in and, of course, they had an excellent team back then. They played a lot of good football, but we performed magnificently that afternoon and won 6-1. What a lovely way to win the title.'

Law smiles at the memory of enjoying his football back then and adds, 'I loved it when Sir Matt Busby gave us our team talks the night before the game – it meant I had forgotten it all by the time I got out on the pitch!'

But Law certainly admired the way Busby went about giving so much pleasure to so many fans. 'His only instruction before a game was to tell us, "Well, I know you can play good football. Go out there and play". If you had given your best, no matter the result at the end of the game, then Busby would say he couldn't have asked for more. It was as simple as that.'

Law, of course, missed out on a European Cup-winners' medal when he was sidelined with injury on the evening United beat Benfica 4-1 at Wembley in 1968. 'Yes, I would have loved to have played,' he says, 'but fate had other ideas. End of story.'

Has he anything special in the pipeline for his 60th birthday? 'Nope, not a thing,' he replies. 'I'm really not that sort of person. We'll have the family around with the assortment of wives, husbands, boyfriends, girlfriends and the like. It will be a good family day.'

At least he knows a nation of grateful football fans will be thinking of him on his big day and sharing many happy memories.

CHAPTER TWENTY-FOUR

DENIS LAW AT SEVENTY

The image is immediately endearing. Denis Law, with his piercing blue eyes and magnetic smile, is laughing while relaxing in the green leather Captain's Chair at Northenden Golf Club near Manchester. The shock of hair, mainly blond, is still a trademark. The man is photogenic, a snapper's dream. On this occasion, his 70th birthday is only three days away and he is posing merrily for the *Scottish Sunday Times*. Douglas Alexander, the newspaper's top sports reporter, is interviewing The King.

A lot has happened over the past decade. Sadly, four of Law's old footballing mates have passed away during the period. Law spent precious moments with George Best before his death in 2005 and has also lost close pals in Jimmy Johnstone, Jim Baxter and Billy Bremner. As Alexander observed, 'They all brought a swagger to football in the sixties.' Law realises he might have joined them if he had not responded swiftly to the advice of his wife, Diana, to see the doctor about an ache that was troubling him in 2003. 'When they confirmed prostate cancer I just conked out. Fainted. The specialist thought I had had a heart attack. That's a Law trait after seeing a doctor with a syringe. All my family are the same. That was traumatic, really traumatic, but it is one of the few on the cancer side that, if it is caught early, there's a great chance you will survive.'

Law also had a brush with the Grim Reaper during his stint in Italy with Torino. He went for a spin in his teammate Joe Baker's brand new Alfa Romeo car. Unfortunately, Baker, still getting used to driving on the right-hand side of the road, went the wrong way on a roundabout. 'Apparently, the car went over three times and flattened the roof. Don't forget we had no seat-belts in those days. If we had seat-belts, I would have been killed because where I was sitting the roof was flush with the headboard. My brother Joe, who was in the back, didn't have a scratch on him and I just got a cut on my hand. Joe [Baker] hit the road and smashed all his face, but his limbs were never touched, so his career was still there.'

Law reflects during an excellent interview with Alexander, 'I was speaking with my brother a few months ago and he said, "I go in the pub now and I don't know anybody because all my pals have gone," and it's a bit like that in the football world. You can't believe they have gone. We were good friends. Jimmy Johnstone and I used to go out on the Clyde in a boat and all that.' He laughs while recalling the Largs incident in 1974 when the Celtic player was cut adrift. 'I had known these guys since my teens or early 20s. It's not the sort of friendship that only lasted a few years. This had been going on for 40 years. With George, lesser people would have passed away weeks, maybe months, before he did. Every time I went down to see him, I just thought, "He's fighting on and on." It was incredible. It is always sad when your friends pass away.'

Law, though, does not cut a morbid figure. He is a happy family man, a proud father of four sons, Iain, Andrew, Robert and Gary, and daughter Di, who works for Manchester United. Of course, there is one story he never tires of telling and that is the day when England won the World Cup in 1966. 'We were at a golf course, one across the road not far from here, at Chorlton. That's where I lived, so I was a member there and a friend of mine, who wasn't a particularly good golfer, had beaten me and said, "Any time you want to have a return, just give me a bell." He was English, so I phoned him and told him I wanted to play him on the Saturday of the World Cup Final.

"Well, you did say any time," I reminded him. We were the only two golfers on the course. I couldn't concentrate and he beat me again. When we came round the corner they were all there, all the English. God, they had won the World Cup. It was a sad day. You just felt that if we had qualified then ... I'm not going to say we would have won it, but we would have done extremely well.'

Denis was asked about a birthday treat. As he had told me a decade earlier, there was nothing special planned. 'A fish supper and deep fried red pudding, although I'll need to go back to Aberdeen for that. It's the same as black pudding, but red, like a sausage, really. When I go home to Aberdeen, that's all I'll eat, fish and chips. It's just the batter and all that. We don't get that down here.'

Today, Law has added work for Cancer Research UK to being the patron of Meningitis UK – he and Diana almost lost Andrew to the illness – and has also succeeded the late Sir Bobby Robson as the figurehead of Football Aid.

A mental picture of Denis Law relaxing by the bank of a river, fishing rod in his hand and half-dozing is not an easy one to deal with. His work never seems to be done.

CHAPTER TWENTY-FIVE

HAIL THE LAWMAN

WILLIE HENDERSON
Twenty-nine caps (19 with Law) 1962-71

Denis Law was the finest Scottish player I have ever had the privilege to play alongside. Absolutely no doubt about it. Everything he did was stamped with class and quality. If I got down the wing and slung over a cross, there was every chance that the blond head of Denis would be there to meet it. The man was lethal in the box. Right foot, left foot, in the air – the guy had the lot.

I remember a game against Northern Ireland at Hampden in November 1962 when we won 5-1. I set up four goals for Denis and scored the other myself. It was just one of those great nights when everything clicked into place. I was up against a very good left-back in Alex Elder, who played for Burnley and they were a top side back then. They had faced Spurs in the FA Cup Final that year and had lost 3-1 to one of the best English teams of that decade. But that night he could do nothing to stop me. Inside, outside – I was beating him all over the place. I'm told he thought about quitting football afterwards, but was talked out of it!

Anything I dropped into the box was gobbled up by Denis. We were both unstoppable that night and it was a joy to be in the same side as him. A month before that Northern Ireland game we had beaten Wales 3-2 on my debut. Denis and I clicked immediately. He scored that night, too, and I was lucky enough

231

to get the winner. We weren't a bad partnership. After the Ireland victory, our next game was against England at Wembley in April the following year. We won again, this time 2-1 with goals from my old Rangers pal Jim Baxter. I was pulled down by Ron Flowers to gain a penalty-kick and Slim Jim popped it into the net for the second of his double. Jim and Denis in the same team – how did we never win the World Cup?

I played alongside Denis on 19 occasions, from 1962 to 1966, and we lost only four times, all by the odd goal, to Norway (3-4), Republic of Ireland (0-1), Northern Ireland (2-3) and Poland (1-2). Interestingly, he scored 18 of his 30 goals in those games and that included another foursome against Norway the year after the meeting with the Irish. I played on the left wing that evening with my Rangers teammate Alex Scott on the right. It didn't matter to Denis; any ball in the danger zone from either left or right was his for the taking.

Another thing about Denis that I must put on record was the fact he was such a nice bloke. There were no airs and graces and he was just one of the guys when we were all together. I'm sure everyone will tell you the same story. He never pulled rank although, of course, he had been there, seen it, done it and had the T-shirt.

He may have been the most expensive player in British football at the time at £115,000, but you wouldn't have known it with his overall demeanour. Remember, Manchester United paid that money in July 1962 and it would be another six years before Rangers broke the Scottish transfer record with the £100,000 signing of Colin Stein from Hibs – still £15,000 short of what Denis had cost all those years beforehand. The man was 100 per cent class and an all-round good guy.

If you couldn't play with Denis Law in the team then you couldn't play at all. He brought the best out in everyone – on and off the field.

LOU MACARI
Twenty-four caps (four plus one sub with Law) 1972-78

I learned a lot from Denis Law and one of the first things was how to take care of myself on a football field. There was a real tough side to Denis and he always told me to give as good as I got. He was a very approachable, likeable guy, but God help the opponent who kicked him. Denis would never accept that from anyone. Let's face it, he had played in Italy and he must have come up against all sorts of uncompromising players in that league. They would hack at you, kick you when the ball wasn't anywhere near you and, sadly, some of them would spit in your face. Denis was still a young man, only 21, when he had to put up with all of that. He was tough before he went to Italy, but even more so when he returned.

People used to ask me what he was like, *really* like. Obviously, I didn't know until I met up with him when we were on international duty. The first time I encountered him was at the training HQ at Largs, my home town. I admit I was excited at the prospect of meeting the Lawman. Given his standing in the game and what he achieved at club and country level, I found him to be a genuine down-to-earth character. You look at that statue that has been erected in his honour at Old Trafford and you don't get things like that just for being a great player. You have got to have other ingredients and Denis had them all; great personality, nice character and a genuine warmth. He has never changed a bit since I first met him all those years ago. I don't know anyone who has got a bad word to say about Denis.

Of course, I first came into his company in 1972 when I was selected for the Scotland squad. I played alongside him for the first time when I came on as a substitute in a 1-0 Home International win over Wales at Hampden. I went on for John O'Hare, of Derby, and played in attack with Denis. There was about half-an-hour or so to go and Peter Lorimer, of Leeds United, got the winner in that period. We must have done enough to convince manager Tommy Docherty to team us up at the start of the next game three days later against England in Glasgow on 27 May. Unfortunately, on this occasion we were on the wrong side of a 1-0 result. But I was learning all the time from playing in the same team as Denis. At the end of June, Scotland played in the Brazilian Independence Cup and I was fortunate enough to line up with Denis on three occasions, a 2-2 draw with Yugoslavia, where I scored both goals, a goalless draw against Czechoslovakia and a narrow 1-0 defeat from Brazil. Every game was a learning curve.

I thought we might have some more time together when I joined Manchester United, but it was brief. I remember I made my debut against West Ham and scored with a toe-poke at the Stretford End. The game finished 2-2. The Doc handed me the No. 10 shirt before the game which, of course, was Denis's number. What I didn't realise, though, was the fact that Denis had worn it for years and years. And he had every right to wear it because he was The King. Denis also played that day, but The Doc had thrown him the No. 4 jersey in the dressing room. When I found out about it later it was another scary thing for me.

I didn't want to be associated with Denis's No. 10 shirt in any shape or form. Who would want the responsibility of even attempting to take over from a legend and wear the number that was associated with him for all those years? He was an unbelievable player and I didn't want to be seen to be replacing Denis. I just wanted to be a player joining Manchester United and, hopefully, go on to do a good job for them and score a few goals into the bargain. I knew all about Best, Law and Charlton and it was one of the reasons that I joined United instead of going to Liverpool. That trio of players were magical, all with very special qualities.

Denis Law fitted perfectly into that threesome.

DANNY McGRAIN
Sixty-two caps (four with Law) 1973-82

My first thought when I was informed that Denis Law was being brought back into the Scottish international squad in 1973 was, 'Wow! I'm going to meet Denis Law.' My second thought was, 'Double wow! I'm going to be playing in the same team as Denis Law!'

Seriously, that's how much it meant to me to meet the player I had adored for such a long time. When the squad of players were told to meet at the old North British Hotel at George Square in Glasgow, I got there early in the hope of introducing myself to Denis and having time for a wee chat. I half-expected him to turn up on a golden chariot pulled along by white horses with horns sounding and all that sort of stuff!

When I arrived, Denis was already in the foyer, drinking a cup of tea. This was the bloke I had idolised from afar and there he was standing right in front of me, the great Denis Law. What a nice, genuine bloke. He may have been a superstar in a lot of people's eyes, including mine, but he was one of the most approachable guys you'll ever meet. It was impossible not to be impressed by him. Back then, we didn't get to see as much football as we do on TV today. I had witnessed Denis in action, of course, and it was obvious he was a very exciting player, but, in most cases, it was only a fleeting glimpse of his ability. Actually getting to play alongside him was something else altogether. Then you really got to see what a class act he truly was.

It was an absolute delight to play alongside him in the team that beat Czechoslovakia 2-1 on that wonderful night that cemented Scotland's place in the 1974 World Cup Finals in West Germany. As a proud nation we had been out in the wilderness for far too long. Denis, as ever, played his part. He really put himself about that evening and all he needed to top it off was a goal. Sadly, that didn't happen, but no-one was complaining as we got the victory we craved and deserved.

It was also a privilege to be in the same team as Denis when we played Zaire in Dortmund in our first game in soccer's most glittering showpiece. What a special, extraordinary evening that was for everyone involved. I didn't know it at the time, but I would be one of his last teammates on a football pitch. I look upon that as an honour and distinction. I wish there had been more, though.

I saw Denis a few years later when we were at a function in Aberdeen. We were sitting at separate tables, but, once again, I was impressed by my old mate. To be honest, he was being pestered by well-meaning fans who wanted autographs and photographs. I don't mind that sort of stuff, but only after I have finished my meal. But there was Denis, halfway through his courses, happily smiling and doing everything that was asked of him.

That, too, was typical of the man.

STEVE ARCHIBALD
Twenty-seven caps 1980-86

In 1980, I chatted to Steve Archibald, then with Aberdeen, for an article that would be seen in the 22nd edition of the prestigious *International Football Book*. He was in good company with star names such as Michel Platini, Karl-Heinz Rummenigge and Roberto Bettega appearing in the same Christmas must-have gift. I knew Denis Law was Archibald's hero. Here's how the interview went:

'Two years ago I was presented with a marvellous and treasured memory. It was not my hat-trick against Celtic or my international call-up, or even being nominated as potentially one of the top strikers in Scotland. No, I'm afraid it's none of those. In fact, it was far removed from the football field … only the opening of a new store in Aberdeen.

'Before you get the impression that I have lost my marbles, let me hastily explain that it was at that store that I finally met my boyhood idol, the player who meant so much to me. The one and only Denis Law. I was really thrilled to shake Denis's hand and, fortunately, there was a photographer in attendance to get a snap of myself and the maestro himself. That photograph has pride of place in my house. I show it to everyone who pops in. The reason I mention the incident with Denis is merely to illustrate what I think football is all about. Denis Law … those two words spell magic to me. Law was a flamboyant character and a menace to rival defences with his incredible acrobatics in the penalty area. His timing was immaculate. How many times did you see him fail to make contact with a high ball when he swooped for it? I remember a goal he scored against England at Hampden in 1966 that typified Law.

'I was still at primary school in Toryglen, virtually a long throw-in from Hampden, but I recall that goal as though it were scored yesterday. A corner-kick was swung over from the left wing to the near post and Denis appeared from nowhere, leapt high above the defence, snapped his head and sent a really fierce header whizzing past the great Gordon Banks, who didn't even get the opportunity to move a muscle. Another great Scot who played that day was little Jimmy Johnstone, the former Celtic wizard of the wing, and he scored two goals from tight angles. But, unfortunately, England still managed to win 4-3.

'Denis Law was a player with a charisma all of his own. He was a showman, a character and an entertainer. I would love to think that when I finally retire – and I hope that day is a long way off considering I have just turned 24 – fans might think of me along similar lines. But, of course, I realise I could never be another Denis Law. There could only ever be one Denis Law.'

Over three decades later, I caught up with Steve Archibald in Barcelona, where he now resides with wife Monica, daughter Kersty and son Elliot. What does he think of Denis Law today? Here's how he now views his all-time football hero.

I rate him even higher than I did back then. I've seen a bit more of life now, of course. I know a bit more about the game. I've since played for Spurs and Barcelona and a whole clutch of other clubs. I've seen management at a lower level with East Fife and I had my experience at Airdrie. I feel a lot more equipped now to air my thoughts on Denis. What he achieved was just awesome; something special. If I am asked, and I am often, who is the best striker of them all, the greatest in the world, one name immediately pops into my mind – Denis Law. It's impossible not to think of him. And it's great that he is Scottish.

You look back at all those spectacular goals and they underline what a fascinating talent he was. That arm in the air salute was really his signature. Denis always possessed that spark and that desire to be successful. His battling qualities were something else altogether. He was an obvious believer that if you don't fight the fight then you won't score the goals. And that man wanted to score goals. People might have misconstrued his style as being slightly arrogant. I don't think he was an arrogant person. I just believe he played with a self-assurance and if your job in the team is to get those goals, then you need to show that composure. Denis had it. He possessed a lot of dig, but he was an accomplished footballer, too. It wasn't all about snarling and snapping at defenders, although he was never afraid to mix it even with the biggest of them. If a defender saw a hint of fear in your eyes their job was half-done. They would never have seen that with Denis. No chance.

A few have tried to copy Denis's style. I used to always play with long sleeves, even in the hottest of conditions, and with my jersey outside my shorts, but that was as far as I would go in attempting to copy Denis. That would have been a total waste of time. He was the original. I've met him a few times since that first introduction in the Aberdeen shop and I have always found him to be a thorough gentleman. A very likeable sort, in fact. Sadly, though, I have lost that treasured photograph from all those years ago. I've moved house about 20 times since then, lived in a few countries and somewhere along the line it has gone missing. It's probably gathering dust in a loft somewhere. If anyone finds it, can they please give me a call!

DEREK JOHNSTONE
Fourteen caps 1973-79

Ball in the net. Arm in the air. Job done. Back to the centre circle. Let's get on with the game. That sums up Denis Law for me. There were no daft antics, like kissing the badge or anything like that. He was out there to score goals and that's what he did with great regularity as his record shows.

For me, he was the best Scottish footballer of all time, bar none. People of my age group will go along with that. There have been several candidates for the accolade, Kenny Dalglish, for one, but Denis is the main man, as far as I am concerned. It's a pity that younger football followers never had the chance to see Denis live in action. He was electric. You can watch all the videos and DVDs you want, but there was nothing like witnessing this guy go about his business in the flesh. I was brought up in Dundee, so it wasn't too easy for me to travel down to see Denis in action at Hampden Park. I think I saw him only twice, but he made the journeys worthwhile. He wasn't just a fabulous footballer, he was also a huge icon. He performed on a different level from anyone else.

I don't think I ever saw him flustered when he was in a crowded penalty box with bodies all over the place and boots flying around. He was also the first player I ever saw actually passing the ball into the net. Others would attempt to rip a hole in the net. How many times have you seen a striker through on the goalkeeper in a one-on-one situation and blast the ball wildly against his opponent's body or legs? But Denis, always calm and assured, was quite content to slip it gently past the keeper. Just so long as the ball crossed the line, it didn't even have to hit the net.

Another thing that impressed me was his energy. He was like a whippet the way he covered the ground. Anything around 30 yards from goal was his territory. I'm not surprised he wanted to play all over the pitch, but was told by Matt Busby, his Manchester United manager, not to come back over the halfway line. He always wanted to be involved. Imagine trying to mark such a player? It must have been impossible for defenders. He also had an inner strength. There wasn't much of him, but no-one knocked him around. There was a real grit about his character.

It's a pity I never got to play alongside Denis. My first cap was against Wales in 1973 and, of course, Denis retired a year later. It would have been brilliant to have played in the same team as him. I have met him plenty of times while we've both been covering World Cups and the like during our media work. He's the type of guy who will sit down and talk football with you for hours on end. It's astonishing to think he never actually played for a Scottish club side, performing all his football across the border apart from that year in Italy. Making it even more difficult to comprehend is the fact he is so passionate about his country; everything about Scotland, not just the football. In short, Denis Law is a great ambassador for Scotland.

FRANK McAVENNIE
Five caps 1985-88

Denis was one of my idols and, okay, I admit I did copy him. So did wee Mo Johnston. Who didn't? The trademark salute with the sleeves pulled right down as far as they would go after scoring another memorable goal. Sheer genius. The man was different class and everyone adored him.

My dad used to take me to Hampden and Parkhead when I was a kid and Denis was my man with Scotland while Kenny Dalglish was my hero at Celtic. What a combination they would have been at their peak. Unstoppable, I would have thought. Imagine being a defender and looking up to see these two guys preparing to kick off. Head-butting a moving train probably would have been more pleasurable.

I was with St Mirren when I won the Young Scottish Player of the Year award in season 1980/81. Old cliché, I know, but you could have knocked me over with a feather when I was told who would present me with the trophy – none other than Denis Law. What a fabulous memory.

I scored a goal against Australia in a World Cup play-off match at Hampden in November 1985. It was the first leg of a double-header against the Aussies that would determine which nation got to the finals in Mexico the following summer. It was crucial that we won in Glasgow and we duly did with myself and the late, great Davie Cooper, with a blistering free-kick, scoring the vital goals.

I had bright blond hair at the time, the shirt outside the shorts doing my Denis Law impersonation. It must have done the trick. One of the national newspapers caught the image of me going through the celebrations after my goal and a pal looked at the photograph and said, 'My God, I thought Denis Law had made a comeback.' I took that as a huge compliment.

Denis is a top bloke and I also recall a time when we were both on the *Terry Wogan Show* during one of my stints with West Ham. It was the number one chat show of its time and what a privilege it was to be invited on with such a legend. There's was a problem, though – Denis had been in a bit of a rush to get from Manchester to London and had brought the wrong pair of shoes. The ones he had collected in his haste had a hole in them. Typical Aberdonian – never threw anything away! He grabbed me before we went on live and said, 'Frank, if you see me crossing my legs give me a nudge. I don't want the nation to think I can't afford a good pair of shoes.'

As we prepared to go out to face the cameras, he pulled me aside and whispered, 'Don't be nervous, Wee Man. There are probably only about 23 million people watching the programme tonight.' I almost fainted at the thought. But that was typical Denis. He enjoyed a joke and he was always marvellous company.

We had a couple of things in common. A lot of what Denis did was completely off the cuff, something that cannot be coached into anyone. I would like to think I could think on my feet, too. Denis always maintained he would never become a football manager and I have to agree with that sort of thinking. Me, a manager? No thanks. I'm quite happy having hair. It would be ripped out by the handful if I was ever in a dug-out. I'm with Denis all the way on this one, believe me.

CHAPTER TWENTY-SIX

WHAT THE PAPERS SAY

IAIN KING, head of sport – *Scottish Sun*

I grew up with posters of Kenny Dalglish on my wall. The Lawman was this fabled figure my dad talked to me about. Then I watched the footage of that back-heel for Manchester City against Manchester United and an image stuck.

I thought then that Denis had the class and integrity of a true legend and that was confirmed when I was lucky enough to meet him in my work on the committee of the Scottish Football Hall of Fame. We had a chat at one of the dinners and smiled about the irony of King Kenny sticking on 30 Scotland goals alongside him.

Denis flashed that mischievous grin and said, 'Aye, son, but it only took me 55 caps, he had 102. Always remember that.'

DON MORRISON, former chief sportswriter – *Sunday Mail*

My abiding memory of Denis has got to be the 1967 Wembley triumph over England. The entire day was just wonderful, of course, and it meant so much to beat the World Cup holders on their home soil. But Denis's antics that afternoon were unforgettable. Not only did he produce yet another magnificent performance in the colours of his country, but it was obvious to everyone he wanted to rub the English noses in it. He was determined to pile on the agony.

He actually looked angry with his great mate Jim Baxter. He was agitated, arms flailing everywhere. You didn't need to be an expert in lip-reading to get the notion he wanted to stick as many behind Gordon Banks as was humanly possible inside an hour-and-a-half. Actually, that was one of Denis's best games for his country and, believe me, I saw a few on my travels with the international team. It was always an honour for Denis to play for Scotland. I've met players who are happy enough to represent Scotland, but it genuinely meant everything to Denis. No-one will be surprised to learn that Denis travelled up to Aberdeen as often as was possible during his playing days. I recall he was sent off twice during his Manchester United career and served two successive suspensions over Christmas periods. He spent that time with his family in his home town. Coincidence or what?

There is also the story that he turned down Arsenal, then the biggest club in England, to sign for Manchester City in 1960 because Manchester was closer to Scotland than London and made the journeys shorter. I could believe that would have been a contributing factor in Denis's decision when he left Huddersfield Town. If you knew the guy, you wouldn't be one bit surprised.

I loved watching Denis in action; he always brought something extra to the proceedings. He was dynamic and must have been hell to play against. Yet, like everyone else, I was always impressed by him when he was away from football. He was always good company and I'm just glad I can say I saw him at his peak. That was that afternoon at Wembley in 1967. Thank God he managed to score at least one goal that day!

DIXON BLACKSTOCK, former sportswriter – *Sunday Mail*

The *Sunday Mail* put together a glossy magazine to celebrate Scotland's feat in reaching the World Cup Finals in Italy in

1990. I knew Denis would be involved in the tournament with ITV and I thought it would be a good idea to have a chat with him about the dangermen to look out for in the competition. I have to say I was very impressed. Denis had the information at his fingertips. I can tell you there are a lot of ex-professional footballers out there who can take the Queen's shilling while working for the media and give back precious little. That wasn't the case with Denis.

Players to watch? The Lawman rattled them out one after another. Ruud Gullit and Marco Van Basten (both Holland), Carlos Valderrama (Colombia), Careca (Brazil), Gianluca Vialli and Roberto Baggio (both Italy), Diego Maradona (Argentina), John Barnes (England) and Scotland's own Mo Johnston and Paul McStay. Those were the guys who got the nod of approval from Denis.

Looking back to 1990, he didn't do too badly, did he? Maradona captained the Argentines to the final where they lost 1-0 to an Andreas Brehme penalty-kick. It wasn't Maradona's fault the game failed to live up to its billing with the Germans well and truly shackling the little genius. And his efforts to lift the trophy again, as he had done four years previously in Mexico, weren't helped when teammates Pedro Monzon and Gustavo Dezotti were ordered off in the second-half. Baggio got the opening goal in the host nation's 2-1 win over England to take third place in the tournament.

Brazilian Careca got off to a storming start with two goals in his country's 2-1 win over Sweden. He was also in the team that knocked out Scotland from Group C, a goal from Muller sending Andy Roxburgh's side tumbling in Turin. Denis tipped Johnston to get the goals for Scotland, but, alas, the striker could only manage one, a penalty-kick winner against Sweden in Genoa. However, overall, not a bad effort at all by Denis.

He was proving to be just as effective off the field as he was on it.

FRASER ELDER, BBC and former sportswriter – *Sunday Mail*

It was always a pleasure and a privilege to be in the company of Denis Law. Not only could he play football, but he was also very knowledgeable about the sport. That's not always the case, you know. I've known a lot of professionals who don't even want to talk about sport when they are away from the ground. There was one former international player who refused to talk about the game, but you couldn't get him to shut up when it came to golf!

I was fortunate enough to be in Perth when Denis made his second debut for Manchester City in 1973. I was covering his debut in a friendly match against St Johnstone at their old Muirton Park ground. The Saints were so excited at the prospect of the Lawman playing in Perth that they asked me to put together a special programme before the match. I was happy to do so and I had to pinch myself when I found myself writing about Denis Law, Francis Lee, Rodney Marsh and Mike Summerbee.

Five years later, Denis was working for the BBC World Service during the World Cup Finals in Argentina when we met up again. He still looked fit enough to pull on the boots and get out there and play. Has this guy never put on weight? As you would expect, he was a first-class and very thorough operator. It is still simply marvellous to think I once teamed up with the Great Man.

Thanks for the memories, Denis – on and off the field.

EPILOGUE

FOREVER THE KING

Denis Law was the showman supreme. Fearless, swashbuckling, elusive, unique. He was more than a mere goalscorer whose cavalier thrusts and menacing darts brought panic and pandemonium to opposing defences. Law was an inspiration to those around him at club and country level; and to street urchins everywhere.

His was a defiance born of a tough upbringing in an Aberdeen tenement, displaying an admirable stoicism while faced with poverty, adversity and even cruelty. Blighted by the deformity of a squint in his eye, he was undaunted as he went about his life with a stubborn, laudable single-mindedness. He snarled at fate. And overcame the obstacles that were strewn across his path.

There is a lot of courage in the Denis Law story. Teammates adored him, opponents feared him, fans revered him. He was a free spirit, an extrovert, a complete one-off, a rare combination of impudence and intelligence, skill and steel. No footballing system is capable of producing a player such as Denis Law. Life chiselled out this character.

Undeniably, he deserved every rapturous applause that greeted yet another spectacular goal, another piece of sorcery. He possessed a certain grace of movement which was to be admired and cherished, artistry to beguile and behold. Every ounce of hero worship was earned, the acclaim thoroughly deserved. The adulation, quite rightly, was his.

Denis Law is, was and always will be The King.

APPENDIX

THAT'S A FACT!

* Denis Law is the only Scotland international to score four goals on two occasions. He claimed a foursome in a 5-1 win over Northern Ireland on 7 November 1962 and followed that up with another four-goal performance against Norway exactly a year later. Both games were at Hampden.

* He was never booked or sent off in his 55 Scottish appearances.

* It took Scotland Under-23s – since replaced by the Under-21s – three attempts to beat their English counterparts. Denis scored the only goal of the game at Ayresome Park, Middlesbrough, in 1961.

* A total of 189 goals were scored during Law's international appearances; 105 for Scotland and 84 against.

* Law only played in two goalless draws; against Spain in a friendly on 8 May 1965 at Hampden (his 30th game) and against Czechoslovakia in the Brazilian Independence Cup on 2 July 1972 in Porto Alegre (his 48th game).

* Only five Scottish keepers had shut-outs in Law's time: Bill Brown, on four occasions, Bobby Clark (3), David Harvey (1), Ally Hunter (1) and Campbell Forsyth (1).

* Law once played AGAINST a Scottish Select. He was in the Italian League team that drew 1-1 with their Scottish counterparts at Hampden on 1 November 1961 in front of 67,000 fans. Rangers' Ralph Brand netted for the Scots with Englishman Gerry Hitchens (Inter Milan) scoring for the visitors. Welsh international John Charles was the third Briton to play for the Italians. Scottish League: Eddie Connachan (Dunfermline); Alec Hamilton (Dundee), Eric Caldow (Rangers); Pat Crerand (Celtic), Ian Ure (Dundee), Jim Baxter (Rangers);

Alex Scott (Rangers), Pat Quinn (Motherwell), Bobby Black (Kilmarnock), Ralph Brand (Rangers) and Davie Wilson (Rangers). Italian League: Albertosi (Fiorentina); David (AC Milan), Pavinago (Bologna); Zaglio (Inter Milan), Charles (Juventus), Colombo (Atalanta); Hamrin (Fiorentina), Maschio (Atalanta), Hitchens (Inter Milan), Law (Torino) and Patris (Fiorentina).

* Law once played FOR England. He was in the English League team that was beaten 4-2 by the Italian League in Milan in 1960. He made his debut alongside his Manchester City teammate Bert Trautmann, the German-born goalkeeper. Law's appearance made him the first Scot to play for an English League Select for 68 years.

* Law and Jim Baxter played for the Rest of Europe team which faced a Scandinavian Select in Copenhagen on 20 May 1964 to celebrate the 75th anniversary of the Danish FA. Law scored in his side's 4-2 win.

* The length of his shirt sleeves were tailored deliberately longer to allow him to clutch the cuffs in his trademark style.

* When Law came off at half-time in the 2-0 defeat against the USSR at Hampden on 10 May 1967, it left Scotland with seven Celtic players on the field. Ronnie Simpson, Tommy Gemmell, John Clark, Billy McNeill, Jimmy Johnstone and Bobby Lennox started the friendly match. Willie Wallace came on for Law. Former Rangers star Jim Baxter, then with Sunderland, captained the side. The other players were Eddie McCreadie (Chelsea), Frank McLintock (Arsenal) and Jim McCalliog (Sheffield Wednesday). The goals came from Gemmell (16 og) and Fedor Medved (41).

* Attendances. Highest: 133,245 witnessed Scotland's 1-0 win over England on 11 April 1964 at Hampden. Lowest: 4,000 attended the 2-2 draw against Yugoslavia in Belo Horizonte during the Brazilian Independence Cup on 29 June 1972. Smallest Hampden crowd was 7,483 for the 1-1 draw with Northern Ireland in the Home International match on 6 May 1969.

* In his 16-year international career, Law faced 16 different countries and lined up against the Home Countries on 25 occasions.

* In 2003 Law was named Scotland's most outstanding player in 50 post-war years and was awarded the Golden Player accolade by the Scottish Football Association.

* Law served a total of 21 managers during his 18-year career between 1956 and 1974 – 12 at club level and nine on the international front. Club bosses: Andy Beattie, Bill Shankly, Eddie Boot (Huddersfield Town 1956-60), Leslie McDowell (Manchester City 60-61), Beniamino Santos (Torino 61-62), Matt Busby, Wilf McGuinness, Frank O'Farrell, Tommy Docherty (Manchester United 62-73), Johnny Hart, Ron Saunders, Tony Book (Manchester City 73-74); International: Matt Busby (58), Andy Beattie (59-60), Ian McColl (60-65), Jock Stein (65), John Prentice (66), Malky MacDonald (66), Bobby Brown (67-72), Tommy Docherty (72-73), Willie Ormond (74).

* In his 55 appearances for Scotland, Law served under eight different captains with Billy Bremner skipper on 13 occasions. Others: Dave Mackay (Spurs), Bobby Evans (Celtic and Chelsea), Eric Caldow (Rangers), Billy McNeill (Celtic), Jim Baxter (Sunderland), John Greig (Rangers) and Davie Hay (Celtic). Law captained Scotland five times.

* Law faced the other two members of the United Trinity – England's Bobby Charlton and Northern Ireland's George Best – in 12 international games, winning five and drawing two.

* Law scored 236 goals in 393 games for Manchester United – 171 in 305 league games, 33 in 44 FA Cup-ties, four in 11 League Cup appearances and 28 from 33 in three European competitions. At Huddersfield, he scored 16 in 81 league games and three in ten FA Cup-ties. At Manchester City, he claimed 30 goals in 66 league games, two in FA Cup (excluding six against Luton in abandoned tie) and one in three League Cup-ties. At Torino, he netted ten in 27 league games. He scored a total of 295 goals at club level. Plus 30 on the international front bringing an overall tally of 325 goals.

* Law scored six goals in an FA Cup-tie against Luton Town at Kenilworth Road – and finished on the losing side. With Manchester City leading 6-2 in January 1961, the match was abandoned due to heavy rain. Law netted again when the tie was replayed, but Luton won 3-1.

* Law made a massive impact on European football as a Manchester United player. He is credited with more hat-tricks than any other Briton at this level. He hit trios on five occasions: against Willem II (Holland) and Sporting Lisbon in the Cup-Winners' Cup in 1963-64, Djurgaarden (Sweden) in the Fairs Cup in 1964-65 and twice against Waterford (Republic of Ireland) in European Cup-ties in 1968-69 (scoring four goals at Old Trafford).

* Between the years 1963 and 1969 Law scored a total of 28 goals in European competitions.

* In Law's 11 years at United, the club played 42 European games and were undefeated in 20 home games with 64 goals scored. In a sequence in 1963-64 they scored 20 goals in four games and Law netted half of them.

* In season 1963-64, Law joined an elite in English football by scoring three hat-tricks in league games for Manchester United.

* In a total of 452 league games in the UK, Law appeared as a substitute only six times, coming off the bench for both Manchester clubs.

* Law appeared as a guest on the BBC's *This Is Your Life* programme in February 1975.

* Law was acknowledged by the University of Aberdeen with an Honorary Doctorate in June 2005.

* In February 2010, Law was appointed a patron of the UK-based charity Football Aid in succession to the late Sir Bobby Robson.

DENIS LAW GOALS

Denis Law scored his 30 goals in 20 games against ten nations. Goals: Norway 7, Northern Ireland 6, Wales 4, England 3, Austria 3, Czechoslovakia 2, Poland 2, Finland 1, Spain 1, Peru 1. Fourteen during the first-half; 16 in the second-half. Nineteen were scored at Hampden. Sequence of goals (Scotland first in scorelines).

WALES 1 (18 Oct 1958: 70 mins: Score: 3-0)
POLAND 1 (4 May 1960: 23 mins: 2-3)
N IRELAND 1 (9 Nov 1960: 8 mins: 5-2)
CZECHOSLOVAKIA 2 (26 Sept 1961: 62, 83 mins: 3-2)
WALES 1 (20 Oct 1962: 63 mins: 3-2)
N IRELAND 4 (7 Nov 1962: 40, 64, 77, 87 mins: 5-1)
AUSTRIA 2 (8 May 1963: 33, 71 mins: Game abandoned
    79 mins: 4-1)
NORWAY 3 (4 June 1963: 14, 22, 76 mins: 3-4)
SPAIN 1 (13 June 1963: 16 mins: 6-2)

NORWAY 4 (7 Nov 1963: 19, 44, 59, 82 mins: 6-1)
WALES 1 (20 Nov 1963: 47 mins: 2-1)
FINLAND 1 (21 Oct 1964: 2 mins: 3-1)
ENGLAND 1 (10 April 1965: 41 mins: 2-2)
POLAND 1 (23 May 1965: 76 mins: 1-1)
ENGLAND 1 (2 April 1966: 42 mins: 3-4)
WALES 1 (22 Oct 1966: 86 mins: 1-1)
ENGLAND 1 (15 April 1967: 27 mins: 3-2)
AUSTRIA 1 (6 Nov 1968: 7 mins: 2-1)
PERU 1 (26 April 1972: 65 mins: 2-0)
N IRELAND 1 (20 May 1972: 86 mins: 2-0)

LAW MINUTES ON PITCH

Denis Law spent 4,675 minutes (78 hours and 32 minutes) playing for Scotland. He was substituted nine times. Alex Young (Hearts) came on after 12 minutes against Austria in 1960. Others: Willie Wallace v. USSR 1967 (46 mins); Alan Gilzean v. Austria 1968 (75 mins); Jimmy Bone v. Yugoslavia 1972 (76 mins); Colin Stein v. Czechoslovakia 1972 (78 mins); Donald Ford v. Czechoslovakia 1973 (58 mins); Joe Jordan v. West Germany 1973 (87 mins); Donald Ford v. West Germany 1974 (59 mins); Joe Jordan v. Northern Ireland 1974 (65 mins).

THEY SERVED WITH THE KING

EXACTLY 113 players performed alongside Denis Law during his 55-game international reign.

Two – Donald Ford, of Hearts, and Norwich City's Jimmy Bone – just missed the privilege of serving with The King. Both were involved in games that also saw Law in action, but they only made their appearances when the iconic frontman was substituted. Bone came on for Law in the 2-2 draw against Yugoslavia during the Brazilian Independence Cup-tie on 29 June 1972 in Belo Horizonte. Ford replaced the Lawman on two occasions – the 1-0 World Cup defeat against Czechoslovakia in Bratislava on 17 October 1973 and in the 2-1 loss against West Germany in a friendly in Frankfurt on 27 March 1974.

Jim Baxter clocked up the most outings alongside Law. The Rangers and Sunderland star played in 23 matches with his great friend.

Twenty-six players started only one game in Law's company: Eddie Connachan (Dunfermline), Jim Cruickshank (Hearts), Jim Herriot (Birmingham City), Thomson Allan (Dundee), Jackie Plenderleith (Manchester City), Davie Provan (Rangers), Ron Yeats (Liverpool), Tom Forsyth (Rangers), John Blackley (Hibs), Erich Schaedler (Hibs), John Hansen (Partick Thistle), Pat Quinn (Motherwell), Jimmy Gabriel (Everton), Willie Hamilton (Hibs), Kenny Burns (Nottingham Forest), Tony Green (Blackpool), Jimmy Smith (Newcastle United), Willie Carr (Coventry City), Bobby Robinson (Dundee), Johnny MacLeod (Hibs), Alex Young (Hearts), George Herd (Clyde), Hugh Robertson (Dundee), Jimmy Robertson (Spurs), Joe McBride (Celtic) and Colin Stein (Rangers).

The full list and number of appearances of players who participated in games alongside Law.

GOALKEEPERS
BILL BROWN (Spurs, 19)
GEORGE FARM (Blackpool, 2)
FRANK HAFFEY (Celtic, 2)
LAWRIE LESLIE (Airdrie, 2)
EDDIE CONNACHAN (Dunfermline, 1)
ADAM BLACKLAW (Burnley, 2)
TOMMY LAWRENCE (Liverpool, 2)
CAMPBELL FORSYTH (Kilmarnock, 4)
JIM CRUICKSHANK (Hearts, 1)
BOBBY FERGUSON (Kilmarnock, 2)
RONNIE SIMPSON (Celtic, 4)
JIM HERRIOT (Birmingham City, 1)
ALLY HUNTER (Celtic, 3)
BOBBY CLARK (Aberdeen, 5)
DAVID HARVEY (Leeds United, 4)
THOMSON ALLAN (Dundee, 1)

DEFENDERS
JOHN GRANT (Hibs, 2)
ERIC CALDOW (Rangers, 16)
WILLIE TONER (Kilmarnock, 2)
TOMMY DOCHERTY (Arsenal, 2)
DUNKY McKAY (Celtic, 6)
ERIC SMITH (Celtic, 2)

BOBBY EVANS (Celtic, Chelsea, 7)
JOHN HEWIE (Charlton, 5)
JOHN CUMMING (Hearts, 3)
JACKIE PLENDERLEITH (Manchester City, 1)
BILLY McNEILL (Celtic, 18)
BOBBY SHEARER (Rangers, 2)
BERT McCANN (Motherwell, 4)
ALEC HAMILTON (Dundee, 21)
IAN URE (Dundee, 9)
DAVIE HOLT (Hearts, 4+1 sub)
JOHN CLARK (Celtic, 2)
DAVIE PROVAN (Rangers, 1)
JIM KENNEDY (Celtic, 6)
JOHN GREIG (Rangers, 18)
RON YEATS (Liverpool, 1)
JACKIE McGRORY (Kilmarnock, 2)
FRANK McLINTOCK (Leicester City, Arsenal, 4+1 sub)
EDDIE McCREADIE (Chelsea, 12)
TOMMY GEMMELL (Celtic, 8)
RONNIE McKINNON (Rangers, 6)
PAT STANTON (Hibs, 3)
WILLIE DONACHIE (Manchester City, 7)
JOHN BROWNLIE (Hibs, 3)
EDDIE COLQUHOUN (Sheffield United, 4)
BOBBY MONCUR (Newcastle United, 4)
MARTIN BUCHAN (Manchester United, 6)
ALEX FORSYTH (Partick Thistle, 3)
SANDY JARDINE (Rangers, 6)
GEORGE CONNELLY (Celtic, 2)
DANNY McGRAIN (Celtic, 4)
TOM FORSYTH (Rangers, 1)
JOHN BLACKLEY (Hibs, 1)
ERICH SCHAEDLER (Hibs, 1)
JOHN HANSEN (Partick Thistle, 1 sub)
JIM HOLTON (Manchester United, 4)

MIDFIELDERS
DAVE MACKAY (Hearts, Spurs, 14)
BOBBY COLLINS (Celtic, Everton, Leeds United, 7)
JOHN WHITE (Falkirk, Spurs, 17)

JIM BAXTER (Rangers, Sunderland, 23)
PAT QUINN (Motherwell, 1)
PAT CRERAND (Celtic, Manchester United, 9)
DAVIE GIBSON (Leicester City, 6)
JIMMY GABRIEL (Everton, 1 sub)
BILLY BREMNER (Leeds United, 18)
WILLIE HAMILTON (Hibs, 1)
BOBBY MURDOCH (Celtic, 4)
ASA HARTFORD (West Brom, Manchester City, 5+1 sub)
ARCHIE GEMMILL (Derby County, Nottingham Forest, 5+1 sub)
GEORGE GRAHAM (Arsenal, Manchester United, 3)
DAVIE HAY (Celtic, 5)
KENNY BURNS (Nottingham Forest, 1)
TOMMY HUTCHISON (Coventry City, 5+1 sub)
TONY GREEN (Blackpool, 1+1 sub)
JIMMY SMITH (Newcastle United, 1+1 sub)
WILLIE CARR (Coventry City, 1)
BOBBY ROBINSON (Dundee, 1 sub)

FORWARDS
GRAHAM LEGGAT (Aberdeen, Fulham, 8)
DAVID HERD (Arsenal, 2)
JACKIE HENDERSON (Arsenal, 2)
WILLIE HENDERSON (Rangers, 19)
BERTIE AULD (Celtic, 3)
ALEX SCOTT (Rangers, Everton, 6)
JOHNNY MacLEOD (Hibs, 1)
IAN ST JOHN (Motherwell, Liverpool, 16+1 sub)
GEORGE MULHALL (Aberdeen, Sunderland, 2)
ANDY WEIR (Motherwell, 3)
ALEX YOUNG (Hearts, 1+1 sub)
GEORGE HERD (Clyde, 1)
RALPH BRAND (Rangers, 2)
DAVIE WILSON (Rangers, 14)
HUGH ROBERTSON (Dundee, 1)
JIMMY ROBERTSON (Spurs, 1)
JIMMY MILLAR (Rangers, 2)
ALAN GILZEAN (Dundee, Spurs, 9+1 sub)
JIMMY JOHNSTONE (Celtic, 8+1 sub)
STEVIE CHALMERS (Celtic, 2)

WILLIE WALLACE (Hearts, Celtic, 4+1 sub)
JOHN HUGHES (Celtic, 4+1 sub)
NEIL MARTIN (Hibs, 2)
WILLIE JOHNSTON (Rangers, 2+1 sub)
JOE McBRIDE (Celtic, 1)
JIM McCALLIOG (Sheffield Wednesday, 3)
BOBBY LENNOX (Celtic, 4)
WILLIE MORGAN (Burnley, Manchester United, 10)
CHARLIE COOKE (Chelsea, 2)
COLIN STEIN (Rangers, 1+1 sub)
JOHN O'HARE (Derby County, 3)
PETER LORIMER (Leeds United, 3+2 sub)
LOU MACARI (Celtic, Manchester United, 4+1 sub)
KENNY DALGLISH (Celtic, Liverpool, 6)
JOE JORDAN (Leeds United, 2+3 sub)

THE LAW LINE-UPS

1958

October 18 v. Wales (Cardiff) 3-0

Brown; Grant, Caldow; Mackay (c), Toner, Docherty; Leggat, Collins, D Herd, Law, J Henderson.
Scorers: Leggat, Law, Collins   *Att*: 59,162

November 5 v. Northern Ireland (Hampden) 2-2

Brown; Grant, Caldow; Mackay (c), Toner, Docherty; Leggat, Collins, D Herd, Law, J Henderson.
Scorers: Herd, Collins   *Att*: 72,732

1959

May 27 v. Holland (Amsterdam) 2-1

Farm; McKay, Caldow; Smith, Evans (c), Hewie; Leggat, Collins, White, Law, Auld.
Scorers: Collins, Leggat   *Att*: 55,000

June 3 v. Portugal (Lisbon) 0-1

Farm; McKay, Caldow; Smith, Evans (c), Hewie; Scott, Collins, White, Law, Auld.
Att: 30,000

October 3 v. Northern Ireland (Belfast) 4-0

Brown; Caldow, Hewie; Mackay, Evans (c), McCann; Leggat, White, St John, Law, Mulhall.
Scorers: Leggat, Hewie, White, Mulhall   *Att*: 59,000

November 4 v. Wales (Hampden) 1-1

Brown; Caldow, Hewie; Mackay, Evans (c), McCann; Leggat, White, St John, Law, Auld.
Scorer: Leggat   *Att*: 55,813

1960

April 9 v. England (Hampden) 1-1

Haffey; McKay, Caldow; Cumming, Evans (c), McCann; Leggat, White, St John, Law, Weir.
Scorer: Leggat   *Att*: 129,783

May 4 v. Poland (Hampden) 2-3

Brown; McKay, Hewie; Mackay, Evans (c), Cumming; Leggat, White, St John, Law, Weir.
Scorers: Law, St John   *Att*: 26,643

May 29 v. Austria (Vienna) 1-4

Brown; McKay, Caldow; Mackay, Evans (c), Cumming; Leggat, White, St John, Law (Young), Weir.
Scorer: Mackay   *Att*: 60,000

November 9 v. Northern Ireland (Hampden) 5-2

Leslie; McKay, Caldow (c); Mackay, Plenderleith, Baxter; G Herd, Law, Young, Brand, Wilson.
Scorers: Law, Caldow, Young, Brand 2   *Att*: 34,564

1961

April 15 v. England (Wembley) 3-9

Haffey; Shearer, Caldow (c); Mackay, McNeill, McCann; MacLeod, Law, St John, Quinn, Wilson.
Scorers: Mackay, Wilson, Quinn   *Att*: 97,350

September 26 v. Czechoslovakia (Hampden) 3-2

Leslie; Shearer, Caldow (c); Crerand, McNeill, Baxter; Scott, White, St John, Law, Wilson.
Scorers: St John, Law 2   *Att*: 51,590

November 29 v. Czechoslovakia (Brussels) 2-4 (After extra-time)

Connachan; A Hamilton, Caldow (c); Crerand, Ure, Baxter; Brand, White, St John, Law, H Robertson.
Scorer: St John 2   *Att*: 7,000

1962
April 14 v. England (Hampden) 2-0

Brown; A Hamilton, Caldow (c); Crerand, McNeill, Baxter; Scott, White, St John, Law, Wilson.
Scorers: Wilson, Caldow (pen)   *Att*: 132,431

October 20 v. Wales (Cardiff) 3-2

Brown; A Hamilton, Caldow (c); Crerand, Ure, Baxter; W Henderson, White, St John, Law, Wilson.
Scorers: Caldow (pen), Law, Henderson   *Att*: 58,000

November 7 v. Northern Ireland (Hampden) 5-1

Brown; A Hamilton, Caldow (c); Crerand, Ure, Baxter; W Henderson, White, St John, Law, Mulhall.
Scorers: Law 4, Henderson   *Att*: 58,734

1963
April 6 v. England (Wembley) 2-1

Brown; A Hamilton, Caldow (c); Mackay, Ure, Baxter; W Henderson, White, St John, Law, Wilson.
Scorers: Baxter 2, 1 pen   *Att*: 98,606

May 8 v. Austria (Hampden) 4-1

(Game abandoned after 79 minutes)
Brown; A Hamilton, Holt; Mackay (c), Ure, Baxter; W Henderson, Gibson, Millar, Law, Wilson.
Scorers: Wilson 2, Law 2   *Att*: 94,596

June 4 v. Norway (Bergen) 3-4

Blacklaw; A Hamilton, Holt; Mackay (c) (McLintock), Ure, Baxter; W Henderson, Gibson, St John, Law, Wilson.
Scorer: Law 3   *Att*: 23,000

June 9 v. Republic of Ireland (Dublin) 0-1

Lawrence; A Hamilton, Holt; McLintock, McNeill, Baxter; W Henderson, Gibson, Millar (St John), Law (c), Wilson.
Att: 26,000

June 13 v. Spain (Madrid) 6-2

Blacklaw; McNeill, Holt; McLintock, Ure, Baxter; W Henderson, Gibson, St John, Law (c), Wilson.
Scorers: Law, Gibson, McLintock, Wilson, W Henderson, St John
Att: 40,000

November 7 v. Norway (Hampden) 6-1

Brown; A Hamilton, Provan; Mackay (c), Ure, Baxter (Gabriel); Scott, White, Gilzean, Law, W Henderson.
Scorers: Law 4, Mackay 2   *Att*: 35,416

November 20 v. Wales (Hampden) 2-1

Brown; A Hamilton, Kennedy; Mackay (c), McNeill, Baxter; W Henderson, White, Gilzean, Law, Scott.
Scorers: White, Law   *Att*: 56,167

1964
April 11 v. England (Hampden) 1-0

Forsyth; A Hamilton, Kennedy; Greig, McNeill (c), Baxter; W Henderson, White, Gilzean, Law, Wilson.
Scorer: Gilzean   *Att*: 133,245

May 12 v. West Germany (Hanover) 2-2

Cruickshank; A Hamilton (Holt), Kennedy; Greig, McNeill (c), Baxter; W Henderson, White, Gilzean, Law, Wilson.
Scorer: Gilzean 2   *Att*: 75,000

October 3 v. Wales (Cardiff) 2-3

Forsyth; A Hamilton, Kennedy; Greig, Yeats, Baxter; Johnstone, Gibson, Chalmers, Law (c), J Robertson.
Scorers: Chalmers, Gibson   *Att*: 37,093

October 21 v. Finland (Hampden) 3-1

Forsyth; A Hamilton, Kennedy; Greig, McGrory, Baxter; J Johnstone, Gibson, Chalmers, Law (c), Scott.
Scorers: Law, Chalmers, Gibson   *Att*: 55,332

November 25 v. Northern Ireland (Hampden) 3-2

Forsyth; A Hamilton, Kennedy; Greig, McGrory, McLintock; Wallace, Law, Gilzean, Baxter (c), Wilson.
Scorers: Wilson 2, Gilzean *Att*: 48,752

1965

April 10 v. England (Wembley) 2-2

Brown; A Hamilton, McCreadie; Crerand, McNeill (c), Greig; W Henderson, Collins, St John, Law, Wilson.
Scorers: Law, St John *Att*: 98,199

May 8 v. Spain (Hampden) 0-0

Brown; A Hamilton, McCreadie; Bremner, McNeill (c), Greig; W Henderson, Collins, Law, Gilzean, Hughes.
Att: 60,146

May 23 v. Poland (Chorzow) 1-1

Brown; A Hamilton, McCreadie; Greig, McNeill (c), Crerand; W Henderson, Collins, Martin, Law, Hughes.
Scorer: Law *Att*: 67,462

May 27 v. Finland (Helsinki) 2-1

Brown; A Hamilton, McCreadie; Crerand, McNeill (c), Greig; W Henderson, Law, Martin, W Hamilton, Wilson.
Scorers: Wilson, Greig *Att*: 20,162

October 2 v. Northern Ireland (Belfast) 2-3

Brown; A Hamilton, McCreadie; Mackay, McNeill (c), Greig; W Henderson, Law, Gilzean, Baxter, Hughes.
Scorer: Gilzean 2 *Att*: 53,000

October 13 v. Poland (Hampden) 1-2

Brown; A Hamilton, McCreadie; Crerand, McNeill (c), Greig; W Henderson, Bremner, Gilzean, Law, Johnston.
Scorer: McNeill *Att*: 107,580

1966

April 2 v. England (Hampden) 3-4

Ferguson; Greig (c), Gemmell; Murdoch, McKinnon, Baxter; J Johnstone, Law, Wallace, Bremner, Johnston.
Scorers: Law, Johnstone 2 *Att*: 123,052

October 22 v. Wales (Cardiff) 1-1

Ferguson; Greig (c), Gemmell; Bremner, McKinnon, Clark; J Johnstone, Law, McBride, Baxter, W Henderson.
Scorer: Law   *Att*: 33,269

1967
April 15 v. England (Wembley) 3-2

Simpson; Gemmell, McCreadie; Greig (c), McKinnon, Baxter; Wallace, Bremner, McCalliog, Law, Lennox.
Scorers: Law, Lennox, McCalliog   *Att*: 99,063

May 10 v. USSR (Hampden) 0-2

Simpson; Gemmell, McCreadie; Clark, McNeill, Baxter (c); J Johnstone, McLintock, McCalliog, Law (Wallace), Lennox.
Att; 53,497

October 21 v. Northern Ireland (Belfast) 0-1

Simpson; Gemmell, McCreadie; Greig (c), McKinnon, Ure; Wallace, Murdoch, McCalliog, Law, Morgan.
Att: 55,000

1968
November 6 v. Austria (Hampden) 2-1

Simpson; Gemmell, McCreadie; Bremner (c), McKinnon, Greig; J Johnstone, Cooke, Hughes, Law (Gilzean), Lennox.
Scorers: Law, Bremner   *Att*: 80,856

1969
April 16 v. West Germany (Hampden) 1-1

Lawrence; Gemmell, McCreadie; Murdoch, McKinnon, Greig; J Johnstone, Bremner (c), Law, Gilzean, Lennox.
Scorer: Murdoch   *Att*: 95,951

May 6 v. Northern Ireland (Hampden) 1-1

Herriot; McCreadie, Gemmell; Bremner (c), Greig, Stanton; W Henderson, Murdoch, Stein, Law, Cooke (Johnston).
Scorer: Stein   *Att*: 7,483

1972
April 26 v. Peru (Hampden) 2-0

Hunter; Brownlie, Donachie; Carr, Colquhoun, Moncur; Morgan, Hartford, O'Hare, Law (c), Gemmill.
Scorers: O'Hare, Law   *Att*: 21,001

May 20 v. Northern Ireland (Hampden) 2-0

Clark; Brownlie, Donachie; Bremner (c), McNeill, Moncur; J Johnstone (Lorimer), Gemmill, O'Hare, Law, Graham.
Scorers: Law, Lorimer   *Att*: 39,710

May 24 v. Wales (Hampden) 1-0

Clark; Stanton, Buchan; Bremner (c), McNeill, Moncur; Lorimer, Green, O'Hare (Macari), Law, Gemmill (Hartford).
Scorers: Lorimer   *Att*: 21,332

May 27 v. England (Hampden) 0-1

Clark; Brownlie, Donachie (Green); Bremner (c), McNeill, Moncur; Gemmill (J Johnstone), Hartford, Lorimer, Macari, Law.
Att: 119,325

June 29 v. Yugoslavia (Belo Horizonte) 2-2

Hunter; A Forsyth (Hansen), Buchan, Colquhoun, Donachie; Morgan, Bremner (c), Hartford, Graham; Law (Bone), Macari.
Scorer: Macari 2   *Att*: 4,000

July 2 v. Czechoslovakia (Porto Alegre) 0-0

Clark; A Forsyth, Colquhoun, Buchan, Donachie; Morgan, Bremner (c), Hartford, Graham; Macari, Law (Stein).
Att: 15,000

July 5 v. Brazil (Rio de Janeiro) 0-1

Clark; A Forsyth, Colquhoun, Buchan, Donachie; Morgan, Bremner (c), Hartford, Graham; Law, Macari.
Att: 130,000

1973
September 26 v. Czechoslovakia (Hampden) 2-1

Hunter; Jardine, Holton, Connelly, McGrain; Morgan, Bremner (c), Hay, Hutchison; Law, Dalglish (Jordan).
Scorers: Holton, Jordan   *Att*: 100,000

October 17 v. Czechoslovakia (Bratislava) 0-1
Harvey; Jardine, T Forsyth, Blackley, McGrain; Morgan, Hay (c), Dalglish, Hutchison; Law (Ford), Jordan.
Att: 15,000

November 14 v. West Germany (Hampden) 1-1
Harvey; Jardine, Holton, Connelly, McGrain; Morgan, Bremner (c), Smith (Lorimer), Hutchison; Dalglish, Law (Jordan).
Scorer: Holton   *Att*: 58,235

1974
March 27 v. West Germany (Frankfurt) 1-2
Allan; Jardine, Buchan, Stanton, Schaedler; Morgan, Hay (c), Burns (Robinson), Hutchison; Law (Ford), Dalglish.
Scorer: Dalglish   *Att*: 62,000

May 11 v. Northern Ireland (Hampden) 0-1
Harvey; Jardine, Holton, Buchan, Donachie (Smith); Morgan, Bremner (c), Hay, Hutchison; Law (Jordan), Dalglish.
Att: 53,775

June 14 v. Zaire (Dortmund) 2-0
Harvey; Jardine, Holton, Blackley, McGrain; Lorimer, Bremner (c), Hay; Dalglish (Hutchison), Jordan, Law.
Scorers: Lorimer, Jordan   *Att*: 25,800

THAT WAS THE YEAR THAT WAS

1940 – DENIS LAW'S BIRTHDAY

Winston Churchill succeeded Neville Chamberlain to become the 13th Prime Minister of Britain in the 20th century.

English international winger Stanley Matthews was permitted to play for Airdrie in the Emergency Cup competition.

Rangers defeated Dundee United in the War Cup Final before 90,000 with an estimated 25,000 locked out of Hampden.

The Football Leagues in the UK were suspended due to the outbreak of the war.

Jimmy Greaves was born on 20 February, four days before Denis Law.

Singer Vera Lynn was voted the Forces' sweetheart.

The radio programme *Music While You Work* was created to entertain factory workers during the war effort.

In the summer, the Battle of Britain was fought out in the skies above southern England.

In June, the British Army was evacuated from Dunkirk by a flotilla of Navy and commercial vessels.

France surrendered and Paris was occupied by German forces.

Coventry was bombed by the Luftwaffe and the cathedral was destroyed.

It cost 3s 9d (18-and-a-half pence) to send 120 Wills' Gold Flake cigarettes to the British Forces in France.

In Hollywood, *Rebecca*, starring Laurence Olivier, won the Oscar for Best Film.

James Stewart won an Oscar for Best Actor in the film *Philadelphia Story*. Ginger Rogers received the female award for *Kitty Foyle*. Other top movies included Walt Disney's *Fantasia*, *Road To Singapore* with Bob Hope, Bing Crosby and Dorothy Lamour and *Strike Up The Band* with Mickey Rooney and Judy Garland.

The most popular film song of the year was 'When You Wish Upon A Star' from Walt Disney's *Pinocchio*.

The Adventures of Superman was one of the top radio shows.

The rail fare from Glasgow to London was £1.10s (equivalent of £1.50p) with return fare £2.10s (£2.50p).

A Daimler 2.5 litre saloon was priced at £485; a Vauxhall saloon cost £169.

A small bungalow could be bought for £250.

A packet of 20 Kensitas cigarettes cost one shilling (five pence).

The average price of a British newspaper was 2d.

John Lennon, Ringo Starr, Tom Jones, Adam Faith, Cliff Richard and Billy Fury, comedian Jimmy Tarbuck and *Only Fools and Horses* actor David Jason were born.

THAT WAS THE YEAR THAT WAS

1958 – DENIS LAW'S INTERNATIONAL DEBUT

The sixth World Cup was hosted by Sweden with Scotland making a second successive appearance in the finals.

Pele exploded onto the world football stage with two goals in Brazil's 5-2 final win over hosts Sweden in Stockholm. He became the youngest scorer in the tournament at the age of 17 years and 239 days when he netted in the 1-0 quarter-final win over Wales. He scored a hat-trick in the 5-2 semi-final victory over France. The two semi-finals, third-place play-off and final yielded a remarkable 27 goals in total.

Hearts won the Scottish First Division championship with Wolves successful in England.

Eight Manchester United players were among the 23 people killed in the Munich Air Disaster.

Bolton Wanderers won the FA Cup for the fourth time in their history, beating Manchester United 2-0 at Wembley. Nat Lofthouse scored both goals.

Mike Hawthorn became the first British world motor racing champion.

Harold Macmillan was the man who occupied 10 Downing Street with Dwight Eisenhower the power in the White House.

Scot Donald Campbell set the world water speed record at 248.62 miles per hour.

In Hollywood, *Gigi* collected nine Oscars as the year's Best Film. David Niven, in *Separate Tables*, and Susan Hayward, in *I Want To Live*, were Male and Female Oscar winners.

Lawman, starring John Russell, *Sea Hunt*, with Lloyd Bridges, *Alfred Hitchcock, What's My Line?*, *Panorama*, *Dixon of Dock Green*, *This Is Your Life* and *Hancock's Half Hour*, starring Tony Hancock, were the favourite TV shows.

Britain's first-ever motorway was opened and the first hovercraft was unveiled.

The top disc was 'Tom Dooley' performed by the Kingston Trio.

Cliff Richard released his debut single 'Move It' which got to No. 2 in the pop charts.

Elvis Presley was recruited into the United States Army.

Sports programme *Grandstand* was first broadcast, as was children's favourite *Blue Peter*.

In Britain's biggest-ever CND protest march, over 12,000 besieged Aldermaston.

The first *Carry On* film was released, *Carry On Sergeant*, starring Bob Monkhouse, Kenneth Williams, Hattie Jacques and Terry Scott.

Chi Chi the giant Panda arrived at London Zoo from China.

In roadside cafes, a full breakfast with tea and toast cost 1/8d (about eight pence).

The world's first-ever computer exhibition was held at Earl's Court in London.

Singers Madonna, Paul Weller and Kate Bush and actors Gary Oldman and Miranda Richardson were born.

THAT WAS THE YEAR THAT WAS

1967 – DENIS LAW'S GREATEST TRIUMPH

Denis Law scored in the 3-2 win over world champions England at Wembley. Law, 'It was a glorious feeling.'

Celtic became the first British club to win the European Cup by beating Inter Milan 2-1 in the final in Lisbon. Tommy Gemmell and Stevie

Chalmers scored the goals. Jock Stein's side won every competition, the League championship, the Scottish Cup, the League Cup and the Glasgow Cup. Rangers lost 1-0 to Bayern Munich in the European Cup-Winners' Cup Final, going down to a Franz Roth extra-time goal in Nuremberg.

Manchester United, with 23 goals from Law, won the English First Division.

Queen's Park Rangers became the first Third Division club to win the English League Cup by beating West Brom 3-2.

Harold Wilson was in residence at 10 Downing Street. Lyndon B Johnson was the United States President.

Muhammad Ali was stripped of his world heavyweight boxing title for refusing to join the US Army.

Top films were *The Graduate*, starring Dustin Hoffman and Anne Bancroft, *Barefoot In The Park*, with Robert Redford and Jane Fonda, *Bonnie and Clyde*, with Warren Beatty and Faye Dunaway, *The Dirty Dozen*, starring Lee Marvin, Donald Sutherland, Charles Bronson, John Cassavetes and Ernest Borgnine, and Clint Eastwood's spaghetti western *For A Few Dollars More*.

'Puppet on a String', sung by Sandie Shaw, won the Eurovision Song Contest for Britain.

The Beatles' *Sergeant Pepper's Lonely Hearts Club Band* was released. Pink Floyd's first album *Piper At The Gates Of Dawn* appeared.

'A Whiter Shade of Pale', by Procol Harum, was one of the biggest hits. Others were 'All You Need Is Love' (The Beatles), 'Something Stupid' (Frank and Nancy Sinatra), 'Ruby Tuesday' (Rolling Stones), 'Brown-Eyed Girl' (Van Morrison) and 'Gimme Some Lovin'' (Spencer Davis Group).

Singer Otis Redding died at the age of 26 in a plane crash, one month before his biggest hit 'Sitting On The Dock Of The Bay'.

Elvis Presley married Priscilla Beaulieu in Las Vegas.

Top TV shows were *Coronation Street*, starring Pat Phoenix, Violet Carson, William Roache and Jack Howarth, *The Saint* (Roger Moore), *The Prisoner* (Patrick McGoohan), *Forsyte Saga* (Nyree Dawn Porter), *Z Cars* (Stratford Johns and Frank Windsor), *Top of the Pops*, *Star Trek* (William Shatner and Leonard Nimoy), *Crossroads* (Noel Gordon) and *Tom and Jerry*.

BBC Radio One, Two, Three and Four were all launched.

The first *Rolling Stone* magazine was published in America.

An average newspaper cost 4d.

The first ATMs were introduced in Barclay's Bank branches in London.

Concorde was introduced.

The average price of a house was £3,840.

A gallon of petrol was priced at 5s 2d.

A new Ford Cortina Mk II saloon sold for £749.

THAT WAS THE YEAR THAT WAS

1974 – DENIS LAW'S RETIREMENT FROM FOOTBALL

Scotland won through to the World Cup Finals in West Germany after an absence of 16 years. Denis Law, making his last-ever appearance, played in the 2-0 triumph over Zaire, Scotland's first win at this level.

The host nation won the World Cup with a 2-1 victory over Holland in Munich. Johan Neeskens scored in the first minute for the Dutch with the first-ever penalty-kick awarded in a final. English referee Jack Taylor awarded another spot-kick 24 minutes later and Paul Breitner equalised. Gerd Muller scored the winner.

Brazilian legend Pele, at the age of 34, made his 605th – and final – appearance for Santos. He signed for New York Cosmos a year later and played 64 times over a two-year period.

Don Revie succeeded Sir Alf Ramsey as manager of England.

Brian Clough was sacked after only 54 days as manager of Leeds United. Bill Nicholson resigned as Spurs boss after 16 years in charge.

Chelsea paid a club record fee of £250,000 for Celtic's Davie Hay. Bob Latchford became British football's most expensive player when Everton paid £350,000 to Birmingham City.

Scotland international skipper Billy Bremner, of Leeds, and Liverpool's Kevin Keegan were each fined £500 and banned for a month after their double sending-off in the showpiece FA Charity Shield game at Wembley. They were also each banned for a month.

The BBC's *Match of the Day* programme celebrated its tenth anniversary.

South African Gary Player won the Open Championship.

Harold Wilson succeeded Ted Heath as British Prime Minister. Richard Nixon resigned as United States President in the wake of the Watergate scandal. Gerald Ford took over. Eva Peron succeeded her late husband as President of Argentina.

The average price for a family-sized house was £10,990.

Olivia Newton-John represented the UK in the European Song Contest with 'Long Live Love'. The No. 1 pop hit of the year was 'Kung Foo Fighting' by Carl Douglas. 'I Shot The Sheriff' by Eric Clapton and 'Band On The Run' by Paul McCartney's Wings were other big sellers. Mama Cass Elliot, of the Mamas and Papas pop group, died at the age of 32.

The Godfather Part Two, starring Al Pacino and Robert de Niro, won the Best Film Oscar. Other top movies were *Murder On The Orient Express*, *The Exorcist*, *Blazing Saddles* and *Death Wish*.

Art Carney was the surprise Best Actor Oscar winner for his performance in *Harry And Tonto* while the Female award went to Ellen Burstyn in *Alice Doesn't Live Here Any More*.

The most-watched TV programmes were *Kojak*, starring Telly Savalas, *The Waltons*, *The Price Is Right*, *Last Of The Summer Wine* and *Six Million Dollar Man*.

A gallon of petrol cost 42 pence.

Tom Baker took over as the fifth *Doctor Who*.

Leonardo di Caprio, Victoria Beckham and Robbie Williams were born.

INDEX